TRANSACTIONS

of the

American Philosophical Society

Held at Philadelphia for Promoting Useful Knowledge

VOLUME 75, Part 1, 1985

Oresme's *Livre de Politiques*
and the France of Charles V

SUSAN M. BABBITT

THE AMERICAN PHILOSOPHICAL SOCIETY

Independence Square, Philadelphia

1985

Library of Congress Catalog
Card Number 84-71076
International Standard Book Number 0-87169-751-3
US ISSN 0065-9746

CONTENTS

To my parents

PREFACE

We might imagine the political world of the Middle Ages as dominated by two paths. The high road is that of ideas, the low road that of practice. Ascending in a roughly parallel way, the paths become increasingly broad and cluttered as they move into the twelfth century and beyond.

Each of these paths has deserved and received careful attention. Less study has been given to the question whether they are truly parallel, or whether there are angles of meeting. Certainly this requires caution: only when we speak of publicists and propagandists can we show that thought and action are related as cause and effect. We can, however, identify a few figures whose circumstances or temperament led them to expose thought and policy to each other. The self-conscious Charlemagne is one example. Stephen Langton may be another. A third is Charles V, a scholarly king who commissioned French versions of ancient and medieval treatises for the express purpose of guiding his government. To translate the *Politics* he chose Nicole Oresme, an ingenious philosopher whose aptitude and attitudes made him an effective supporter of the Valois monarchy.

It was the task of Oresme to take his text out of the language of a small but international community of scholars, and adapt it to serve the French people. He had to make something new of his native language, to invent a vocabulary for serious discourse. At the same time, he had to make something new of the *Politics*, to make it accessible to a new and broad audience. For this reason he interrupted his translation to make interpolations ranging from (sometimes ill-considered) identifications and etymologies to miniature treatises on Aristotle's view of apostolic poverty, or why an empire cannot be a *communitas perfecta*.

Nowhere in these glosses do we find the boldness or eccentricity of Oresme's near predecessors Marsilius of Padua and William of Ockham. No study of the *Livre de Politiques* is likely to disturb the judgment that Oresme gave his best to science. Nor will such a study prove that his glosses altered the course of political life. But we can claim for this commentary a rare value as a reflecting device. If it is worthwhile to ask, when reading the *Politics*, how this text would have struck an intellectual living at the center of political life in fourteenth-century France, we have one answer here. No occasional treatise follows the ancient text so closely. No university commentary takes the reader so close to the life of the time.

* * *

I should like to express thanks for the assistance of Marshall Clagett, Jürgen Deininger, Kenneth M. Setton, and Brian Tierney.

I. ORESME AND HIS VERSION OF THE *POLITICS*

The Life and Achievements of Nicole Oresme

Oresme was well fitted to stand at the crossroads of political thought and political life. At the least estimate an exceptionally intelligent man, he was a scholar at the center of European intellectual life, an adviser to one of the most learned and statesmanlike of medieval monarchs, and a bishop besides.

These are the outlines of his life. There are other, more oblique, aspects of Oresme's life which are not without importance. It is a matter of interest to us (and a matter of obvious pride to Oresme) that he was a Norman, that he came from a province which, having lately become a part of France, showed a paradoxically heightened loyalty to the crown.[1] Also, we should keep in mind that Oresme was one of the great scientists of his century.

During his life Oresme rose from obscurity to preeminence. In death, he returned to obscurity until the latter part of the nineteenth century, when interest in his work was revived.[2] Unless new evidence is found we shall

---

[1] See Joseph R. Strayer, "Normandy and Languedoc," *Medieval Statecraft and the Perspectives of History* (Princeton, 1971), 57–59. This article also appears in *Speculum* 44 (1969): 1–12.

[2] The most recent monograph on the life of Oresme is Paul Target's "Notice Biographique sur Nicolas Oresme," published in 1868 for the Société d'Émulation of Lisieux. This is approximately twelve pages long. More detailed is Francis Meunier's *Essai sur la vie et les ouvrages de Nicole Oresme* (Paris, 1857). For an account of Oresme's career as bishop of Lisieux, see H. de Formeville, *Histoire de l'ancien évêché-comté de Lisieux*, 2 vols. (Lisieux, 1873), 2: 139–146. Pierre Feret contributed an article of several pages (which disputes some of the conclusions of Meunier) to *La Faculté de théologie de Paris et ses docteurs les plus célèbres*, 4 vols. (Paris, 1894–1897), 3: 289–304. The enormous book of Émile Bridrey, *La théorie de la monnaie au XIVe siècle. Nicole Oresme. Étude d'histoire des doctrines et des faits économiques* (Paris, 1906) has a much broader scope than the title indicates and contains a formidable amount of information. The article by É. Amann in the *Dictionnaire de théologie catholique*, 15 vols. in 23 (Paris, 1903–1950), 11²: cols. 1405–1410, contains a concise account of the career and writings of Oresme.

The introductions of Albert Douglas Menut to his editions of the translations of Oresme provide a synthesis of old and new material as well as the background for each translation: *Le Livre de Ethiques d'Aristote* (New York, 1940); "Le Livre du ciel et du monde," edited in collaboration with Alexander J. Denomy and published in *Mediaeval Studies* 3 (1941): 185–280, 4 (1942): 159–297, and 5 (1943): 167–333, and also published by the University of Wisconsin (Madison, 1968); "Le Livre de Yconomique d'Aristote," *Transactions of the American Philosophical Society* 47 (1957): 783–853; and *Le Livre de Politiques d'Aristote. Transactions of the American Philosophical Society*, n. s. 60, pt. 6 (1970).

For the career of Oresme at the court of Charles V, the best sources are those on Charles himself. These will be examined below, chap. 3, n. 1.

The literature on the works of Oresme has been largely (and not unreasonably) devoted to his achievements in economics and science. This will be described below. Menut has compiled "A Provisional Bibliography of Oresme's Writings," for *Mediaeval Studies* 28 (1966): 279–299, with a supplementary note, ibid., 31 (1969): 346–347. Raphael Levy has described "Recent Studies of Nicole Oresme," in *Symposium* 13 (1959): 135–139.

1

never know much about the early life of Oresme. The year of his birth can be estimated on the basis of his progress at the University of Paris, where there were age requirements for the granting of degrees: a date in the early 1320s seems likely.[3] Of his childhood we know with certainty only that he was born in Normandy, probably in the region of Caen,[4] and of his family we know only that his surname comes from relation rather than location.[5] We may note the appearance of one Guillaume Oresme on the list of the College of Navarre for 1348.[6] There seems to have been a nephew of Nicole named Henri Oresme, who was a canon of Bayeux.[7]

Our first direct documentary evidence of Oresme comes from 1348, when he entered the College of Navarre at the University of Paris to study theology as a *boursier* or scholarship student.[8] He must by this time have completed several years of study in the Arts Faculty, and obtained his Master of Arts degree there.[9] During this period he probably met and studied with the celebrated rector of the University, Jean Buridan, who shared his scientific interests.[10] In 1356 Oresme took his degree in theology, and became grand master of his college.[11]

Oresme's career at the College of Navarre had ended by 23 November 1362, when he received his first benefice, a canonry at the cathedral of Notre Dame in Rouen.[12] This appointment was followed by others: a semi-prebend as canon at the Sainte-Chapelle (10 February 1363); a deanery at

---

[3] See Meunier, *Essai,* p. 3. Menut notes in his introduction to *Le Livre du ciel et du monde* (1968 publication), p. 8, n. 14, that a date of 1323 or later would not be consistent with the age requirement (35) for the master of theology degree Oresme received in 1356.

[4] Pierre Daniel Huet, *Les origines de la ville de Caen,* 2nd ed. (Rouen, 1706), 331, cited in Menut, *Le Livre de Politiques,* 13b. Allemagne, a (supposed) village near Caen, has been suggested as the site of Oresme's birth.

[5] Menut, *Le Livre de Politiques,* 13b–14a. For this reason the designation "Nicole de Oresme" is incorrect.

[6] Menut, *Le Livre du ciel et du monde* (1968), 8. Unfortunately, Guillaume, whose presence is also recorded at the College of Navarre in 1352 and 1353 and at Bayeux in 1376 (Menut, *Le Livre de Politiques,* 16b) has not been identified with certainty as a relative of Nicole.

[7] Menut, *Le Livre de Politiques,* 34a. Target ("Notice Biographique," p. 4, n. 1, cited ibid., p. 14a) gives other examples of men bearing this name, and writes that Oresmes were his contemporaries in Caen.

[8] Heinrich Denifle and Émile Chatelain, *Chartularium universitatis parisiensis, 1200–1452,* 4 vols. (Paris, 1891–1897), 2 (1891), 641, n. 3. See also C. E. Du Boulay, *Historia universitatis parisiensis,* 6 vols. (Paris, 1665–1673), 4 (1668): 977.

[9] Menut, *Le Livre du ciel et du monde* (1968), 8.

[10] Menut, *Le Livre de Politiques,* 14a. For the life of Buridan, see Edmond Faral, *Jean Buridan, Maître ès arts de l'Université de Paris,* from *Histoire littéraire de la France,* 38 (Paris, 1950). Oresme does not mention Buridan, but Buridan speaks in his *Quaestiones super tres libros Metheorum* of an observation made to him by "Reverendus Nicholaus Oresme" (see Jean Bulliot, "Jean Buridan et la mouvement de la terre," *Revue de Philosophie* 25 [1914]: 12).

[11] Denifle and Chatelain, *Chartularium,* 2: 641, n. 3.

[12] For Oresme's career in the church, see Denifle and Chatelain, *Chartularium,* 2: 641, n. 3, and Feret, *La Faculté de théologie,* 3: 295; Jean de Launoy, *Regii Navarrae gymnasii parisiensis historia,* 2 vols. (Paris, 1677), 1: 71–72; *Gallia christiana,* 16 vols. (Paris, 1759), 11: 788–789. On 23 May 1361, Oresme was granted a prebend as archdeacon at Bayeux. He lost this position as the result of a challenge set before the Parlement of Paris and based on a university regulation forbidding officials receiving sixty pounds a year to have additional income. The challenge came from one Simon Freron, a rather suspicious character who subsequently gathered the archdeaconry unto himself (Menut, *Le Livre de Politiques,* 17b).

Notre Dame in Rouen (18 March 1364); and finally his nomination to the see of Lisieux (16 November 1377), which he held until his death on 11 July 1382.

This is an impressive career, but Oresme is not remembered primarily as a grand master or bishop. He attained his greatest standing and influence as a royal servant. At some time before 1356, Oresme had attracted the attention of Jean II. The misfortunes of this king, who was soon to be defeated at the battle of Poitiers and carried off as a prisoner to England, included serious shortages of money, owing in large part to frequent changes in the value of the currency.[13] Jean asked Oresme for advice: the result was a sensible treatise whose counsels against the alteration of currency were followed in the absence of the king by his son and regent, the future Charles V.

It was Charles, an unheroic but conscientious king, who became the great patron of Oresme. For centuries Oresme was said to have been the *precepteur* of Charles the dauphin.[14] This designation, accurate or not, suggests the quality of the friendship between the king and his counselor, a friendship which lasted until the king's death in 1380. In addition to being the "amé et feal conseillier"[15] of Charles, Oresme described himself as "secretaire du roy" during the regency,[16] and as the "humble chapellain" of Charles during the latter's reign.[17]

Oresme also acted on occasion as a royal agent. Charles, while regent, sent him to negotiate a loan in Rouen,[18] and to preach before the pope in Avignon (Christmas Eve 1363).[19] Oresme was part of a delegation sent to escort the emperor Charles IV to Vincennes in early 1378,[20] and was a prominent participant in the funeral of the queen, Jeanne de Bourbon, in the same year.[21] Even as dean at Rouen, he was perhaps expected to serve the king by observing the possibly disloyal archbishop, Philippe d'Alençon.[22]

---

[13] Amann, in his article in the *Dictionnaire de théologie catholique* 11², col. 1408, says that between 1351 and 1360, the *livre tournois* changed value seventy-one times.

[14] See Charles Jourdain, "Nicole Oresme et les astrologues de la cour de Charles V," *Excursions historiques et philosophiques à travers le moyen âge* (Paris, 1888), 582, for a citation of a fifteenth-century manuscript (B.N. MS. fr. 1223, fol. 116rº–vº), containing the first use of this title: "son instructeur."

[15] From an act of 26 January 1377 (Léopold Delisle, *Mandements et actes divers de Charles V* [1364–1380], recueillis dans les collections de la Bibliothèque Nationale [Paris, 1874], 804, #1619).

[16] This description comes from an act of the Chambre des Comptes of 2 November 1369 (Bridrey, *Nicole Oresme*, 449, and Abraham Tessereau, *Histoire chronologique de la grande Chancellerie de France*, 2 vols. [Paris, 1705–1710], 1: 22).

[17] See the *prohemium* to Oresme's translation of the *Politics* (fol. 3c, p. 44a of Menut's edition).

[18] Bridrey, *Nicole Oresme*, 449.

[19] See, among several printed editions of the "Sermo coram papa Urbano V," "Juxta est salus mea ut veniat, et justitia mea ut reveletur," that in the *Catalogus testium veritatis* of Matthias Illyricus Flaccius (Basel, 1556).

[20] Roland Delachenal, *Chroniques des règnes de Jean II et de Charles V*, 4 vols. (Paris, 1910–1920), 2: 205; Louis Dubois, *Histoire de Lisieux*, 2 vols. (Lisieux, 1845), 1: 217–230.

[21] Delachenal, *Chroniques* 2: 281.

[22] Menut, *Le Livre de Politiques*, 18a with reference to Pierre Adolphe Cheruel, *Histoire de Rouen pendant l'époque communale 1150–1382*, 2 vols. (Rouen, 1843–1844), 2: 411–430.

We can only speculate about the less obvious services peformed by Oresme for the king, for example the influence of his advice on governmental practice.[23]

Science and economics are the two areas in which Oresme is often seen in his customary and peculiar role of precursor. One might propose as his sobriquet *Doctor anticipator,* for it has been his fate seldom to be discussed for his own sake, but rather in relation to someone other and greater than himself.[24] Some Oresme scholars have a wall-eyed aspect, turning one eye toward their subject and the other toward his more celebrated successors. His reputation soars when anticipation is admitted, and plummets when it is denied. In both cases little attention is paid to the value of the work itself. Time, however, is restoring the equilibrium of Oresme's position without any loss of praise.

A modest anticipation of Oresme by Oresme may be seen in his treatise on currency, which like the *Livre de Politiques* adapts Aristotle to serve practice as well as theory.[25] He tends to object to Aristotle's description of money as an artificial convention,[26] a description which could lead to what Bridrey calls the *théorie signe.*[27] This theory suggests that money need not be kept at an absolute value,[28] while the opposing *théorie marchandise,*[29] later asso-

---

[23] Oresme's translations of Aristotle might have influenced Charles to make changes in his government, specifically the choice of chancellors by election. See Siméon Luce, "De l'élection au scrutin de deux chanceliers de France sous le règne de Charles V," *Revue Historique* 16 (1881): 91–102.

[24] For example, see Jan Dijksterhuis, *The Mechanization of the World Picture* (Oxford, 1961), 164. For him Oresme was "the very medieval thinker whose affinity with later scientists was greatest" (ibid., p. 204). Similarly, Olaf Pedersen says that he was a figure who "can only be compared with the great geniuses of the early Renaissance" ("The Development of Natural Philosophy 1250–1350," *Classica et mediaevalia* 14 [1953]: 150).

[25] Modern study of this subject began with Louis Wolowski's *Traictie de la première invention des monnaies de Nicole Oresme: textes français et latin* (Paris, 1864). We have already mentioned Émile Bridrey, *La Théorie de la monnaie au XIVe siècle. Nicole Oresme. Étude d' histoire des doctrines et des faits économiques* (Paris, 1906). Other studies include: Charles Jourdain, "Mémoire sur les commencements de l'économie politique dan les écoles du moyen âge," in his *Excursions historiques et philosophiques à travers du moyen âge* (Paris, 1888): 421–462; Henry Hertrich, *Les Théories monétaires au XIVe siècle: Nicolas Oresme* (Lyons, 1899); T. W. Balch, *The Law of Oresme, Copernicus, and Gresham* (Philadelphia, 1908); Constantin Miller, *Studien zur Geschichte der Geldlehre: die Entwicklung im Altertum und im Mittelalter bis auf Oresmius* (Stuttgart and Berlin, 1925); Henri Laurent, *La Loi de Gresham au moyen âge: essai sur la circulation monétaire entre la Flandre et le Brabant á la fin du XIVe siècle* (Brussels, 1933); Hector Estrup, "Oresme and Monetary Theory," *Scandinavian Economic History Review* 14 (1966): 97–116.
A recent edition of Oresme's treatise has been produced by Charles Johnson, *The De moneta of Nicholas Oresme and English Mint Documents* (London, 1956). Johnson provides an English translation, which faces the Latin text. Wolowski (see above) is still the source for the French text. For the connection between the doctrines of Buridan and Oresme, see Rudolf Kaulla, "Der Lehrer des Oresmius," *Zeitschrift für die gesamte Staatswissenschaft* 60 (1904): 453–461. For a detailed bibliography on all aspects of Oresme's work, see Charles Lohr, "Medieval Latin Aristotle Commentaries," *Traditio* 28 (1972): 290–295.

[26] For Aristotle's theory of currency, see *Politics* 1. 9–10. 1256b–1258b. The purpose of money is also discussed in *Ethics* 5. 5. 1132b–1134a.

[27] *Nicole Oresme,* 110–113.

[28] *Ethics* 5.5. 1133a.

[29] *Nicole Oresme,* 110.

ciated with Oresme, makes of money a *natural* convention[30] which, having an intrinsic value,[31] is more than a sign.[32]

This is the basis of Oresme's advice,[33] to which he adds a list of the practical disadvantages of the alteration of currency.[34] His condemnation of all mutation save that required by emergency[35] doubtless influenced Charles's decision to return the coinage to a fixed ratio of silver and base metal (5 December 1360).[36] This was Oresme's immediate reward. Since then he has been granted, and then denied, the precursorship of Gresham,[37] criticized for lack of originality,[38] and admired for the skill of his borrowing and combining.[39]

This pattern is followed on a larger scale in the story of Oresme the scientist.[40] His graph-like figures are no longer seen as early examples of

[30] Ibid., 203.

[31] Ibid., 201.

[32] Ibid., 201.

[33] See Ernest Barker, *The Political Thought of Plato and Aristotle* (New York, 1906), 388–389, for a comparison between Oresme and Marsilius of Padua.

[34] Johnson, *The De moneta*, 30–35 (chaps. 19–21). This is the *locus* of Oresme's alleged anticipation of Gresham's Law. There is an addition to one of the manuscripts of the French version (Paris, B. N. MS. fr. 23926), an apparently later interpolation which contains a formula resembling this law. See Laurent, *La Loi de Gresham*, 89, and his "Le problème des traductions françaises du 'Traité des monnaies' de Nicole Oresme dans les Pays-Bas bourguignons," *Revue d'Histoire économique et sociale* 21 (1933): 13–24. See also chapter 20 of Oresme's treatise, for a notion similar to that of "bad money driving out good" (Johnson, 32).

[35] Oresme also opposed revenue from taxation (especially indirect taxes like the *gabelle*). See the *Livre de Politiques* 5. 4. (fol. 169a, p. 208a), and chapter 4 below.

[36] See François André Isambert, *Recueil général des anciennes lois françaises, depuis l'an 420 jusqu'à la révolution de 1789*, 29 vols. (Paris, 1821–1833), 5: 105–112. This policy was ended early in the reign of Charles's son. For evidence that Philip of Burgundy, brother of Charles V, made a copy of a French version of Oresme's treatise, for the use of his accounting officers, see Laurent, "Le problème des traductions."

[37] For references, see Menut's introduction to the *Livre de Politiques*, 15b, n. 14.

[38] Wilhelm Endemann, *Die nationaloekonomischen Grundsätze der canonistischen Lehre* (Jena, 1863), lists Bartolus, Hostiensis, Panormitanus and Innocent III among the contributors to Oresme's "half-canonist, half-civilian" doctrine.

[39] Bridrey, *Nicole Oresme*, 5.

[40] A bibliography should begin with the works of Pierre Duhem: *Études sur Léonard de Vinci*, 3 vols. (Paris, 1906–1913) and *Le système du Monde*, 10 vols. (Paris, 1913–1959). Anneliese Maier is less enthusiastic: *Die Impetustheorie der Scholastik* (Vienna, 1940); *An der Grenze von Scholastik und Naturwissenschaft* (Essen, 1943; revised, Rome, 1952); *Die Vorläufer Galileis im 14. Jahrhundert* (Rome, 1949) and *Metaphysische Hintergründe der spätscholastischen Naturphilosophie* (Rome, 1955). More recent work includes: Dana B. Durand, "Nicole Oresme and the Mediaeval Origins of Modern Science," *Speculum* 16 (1941): 167–185; Ernest A. Moody, "Laws of Motion in Medieval Physics," *Scientific Monthly* 72 (Jan.–June 1951): 18–23; Marshall Clagett, *The Science of Mechanics in the Middle Ages* (Madison, Wis., 1959); Edward Grant, "Late Medieval Thought, Copernicus, and the Scientific Revolution," *Journal of the History of Ideas* 23 (1962): 197–220; Marshall Clagett, "Nicole Oresme and Medieval Scientific Thought," *Proceedings of the American Philosophical Society* 108 (1964): 298–309; A. George Molland, "Oresme Redivivus," *History of Science* 8 (1969): 106–119; idem, "Nicole Oresme and Scientific Progress," *Miscellanea Mediaevalia* 9 (1974): 206–220; Stefano Caroti, "Nicole Oresme precursore di Galileo e di Descartes?" *Rivista critica di storia della filosofia* 32 (1977): 11–23, 413–435; and Edward Grant, "Scientific Thought in Fourteenth-Century Paris: Jean Buridan and Nicole Oresme," in Madeleine Pelner Cosman and Bruce Chandler, eds., *Machaut's World: Science and Art in the Fourteenth Century. Annals of the New York Academy of Sciences* 314 (New York, 1978): 105–124. See also the items mentioned above in n. 24.

analytical geometry:[41] we need only note that in the *Livre de Politiques* such figures occur.[42] Oresme's work on uniformly accelerated motion is acknowledged to fall far short of Galileo's,[43] but to be "clearly superior" to the work of the former's contemporaries.[44] Similarly, Oresme approaches the conclusions of Copernicus on the diurnal rotation of the earth,[45] but at last agrees with the Bible,[46] retreating (as some see it) into the role of a theologian.[47] Still, his arguments have been called worthy of Copernicus.[48]

Somewhere between this scientific study and the practical translations from Aristotle are Oresme's writings against astrology. In his attempts to cure Charles of his dangerous love of divination,[49] his counselor used traditional arguments[50] reinforced by an original and admirably abstruse demonstration based on irrational ratios.[51] Paradoxically, he was less skeptical of the possibilities of alchemy and witchcraft.[52]

When Oresme's reputation is not subjected to anachronistic praise or prejudice, he stands securely,[53] as "a significant figure in his own right."[54]

---

[41] Dijksterhuis, *Mechanization*, 194–195.

[42] For example in 5. 33. (fol. 212c, p. 254a), and in the *Livre de Ethiques* (ed. Menut [New York, 1940]), 5. 7. (fol. 95b, p. 286); 5. 10. (fol. 99a, p. 293); 5. 11. (fol. 100c, p. 296).

[43] John H. Randall, "The Medieval Roots of Galilean Science," from his *The Career of Philosophy*, 2 vols. (New York, 1962), 1: 278–279.

[44] Marshall Clagett, "Nicole Oresme and Medieval Scientific Thought," 304.

[45] Konstanty Michalski, "La physique nouvelle et ses différents courants philosophiques au XIVᵉ siècle," *La philosophie au XIVᵉ siècle: six études* (Frankfurt, 1969), 263.

[46] See *Le Livre du ciel et du monde* 2. 25. (1968 edition, 536–538).

[47] Edward Rosen, "Renaissance Science as seen by Burckhardt and his Successors," in *The Renaissance: A Reconsideration of the Theories and Interpretations of the Age*, ed. Tinsley Helton (Madison, Wis., 1961), 92.

[48] Dijksterhuis, *Mechanization*, 297.

[49] Gaston Dodu, "Les idées de Charles V en matière de gouvernement," *Revue des questions historiques*, 3rd ser. 14 (1929): 14, n. 7, says that there were around 300 books on divinatory science in Charles's library at the Tour du Louvre. For a list of astrological works copied for Charles, see George W. Coopland, *Nicole Oresme and the Astrologers. A Study of his Livre de divinacions* (Liverpool, 1952), 184–185. One of Oresme's three Latin tractates against astrology (see Menut, "A Provisional Bibliography," 288–289) begins: "Multi principes et magnates, noxia curiositate solliciti, vanis nituntur artibus occulta perquirere et investigare futura" (from *Tractatus contra astronomos*, in Coopland, *Oresme and Astrologers*, 123). The *Livre de Divinacions* was written for "personnes d'estat comme sont princes et seigneurs auxquels appartient le gouvernement publique" (Coopland, 50). Oresme's distrust of divination creeps into his *Livre de Ethiques*: "Il entent par Sophistes ceulz qui veulent apparoir et faignent que ilz scevent pluseurs grans choses, et il n'est pas ainsi; si comme sont divineurs et ceuls qui se dient savoir experimenz et choses merveilleuses" (9. 1. [fol. 178c, p. 453]). The fact that Oresme said such things while enjoying royal support has suggested to some that Charles was not really serious about astrology (see Victor LeClerc in *Histoire littéraire de la France* 24 [Paris, 1862]: 187).

[50] Coopland, *Oresme and Astrologers*, 39. Aristotle, Augustine, Cicero, Pliny, Seneca and Ptolemy are among the authors Oresme most frequently cited (ibid., 216).

[51] Edward Grant discusses this mathematical work in "Nicole Oresme and his *De proportionibus proportionum*," *Isis* 51 (1960): 311–313. See also Clagett, "Nicole Oresme and Medieval Scientific Thought," 302–303, for a description of this argument.

[52] Coopland, *Oresme and Astrologers*, 37–38. In the *Livre de Politiques* 2. 21., for example, Oresme mentioned bewitched persons among those who should be excluded from succession to kingdoms (fol. 65d, p. 109a).

[53] Maier has called him the greatest genius among fourteenth-century scientists (*An der Grenze von Scholastik und Naturwissenschaft*, 270). Pedersen has called him "the most prominent natural philosopher of the period immediately preceding the early renaissance" ("The Development of Natural Philosophy," 90).

[54] Clagett, "Nicole Oresme and Medieval Scientific Thought," 309.

Finally, what Durand has said about Oresme's habits of mind as a scientist may be applied to him as the author of the *Livre de Politiques*:

The commentator of this late period . . . was either reduced to the sterile repetition of familiar points, or impelled to wrest new and subtler interpretations from his text. To a thinker as fertile and ingenious as Oresme the second alternative was naturally the more attractive. . . . The genius of Oresme's mind lay in its facility for combining ideas, for detecting inter-relations between fields of thought which more pedestrian thinkers had failed to note.[55]

The Making of the *Livre de Politiques*[56]

Nicole Oresme lent his talents to the tradition of the *Politics* because his king saw in Aristotle an inspiration to good government. The *Livre de Politiques* is not an exercise intended for the university. Like the translations of *The City of God* made for Charles by Raoul de Presles, and Denis Foulechat's version of the *Policraticus* of John of Salisbury,[57] it is meant to supply the practical wisdom needed by a ruler.[58] The *Songe du Vergier* mentions

---

[55] "Nicole Oresme and the Mediaeval Origins of Modern Science," 178.

[56] For material on the *Livre de Politiques*, see Menut's introduction to his edition; Bridrey's *Nicole Oresme*, passim; Léopold Delisle, "Les Ethiques, les Politiques, et les Économiques d'Aristote traduites et copiés pour le roi Charles V," *Mélanges de paléographie et de bibliographie* (Paris, 1880): 257–282; Mario Grignaschi, "Nicole Oresme et son commentaire à la 'Politique' d'Aristote," *Album Helen Maud Cam*, 2 vols. (Louvain and Paris, 1960–1961), 1: 97–151, and Shulamith Shahar, "Nicolas Oresme, un penseur politique indépendant de l'entourage du roi Charles V," *L'Information historique* 32 (1970): 203–209. Shahar makes valuable comments about Oresme's opposition to the authority of Roman law and his relation to the other political writers around Charles V, but she seems, when speaking of Oresme's citation of the *Defensor Pacis*, to mistake quotation for approbation, and to describe as borrowings from Marsilius the use of ideas taken by both from Aristotle (204). Her view is accepted by Bernard Guenée, "Y a-t-il un État des XIVᵉ et XVᵉ siècles?" *Annales* 26. 1. (1971): 404. The book of Jeannine Quillet, *La Philosophie politique du Songe du Vergier* (1378). *Sources doctrinales* (Paris, 1977) contains extensive discussion (123–160) of the *Livre de Politiques*.

[57] See Léopold Delisle, *Le Cabinet des manuscrits de la Bibliothèque Nationale*, 4 vols. (Paris, 1868–1881), 1: 38–43, and Gaston Dodu, "Les ideés de Charles V en matière de gouvernement," *Revue des questions historiques*, 3rd ser. 14 (1929): 16, n. 4.

[58] The *Songe du Vergier* cites the ruler's need for learning: ". . . [the king of France] ayme science en laquelle il fait introduire et enseigner son aisné filz, affin qu'il ne gouverne pas son peuple par tyrannie" (ed. Jean Louis Brunet, in vol. 2 of Pierre Dupuy, *Traitez des droits et libertez de l'église gallicane*, rev. ed., 4 vols. [Paris, 1731–1751] : 134, *Songe* 1. 132.).

The royal translators themselves explained the purpose of their work. Pierre Bersuire, the "petit serviteur" of Jean II, said in the preface to his translation of Livy: "C'est tout certain . . . que tous excellens princes, de tant comme il ont l'enging plus clervoiant et de plus noble et vive qualité, de tant veul[en]t il plus volentiers encerchier et savoir les vertueus faiz et les notables oeuvres des princes anciens, et les senz d'armes, raisons et industries par lesquelles ilz conquistrent jadis les pays et les terres et ediffierent empires et royaumes . . . "(quoted in Charles Samaran's article on Bersuire in *Hist. litt. de la France* 39 [Paris, 1962]: 359). Raoul de Presles addressed Charles V in the *Cité de Dieu*: "Vous avez fait translater pluseurs livres, tant pour plaire à vous, comme pour proufiter à vos subgéz. . . . pour le proufit et utilité de vostre roiaume, de vostre pueple et de toute la chrestienté . . . " (quoted in Léopold Delisle, *Le Cabinet des manuscrits*, 1: 39).

For modern discussions of the motives of the translation project, see Dodu, "Les idées de Charles V," p. 17, and Jacques Monfrin, "Humanisme et traductions au Moyen Age," *Journal des savants*, July–September 1963, 172–177, who has remarked (176): ". . . l'oeuvre de Charles V est une oeuvre de politique, non d'humaniste; la notion d'utilité publique domine."

Charles's interest in the works of practical philosophy which were read to him each day.[59]

But why was a translation necessary?[60] Christine de Pisan assures us that Charles could read Latin, saying that he understood it well.[61] Indeed, he was among the most scholarly of medieval monarchs. We will see, however, that the chief virtue of Moerbeke's translation was fidelity, not clarity. Oresme, who admitted that he was more at ease with Latin than with French,[62] had trouble with this text.[63] Thus the version of Moerbeke was difficult to master for one with university training and a century of commentary available to him. For Charles it would have presented even greater problems.[64] Moreover, even if Charles was able to master the Latin *Politics* himself, he wished to make "les plus notables livres"[65] available to his counselors and to others who needed a French version.[66]

Oresme explains the purpose of his translations in the prologue to the *Livre de Ethiques*:

But because the ethical works of Aristotle were written in Greek, while we have them in a Latin version which is very hard to understand, the king has wished, for

---

[59] Brunet, p. 134, *Songe* 1. 132.

[60] *The Livre de Politiques* was not the first attempt to produce a French version of the *Politics*. A version had been made from Moerbeke's Latin in about 1305, by Pierre de Paris. This has been lost, but perhaps fortunately, according to Mario Roques, who wrote about Pierre de Paris for the *Hist. litt. de la France* (vol. 37 [Paris, 1938]), and had no high opinion of Pierre's prose (". . . [considering the work of Oresme] nous sommes presque tentés de bénir le hasard qui, en détruisant l'oeuvre de Pierre de Paris, nous épargne un spectacle qui n'aurait pu être qu'affligeant" [449]).

[61] ". . . non obstant que bien entendist le latin et que ja ne fust besoing que on lui exposast . . ." (*Le Livre des fais et bonnes meurs* 3. 12. [Solente 2: 43]). On the other hand, she said that his Latin was not "si en usage comme la lengue françoise" because of the "termes soubtilz" in the former language (ibid., 3. 3. [Solente 2: 13]).

[62] "Toutesvoies, quoique je dy, je le soubmet a la correction de ceulx a qui il appartient et supplie que on me ait pour excuse de la rude mainere de parler, car je n'ay pas aprins de (estre) acoustume de riens bailler ou escripre en francois" (from the prologue to the *Livre de Divinacions*, fol. 39 r2, from Coopland, *Oresme and Astrologers* [Liverpool, 1952], 50). See also *Le Livre de Politiques* 5. 18. (fol. 191d, p. 232b).

[63] In the *Livre de Politiques* 4. 6. (fol. 135b, p. 174a), he concludes a gloss by saying "Ce est ce qu'il me semble sans affermer; car le texte est obscur et les expositeurs ne sunt pas d'un acort." In 5. 15. (fol. 186c, p. 227a) he said that his text was obscure, poorly understood by the expositors, and "par aventure mal translaté en latin."

[64] A few generations before Oresme made his translations, Jean de Meun delicately explained to Philip IV why a translation of Boethius would be useful to that monarch: ". . . Boece de Consolacion, que je t'ay translaté de latin en françoys, jasoit ce que tu entendes bien latin; mais toutesvoies est moult plus legier à entendre le françoys que le latin" (from the article on Jean de Meun by Paulin Paris in the *Hist. litt. de la France* 28 [Paris, 1881]: 409).

[65] Christine de Pisan, *Le Livre des fais et bonnes meurs* 3.12. (ed. Solente, 2: 43).

[66] Earlier one might have expected that the majority of the king's counselors would be clergymen at ease with Latin as well as the vernacular. Charles's translation program reminds us of the process described by Joseph Strayer in "The Laicization of French and English Society in the Thirteenth Century" (*Speculum* 15 [1940]: 76–86; also in *Medieval Statecraft and the Perspectives of History* [Princeton, 1971]: 251–265; see also the foreword to this book by Gaines Post, xi). Whatever the reason, it seems that at the time of Charles V "le latin était en voie de disparition à la cour" (Josette A. Wisman, "L'éveil du sentiment national au Moyen Age: le pensée politique de Christine de Pisan," *Revue historique* 257 [1977]: 297).

the common good, to have them translated into French, in order that his counselors and others may be enabled better to understand them.[67]

In the same prologue he mentions the remark of Cicero that weighty works are most agreeable when written in the language of one's country, and praised the French language and people.[68] He also spoke in general terms of the usefulness of knowledge to the ruler.[69]

The interest of his ruler in Oresme's translation project[70] is clear from the royal records. In a letter from the king to the canons of Rouen, where Oresme had been appointed dean, he asks their indulgence while their new superior remained in Paris to finish this project.[71] Regular payments were made to Oresme from 1370 to 1374.[72] His appointment to the see of Lisieux may be regarded as a final reward for his work on Aristotle.[73] The extent of the royal supervision is not clear: Oresme did say that the *Livre de Politiques* had been brought from obscurity to clarity under the guidance of the king.[74]

In making his translations Oresme confronted problems which, while not unprecedented, made his task more difficult than that of a Latin commentator.[75] He was obliged to give a new form not only to Aristotle but to the

---

[67] Fol. 1d, p. 99, in the edition of Menut.

[68] "Et, pour certain, translater telz livres en françois et baillier en françois les arts et les sciences est un labeur moult proffitable; car c'est un langage noble et commun a genz de grant engin et de bonne prudence. Et comme dit Tulles en son livre de *Achademiques*, les choses pesantes et de grant auctorité sont delectables et bien aggreables as genz ou langage de leur païs" (ibid., fol. 2a, p. 101). See also the prologue to the *Livre de Politiques* (fol. 4a–b, p. 44b). Perhaps the Cicero he mentions is actually *De natura deorum* 1. 3. 7. (p. 10 in the Loeb edition with trans. by H. Rackham [London and New York, 1933]) ". . . ipsius rei publicae causa philosophiam nostris hominibus explicandum putavi, magni existimans interesse ad decus et ad laudem civitatis res tam gravis tamque praeclaras Latinis etiam litteris contineri."

[69] *Le Livre de Ethiques*, fol. 1b, p. 98.

[70] See Menut, *Le Livre de Ethiques*, introd., 15–18. In his introduction to *Le Livre de Politiques* (p. 19b) Menut uses the prologue of the *Ethiques* to show that the first redaction of that work (which was done before the *Livre de Politiques*) was finished in 1370. Only a short time would have been required for revisions on the *Ethiques*; the work on the *Livre de Politiques* was probably begun early in 1371, with the first redaction done by 21 February 1372. This is the date of the first election of a royal chancellor, an experiment Menut feels was influenced by the *Livre de Politiques*. The first redaction was amended at least two times (see Menut's introduction, 19–20).

[71] See Bridrey, *Nicole Oresme*, 454–455, n. 5, from *Reg. capitulaires de Notre-Dame de Rouen* (Arch. Seine-Inférieure, G. 2118), a deliberation of 28 August 1372.

[72] A gift to Oresme of two hundred *franz d'or* was made on 31 August 1374 (Léopold Delisle, *Mandements et actes divers de Charles V* [1364–1380] [Paris, 1874], p. 552, # 1061; see also p. 458). This is the last time this work (along with the *Livre de Yconomique*) is mentioned in the treasury accounts (Menut, introduction to the *Livre de Politiques*, 20a). See also Delisle, *Le Cabinet des manuscrits* 1: 41–42, and his *Recherches sur la librarie de Charles V, Roi de France*, 2 vols. (Paris, 1907), 1: 104–105 and appendix X (p. 379).

[73] Oresme said in the conclusion of his translation of *De caelo et mundo*, the last (1377; Menut, *Le Livre de Politiques*, 20a) to be completed of his commented translations: "Et ainsi à l'aide de Dieu, je [ay] acompli le livre *Du Ciel et du monde* au commandement de tres excellent prince Charles, quint de ce nom, par la grace de Dieu roy de France, lequel en ce faisant m'a fait evesque de Lisieux" (4. 12. [fol. 203c, p. 730], from the 1968 edition by Menut and Denomy).

[74] Fol. 4b, p. 45a.

[75] Menut, in his introduction to the *Livre de Politiques*, 28b–29b, mentions examples of vernacular translations made before the time of Oresme. For further information, see Paulin

French language, which lacked the style and vocabulary appropriate to reasoned discourse.[76] In spite of these handicaps Oresme achieved a remarkable clarity and precision of expression[77] while conserving the habits of writing which he had acquired in his university training.[78] In doing so he enriched the vocabulary of the French language by hundreds of words, even at the lowest estimate,[79] and aided his readers by appending to his translation a "Table des expositions des fors mos de *Politiques*," "qui ne sunt pas en commun parler."[80]

A flexible form suited his purpose, allowing him to interrupt his text for necessary explanations or when he reached a point of departure for a short (or long) essay. His glosses vary greatly in content, and vary in length from mere phrases to discourses covering several folios in manuscript. A list of

---

Paris's article on Jean de Meun (n. 64, above); R. R. Bolgar, *The Classical Heritage and its Beneficiaries* (Cambridge, 1954), for its appendix 2, which contains lists of "Translations of Greek Authors into the Vernaculars before 1600" (508–525) and "Translations of Latin Authors into the Vernaculars" (526–541); Jean Rychner, "Observations sur la traduction de Tite-Live par Pierre Bersuire," *Journal des savants,* October–December 1963, 242–267, which contains a detailed discussion of Bersuire's methods of translation; and two articles by Jacques Monfrin, "Humanisme et traductions au Moyen Age," *Journal des savants,* July–September 1963, 161–190, and "Les Traducteurs et leur public au Moyen Age," ibid., January–March 1964, 5–20.

[76] Mahieu le Vilain, who translated Aristotle's *Meteorologica* into French in the mid-thirteenth century, made a complaint which might have come from Oresme: "Mes sachiés: l'en ne puet pas si proprement translater science en franchois comme en latin" (cited in Menut's introduction to the *Livre de Politiques,* 28b, from the edition of Rolf Edgren, *Mahieu le Vilain, Les Metheores d'Aristote* [Uppsala, 1945], fol. 1ᵛ, p. 1). Pierre Bersuire joined the chorus: ". . . n'avons en langage françois nulz propres mos semblables qui toutes cestes choses puissent segnefier" (from his preface to the Livy translation, quoted in Charles Samaran's article in the *Hist. litt. de la France* 39 [Paris, 1962]: 360).

[77] Meunier, *Essai sur la vie . . . de Nicole Oresme,* p. 100, calls his style "sain, ferme, vigoreux." Oresme is praised by Victor LeClerc (in the *Hist. litt. de la France* 24 [Paris, 1862]: 182) for his "concision et . . . fermété de style," and described as one of the first writers who gave to French prose "son caractère exact et précis" (572).

[78] ". . . son style restera latin, le tour sera calqué sur la syntaxe latine, il traduira Aristote sur le texte latin, ou plutôt il ne traduira pas, il transposera" (Louis Petit de Jullevile, "Les origines de la Renaissance en France. Nicolas Oresme," *Revue des cours et conférences,* 2nd ser. 4 [April–July 1896]: 208–209). See also Meunier, *Essai,* 144–161, and Menut's edition, 27–33.

[79] Menut attributes to Oresme the introduction of a thousand words (introduction to the *Livre de Politiques,* 11a, 28a), and estimates that nearly thirty percent of the words he coined are still in use today (ibid., 28a). On the other hand, Robert A. Taylor, "Les Néologismes chez Nicole Oresme, traducteur du XIVᵉ siècle," *Actes du Xᵉ Congrès International de Linguistique et Philologie Romanes,* part 4, vol. 2 (Paris, 1965): 727–736, has disagreed with Menut, and suggested 450 as a more likely figure. (He provides a list as well.) Meunier, *Essai,* 161–205, gives a lexicon of Oresme's usage, without reference to the place where each word appears in Oresme's works.

[80] Fols. 325c–329d, 369b–374b in Menut. Oresme was not the first translator to add such a glossary. Pierre Bersuire was perhaps the first to do this, in his Livy translation. (See Samaran's article, 382–384, which lists other examples, including Oresme, on pp. 382–383, n. 1.) Jean Daudin, who translated Petrarch's *De remediis utriusque fortunae* for Charles V, directed his readers to Bersuire's lexicon for words not found in his own: "Neantmoins, en laisse je plusieurs a exposer, pour ce que on les pourra trouver au commencement dela translacion que le prieur de Saint Eloy fist sur le livre de Titus-Livius" (see the Samaran article, 382–383, n. 1, Monfrin's article "Les Traductuers et leur public," p. 10, and Léopold Delisle, "Anciennes traductions françaises du traité de Pétrarque sur les remèdes de l'une et l'autre fortune," in *Notices et Extraits* 34. 1 [1891]: 295).

the types of glosses used by Oresme appears below, beginning with the most superficial:

1. *Directions to the text.* In one variety, Oresme indicates the purpose of a bit of the text. Another subspecies gives a cross-reference within the *Politics*. Another is the recapitulation of items from the text. Sometimes he uses short glosses to finish a sentence which seems incomplete (or was incomplete, in the Latin translation he used).

2. *Identifications and definitions.* Oresme has some difficulty here, especially when contending with transliterated Greek words from one of his Latin texts. His sense of geography is occasionally very confused (as we shall see by comparing his work with that of earlier commentators). Most of the notes, however, are sound and useful.

3. *Etymologies.* Oresme knew almost no Greek, but, continuing the tradition of Isidore of Seville, he produced explanations which Menut describes as "ridiculous"[81] and "fantastic."[82] He derived the name of Megara from the Greek *mega*, "because it was large."[83]

4. *Explanatory examples.* Most of Oresme's references to contemporary life occur here. For example, while discussing the disadvantages of lifetime tenure for officials, he mentioned the cases of *bailliages* and *prevostés*.[84] While considering the problem of succession in the Carthaginian constitution, he referred (though not by name) to the Salic law and its provision excluding succession through females, a matter of some importance to France during the Hundred Years War.[85]

5. *Parallel texts.* Many short glosses introduce verses from the Bible, or extracts from classical works, as parallels to, or support for, Aristotle.[86] Sometimes he used a gloss to compare an idea expressed in the *Politics* with one found in another work of Aristotle, as in 2. 3., where he reconciled an apparent contradiction between two statements about the preeminence of the common good.[87] Sometimes Oresme used a gloss to draw together citations from a variety of sources, as in 3. 4., where he cited Euripides, Sallust, Virgil and Isaiah on the knowledge necessary for rulers and subjects.[88]

6. *Textual explanations.* Often with the aid of material from earlier commentaries, Oresme explained the meaning of obscure or ambiguous sentences or phrases. Sometimes he introduced without criticism an opinion

---

[81] *Le Livre de Politiques* 4. 7. (fol. 135b, p. 174a).

[82] Ibid., 4. 21. (fol. 157b, p. 196b).

[83] Ibid., 5. 8. (fol. 175d, p. 215b).

[84] Ibid., 2. 17. (fol. 60c, p. 103a).

[85] Ibid., 2. 21. (fol. 65d, p. 109a).

[86] E. g., 3. 14. (fols. 97d–98a, p. 138a), from *Politics* 3. 11. 1282b (Barker, p. 127). The gloss reads: "Aussi comme se les gouverneurs de teles policies deissent en leur cuer ce que est escript, Sapientie .ii? capitulo: Sit fortitudo nostra lex injusticie." The reference is to verse 2: 11, which speaks of "iustitiae."

[87] Fol. 35c–d, p. 78b. (See *Politics* 2. 3. 1261b.)

[88] Ibid., 3. 4. (fol. 80b–d, p. 121b).

which differed from his own, as in 2. 15., where he tried to explain *fer au marché*.[89] At other times, he made objections, especially against the exposition of Albertus Magnus.[90] Oresme did not always identify his sources. In 1. 7., for example, there is a reference to the opinions of "aucuns docteurs."[91]

7. *Critical observations.* Occasionally Oresme went beyond the explication of his text to interject his own opinions. In 3. 19., he objected to Aristotle's apparent suggestion that in the ideal state men can be banished for having "political strength, or wealth, or an abundance of connexions," although saying that his response suited the intention of Aristotle.[92]

8. *Small treatises or essays.* These differ from the glosses in the previous categories in that they are longer and more elaborately constructed; they resemble scholastic *quaestiones*. (Some of those listed below, as numbers 3, 8, 9, 11 and 13, are described as "question[s]" in Oresme's "Table des Notables.") In the manuscript used by Menut for his edition of the *Livre de Politiques*,[93] there are thirteen glosses which cover the equivalent of one folio or more. (This is a purely arbitrary division-point between observations, explanations, treatises and essays, but some choice must be made.) The locations and subjects of these glosses are listed below:

	Pages (Menut)	Folios	Subject
1.	83a–83b	40c–42a	Voluntary poverty
2.	149a–150b	108d–110d	Kingship in the Old Testament
3.	153a–156b	112d–117b	Election vs. succession
4.	159a–161b	119d–125a	Rule by law (in the church)
5.	189a–b	149c–150c	The church and Aristotle's middle polity
6.	203b–205a	164d–166b	Sedition
7.	242b–244b	201a–203d	Moderate kingship
8.	285a–286b	242c–244d	The active and contemplative lives
9.	289b–294b	247c–253b	Universal monarchy (the longest of his glosses)
10.	297a–299a	255c–257c	Geography and the distribution of power
11.	302a–304b	260b–263a	The necessity of a sacerdotal element in the state
12.	306b–308b	264d–266d	Voluntary poverty
13.	311a–314a	269a–272b	Property and jurisdiction in the church

[89] Ibid., fol. 55a, p. 97b. The exposition is in fact that of Thomas Aquinas (see Menut's note and the edition of Spiazzi, p. 95, #291).

[90] A typical conclusion to one of these glosses, from 3. 20. (fol. 108a, p. 148a), is "Et Albert l'expose autrement, mes il ne se acorde pas ou texte."

[91] Ibid., fol. 17a, p. 59a.

[92] Fols. 104d–105a, p. 145a. The text of *Politics* 3. 13. 1284b is from Barker, 136.

[93] Avranches, Bibliothèque Municipale, MS. 223.

Two long glosses which miss the one-folio length should be added because of the importance of their subjects:

14.	59a–60a	16d–17d	Natural slavery
15.	319a–320a	276d–277c	Aristotelian ecclesiology

This list gives a hint of the subjects to be considered after a brief description of Oresme's place in the commentary tradition of the *Politics*.

II. ORESME AND THE COMMENTARY TRADITION OF THE *POLITICS*

The Predecessors of Oresme

When Oresme began his translations, the Aristotelian revival in the West was over two centuries old.[1] The twelfth century had seen the greatest progress in translation since Boethius:[2] by 1200, the greater part of the treatises had been rendered into Latin.[3] The thirteenth century brought, along with the contributions of Robert Grosseteste and William of Moerbeke, Latin versions of the commentaries of Averroës, which did much to enliven academic life. But by the middle of the fourteenth century, Aristotelianism was less a censored heresy than a compromised orthodoxy.[4]

---

[1] See Martin Grabmann, "Forschungen über die lateinischen Aristotelesübersetzungen des 13. Jahrhunderts," *Beiträge zur Geschichte der Philosophie des Mittelalters* 17 (1916), pts. 5–6; E. K. Rand, "The Classics in the Thirteenth Century," *Speculum* 4 (1929): 249–269: Martin Grabmann, "Studien über den Einfluss der aristotelischen Philosophie auf die mittelalterlichen Theorien über das Verhältnis von Kirche und Staat," *Sitzungsberichte der Bayerischen Akademie der Wissenschaften zu München. Philosophisch — historische Abteilung* (hereafter known as *SBAW*), 1934, pt. 2: 3–163; Georges de Lagarde, review of this article, in *Revue historique de droit français et étranger*, 4th ser. 15 (1936): 360–364; Martin Grabmann, "Methoden und Hilfsmittel des Aristotelesstudiums im Mittelalter," *SBAW* 1939, part 5: 3–198; George Lacombe, *Aristoteles latinus, codices descripsit* . . . , 26 vols. (Rome, 1939), and additions to this including the *Supplementa altera* by Pierre Michaud-Quantin (Paris and Bruges, 1961); Richard McKeon, "Aristotelianism in Western Christianity," in John Thomas McNeill, Matthew Spinka, and Harold T. Willoughby, eds., *Environmental Factors in Christian History* (Chicago, 1939): 207–231; Daniel Callus, "The Introduction of Aristotelian Learning at Oxford," *Proceedings of the British Academy* 29 (1943): 229–281; Martin Grabmann, *Guglielmo di Moerbeke, O. P. il traduttore delle opere di Aristotele* (Rome, 1946); Fernand Van Steenberghen, *Aristote en Occident. Les origines de l'aristotélisme parisien* (Louvain, 1946), and the revised version, in the English translation of Leonard Johnston, *Aristotle in the West. The Origins of Latin Aristotelianism* (Louvain, 1955); Jean Dunbabin, "Aristotle in the Schools," in Beryl Smalley, ed., *Trends in Medieval Political Thought* (Oxford, 1965): 65–85; Marie-Thérèse d'Alverny, "Les Traductions d'Aristote et de ses commentateurs," *Revue de synthèse*, 3rd ser. 49 (1968): 125–144. For extremely detailed bibliography, see the series of articles by Charles Lohr on "Medieval Latin Aristotle Commentaries," in *Traditio*: 23 (1967): 313–413, for authors A–F; 24 (1968): 149–245, for G–I; 26 (1970): 135–216, for Jacobus-Johannes Juff; 27 (1971): 251–351, for Johannes de Kanthi-Myngodus; 28 (1972): 281–396, for Narcissus-Richardus; 29 (1973): 93–197, for Robertus-Wilgelmus, and 30 (1974): 119–144, for a supplement.

[2] McKeon, "Aristotelianism," 213–214.

[3] Steenberghen, *Aristotle in the West*, 62–63.

[4] By this time, for example, inceptors in the Faculty of Arts at the University of Paris had to swear to teach nothing contrary to the doctrines of Aristotle. See Hastings Rashdall, *The Universities of Europe in the Middle Ages*, revised edition in 3 volumes, edited by F. M. Powicke and A. B. Emden (Oxford, 1936), 1: 369, n. 2., with reference to C. E. Du Boulay, *Historia universitatis parisiensis*, 6 vols. (Paris, 1665–1673), 4 (1668): 275.

As Rand says ("The Classics in the Thirteenth Century," 260), Aristotle was "first ostracized, then tolerated, then prescribed."

Aristotle's *Politics* reached western Europe later than his other works. Islamic writers knew it only in fragments, and produced no commentary.[5] Latin writers mentioned[6] and tried to describe[7] it. By about 1270 William of Moerbeke had made available to them the treatise promised at the end of the *Ethics*.[8] His work on the *Politics* may have been done in two stages.[9] Three manuscripts of a translation of the first two books have been found, each ending with the explanation that the rest of the work was not available.[10] This first attempt seems to date from 1264, while the complete version was done around 1269. The latter was an entirely new effort, which showed a greater tendency to Latinize words which had merely been transliterated in the incomplete version. (Oresme used both. His attempts to explain half-Greek words from "l'autre translacion" are sometimes bizarre.[11]) The second version, though shorn of Greek terms, was made with such scrupulous fidelity to the original syntax that it frustrated Latin-trained readers.[12]

The new translation was followed almost immediately by commentaries,[13] each written in a form suited to the purposes of the author, and

---

[5] Richard Walzer, *Greek into Arabic. Essays on Islamic Philosophy* (Oxford, 1962), 243. Averroës said that he had been unable to find a copy of it (Émile Bridrey, *La théorie de la monnaie au XIVᵉ siècle. Nicole Oresme. Étude d'histoire des doctrines et des faits économiques* [Paris, 1906], 353, n. 1, citing the *Commentar. in Platonis Rempublicam* [Venice, 1562], in-4, fol. 336).

[6] Martin, "Some Medieval Commentaries," 30, n. 7, with reference to L. Baur, "Dominicus Gundissalinus, De Divisione Philosophiae," *Beiträge zur Geschichte der Philosophie des Mittelalters* 4 (1903), pts. 2–3: 136.

[7] Martin Grabmann, "Die mittelalterlichen Kommentare zur Politik des Aristoteles," *SBAW*, 1941, 2, pt. 10: 9.

[8] *Ethics* 10. 9. 1181b.

[9] See Grabmann, *Guglielmo di Moerbeke*, and, for Moerbeke's translation of the *Politics*, see Franz Susemihl, *Aristotelis Politicorum libri octo, cum vetusta translatione Guilelmi de Moerbeka* (Leipzig, 1872).

[10] Concerning the manuscripts of the *translatio prior*, see Pierre Michaud-Quantin, *Politica. Translatio prior imperfecta interprete Guillelmo de Moerbeka (?)*. *Aristoteles Latinus* 29¹ (Bruges, 1961).

[11] See Albert Douglas Menut, *Maistre Nicole Oresme. Le Livre de Politiques d'Aristote. Transactions of the American Philosophical Society*, n. s. 60, pt. 6 (Philadelphia, 1970), 25b–26a. (Column letters have been added for easier consultation of Menut.)

[12] The conscientious work of Moerbeke, which has been useful to modern scholars seeking to reconstruct the text of Aristotle (Mario Grignaschi, "Nicole Oresme et son commentaire à la 'Politique' d'Aristote," *Album Helen Maud Cam*, 2 vols. [Louvain-Paris, 1960–1961], 1: 98; Menut, *Le Livre de Politiques*, 24), was not received with universal approbation, and was even attacked for inaccuracy. Roger Bacon complained: "Wilielmus iste Flemingus, ut notum est omnibus Parisiis literatis, nullam novit scientiam in lingua graeca, de qua praesumit, et ideo omnia transfert falsa et corrumpit sapientiam Latinorum" (cited in W. L. Newman, *The Politics of Aristotle*, 4 vols. [Oxford, 1887–1902]; 2: xliv–xlv, n. 3). Newman also cites the judgment of Sepulveda: "vix enim eos in numero interpretum habendos puto, qui verbum verbo inepta quadam fidelitate reddunt."

[13] For general treatments of the commentaries on the *Politics*, see: Ferdinand Edward Cranz, "Aristotelianism in Medieval Political Theory. A Study of the Reception of the Politics" (Ph.D. dissertation, Harvard University, 1938); Martin Grabmann, "Die mittelalterlichen Kommentare zur Politik des Aristoteles," *SBAW*, 1941, 2, pt. 10; Conor Martin, "The Commentaries on the *Politics* of Aristotle in the Late Thirteenth and Early Fourteenth Centuries" (Ph.D. dissertation, Oxford University, 1949); idem, "Some Medieval Commentaries on Aristotle's *Politics*," *History* 36 (1951): 29–44; Pawel Czartoryski, "Gloses et commentaires inconnus sur la Politique d'Aristote d'après les Mss. de la Bibliothèque Jagellone de Cracovie," *Mediaevalia Philoso-*

bearing the impress of his personality. One of the most complete descriptions of these forms is found in the preface to Charles Lohr's "Medieval Latin Aristotle Commentaries."[14] Under the heading "commentaries proper," whose purpose is to explain the text, he lists the *glossa*, used for difficult passages, the *commentum* or *expositio*, in which the text is analyzed bit by bit, and the paraphrase. A second form is the series of *quaestiones*, based on controversial points in the text. A third is the treatise independent of the commented text.[15] Although treatises are not commentaries, strictly speaking, they may lean heavily upon a particular source. Thus the first section of the *Defensor Pacis* of Marsilius of Padua might be called a commentary on the *Politics*.[16] Other important Aristotelian treatises are the *De Regimine Principum* begun by Thomas Aquinas and finished after his death (1274) by Ptolemy of Lucca,[17] the *De Regimine Principum* of Giles of Rome, written ca. 1285,[18] the *De regia potestate et papali* of John of Paris (John

---

phica Polonorum 5 (1960): 3–44; Mario Grignaschi, "La Définition du 'civis' dans la scolastique," *Anciens pays et assemblées d'états* 35 (1966): 70–100, and Lowrie J. Daly, "Medieval and Renaissance Commentaries on the *Politics* of Aristotle," *Duquesne Review* 13 (1968): 41–55. Bibliography for the individual commentaries will appear below.

[14] *Traditio* 23 (1967): 313.

[15] It would be difficult to bring these treatises into a discussion of the commentaries, which bear a quite different relation to the text of Aristotle. We can guess that the commentator's remarks have been suggested by his text although we cannot be sure that we are reading his own opinion. We are more certain of the opinions of the author of a treatise, but less certain of their source. Nevertheless, these works must be introduced here, because they equal or surpass the commentaries in quality of thought and in influence.

[16] The Latin text of the *Defensor Pacis* (ca. 1324) is available in editions by Charles W. Previté-Orton (Cambridge, 1928), and Richard Scholz (Hanover, 1932). There is an English translation by Alan Gewirth, *Marsilius of Padua. The Defender of Peace*, 2 vols. (New York, 1951–1956) and a French translation with commentary by Jeannine Quillet, *Le Défenseur de la paix* (Paris, 1968). For Marsilius and Aristotle, see M. Guggenheim, "Marsilius von Padua und die Staatslehre des Aristoteles," *Historische Vierteljahrschrift* 7 (1904): 343–360, who emphasizes Marsilius's adaptation of Aristotle; John W. Allen, "Marsilio of Padua and Mediaeval Secularism," *The Social and Political Ideas of Some Great Mediaeval Thinkers*, ed. F. J. C. Hearnshaw (London, 1923): 167–191; C. W. Previté-Orton, "Marsiglio of Padua. Part II: Doctrines," *English Historical Review* 38 (1923): 1–21; Georges de Lagarde, "Une adaptation de la Politique d'Aristote au XIVᵉ siècle," *Revue historique de droit français et étranger*, 4th ser. 11 (1932): 227–269; and Mario Grignaschi, "Le rôle de l'aristotélisme dans le 'Defensor Pacis' de Marsile de Padoue," *Revue d'histoire et de philosophie religieuses* 35 (1955): 301–340, who says that Marsilius deliberately misused Aristotle to create a social contract theory. See also Jeannine Quillet, *La Philosophie politique de Marsile de Padoue. L'Église et l'État au Moyen Age* 14 (Paris, 1970).

[17] This is available in Latin editions by Joseph Mathis (Turin, 1924) and Raymond M. Spiazzi (in the *Opuscula Philosophica* [Turin, 1954], 253–358). The section by Aquinas is available in English translation by Gerald B. Phelan, with an introduction and notes by I. Th. Eschmann: *On The Governance of Rulers* (Toronto, 1949). See also Joseph Anton Endres, "De regimine principum des hl. Thomas von Aquin," *Festschrift Clemens Baeumker* (Münster, 1913): 261–267, and Ezio Flori, "Il trattato 'De regimine principum' e le dottrine politiche di S. Tommaso," *Scuola cattolica*, 7th ser. 4 (1924): 134–169, for a denial of the dual authorship of the treatise. On Ptolemy, see Karl Krüger, *Des Ptolemäus Lucensis Leben und Werke* (Göttingen, 1874), and Alfred O'Rahilly, "Notes on St. Thomas. IV. 'De Regimine Principum'; V. Tholomeo of Lucca, the Continuator of the 'De Regimine Principum,'" *Irish Ecclesiastical Record*, 5th ser. 31 (1928): 396–410, 606–614.

[18] There is no modern edition of this treatise. Samuel P. Molenaer published a French version from the thirteenth or fourteenth century, *Li livres du gouvernement des rois* (New York, 1899), which includes a list of old Latin editions.

Quidort), written ca. 1301–1302,[19] the *De bono communi* of Remigio da Girolami (d. 1319),[20] and the *De monarchia* of Dante (d. 1321).[21] The other forms of commentary are briefer, and scarcely figure in a comparison with the *Livre de Politiques.*[22]

The commentaries on the *Politics* available both to Oresme and to us are those of Albertus Magnus (ca. 1200–1280), Thomas Aquinas (ca. 1225–1274)/Peter of Auvergne (d. 1304),[23] Walter Burley (ca. 1275–at least 1344), and Jean Buridan (ca. 1300–after 1358).[24]

The commentary of Albertus Magnus[25] is for the most part a literal exposition of the text,[26] which is analyzed part by part, with a *commentarius*

---

[19] For the Latin text see Melchior Goldast, *Monarchia s. Romani imperii*, 3 vols. (Hanover, 1611–1642), 2: 108–147, and Jean Leclerq, *Jean de Paris et l'ecclésiologie du XIIIᵉ siècle* (Paris, 1942): 173–260. For a critical edition and German translation, see Fritz Bleienstein, *Über königliche und päpstliche Gewalt* (Stuttgart, 1969). There is an English translation by John Watt, *On Royal and Papal Power* (Toronto, 1971). See also M. F. Griesbach, "John of Paris as a Representative of Thomistic Political Philosophy," *An Étienne Gilson Tribute*, ed. Charles J. O'Neil (Milwaukee, 1959): 33–50, and Thomas Renna, "The Populus in John of Paris' Theory of Monarchy," *The Legal History in Review* 42 (1974): 243–268.

[20] For excerpts see Richard Egenter, "Gemeinnutz vor Eigennutz: Die soziale Leitidee im 'Tractatus de bono communi' des Fr. Remigius von Florenz (*1319)," *Scholastik* 9 (1934): 79–92. See also Lorenzo Minio-Palluelo, "Remigio Girolami's *De bono communi*: Florence at the Time of Dante's Banishment and the Philosopher's Answer to the Crisis," *Italian Studies* 11 (1956): 56–71; Charles T. Davis, "Remigio de' Girolami and Dante: a comparison of their conceptions of peace," *Studi Danteschi* 36 (1959): 105–136, and idem, "An Early Florentine Political Theorist: Fra Remigio de' Girolami," *Proceedings of the American Philosophical Society* 104 (1960): 662–676.

[21] Citations here will be from the edition of L. Bertalot (Florence and Rome, 1920). For Dante's use of Aristotle, see Allan A. Gilbert, "Had Dante Read the *Politics* of Aristotle?" *Publications of the Modern Language Association* 43, no. 3 (1928): 602–613, and Larry Peterman, "Dante's *Monarchia* and Aristotle's Political Thought," *Studies in Medieval and Renaissance History* 10 (1973): 1–40.

[22] These include the *abbrevatio* or *compendium*, containing summaries of the material in the subject book; the *conclusiones*; the compilations of excerpts called *flores* or *auctoritates*, and the *tabulae*, or alphabetical lexicons.

[23] There also exist unpublished questions on the *Politics* by Peter of Auvergne, which have not been much studied. See Lohr, "Medieval Latin Aristotle Commentaries," *Traditio* 28 (1972): 343.

[24] For evidence of other commentaries, see the Lohr articles in *Traditio* 23 (1967)–31 (1975). For evidence of a commentary by Giles of Rome, see Pawel Czartoryski, "Quelques éléments nouveaux quant au commentaire de Gilles de Rome sur la Politique," *Mediaevalia Philosophica Polonorum* 11 (1963): 43–48, and, in the Lohr articles, p. 336 of the first section (*Traditio* 23). The brief *quaestiones* of John Vate are mentioned in Martin, "Some Medieval Commentaries," 32, and in Lohr, *Traditio* 27 (1971): 290.

[25] *Opera omnia*, 38 vols. (Paris, 1890–1899) 8 (1891): 1–856. See also A. M. Rohner, "Kommentar des hl. Albertus Magnus zur Einführung in die Politik des Aristoteles," *Divus Thomas* 10 (1932): 95–108, and Gianfranco Fioravanti, "Politiae Orientalium et Aegyptiorum. Alberto Magno e la *Politica* aristotelica," *Annali della Scuola normale superiore di Pisa. Classe di lettere e filosofia*, 3rd ser. 9 (1979): 195–246. Georg von Hertling, "Zur Geschichte der Aristotelischen Politik im Mittelalter," *Rheinisches Museum für Philologie*, n. s. 39 (1884): 446–457, discusses the relation of the commentary to that of Thomas Aquinas/Peter of Auvergne.

[26] The difficulty of the Moerbeke version made any more ambitious plan impractical, at least for the first expositors. Albert himself was proud of his faithfulness to the text, and said: "Sicut enim in omnibus libris physicis, numquam de meo dixi aliquid, sed opiniones Peripateticorum quanto fidelius potui exposui" (*Opera omnia* as cited, 8: 803). In his commentary on the *Metaphysics* he said: "Hic igitur sit finis disputationis istius, in qua non dixi aliquid secundum

concluding each chapter. The *expositio literalis* was not the usual method of Albertus, who, in his attempts to "make Aristotle intelligible to the Westerners,"[27] typically emulated the paraphrase of Avicenna.[28] As we shall see, this anomaly has caused doubt about the precedence of his commentary over that of Thomas Aquinas. In any case, the style of Albertus is his alone. He has been called "vivid, rather uncouth" and "inclined to be wild with his etymologies and to guess at a meaning."[29] Conor Martin calls him "personal, self-revealing, even chatty," and mentions a recipe (of sorts) given in one of the explications.[30] Albertus is last seen denouncing the enemies of philosophy.[31]

The exposition of Thomas Aquinas/Peter of Auvergne[32] is similar in form to that of Albertus Magnus. The commentator presents one chapter at a time, and follows this with a *lectio*, usually at least twice as long as the chapter itself, which explains the purpose of the chapter and its place in the scheme of the *Politics*. Frequently the *lectio* introduces material from other works of Aristotle, for comparison and reconciliation. Thus the explication, while not paralleling the text on a sentence-to-sentence basis, makes clear

---

opinionem meam propriam, sed omnia dicta sunt secundum positiones Peripateticorum" (ibid., 6: 751–752).

[27] ". . . nostra intentio est omnes dictas partes . . . facere Latinis intelligibiles" (*Opera omnia*, 3: 2, from the commentary on the *Physics* 1. 1. 1.).

[28] Grabmann, "Die mittelalterlichen Kommentare," 12.

[29] Thomas Gilby, *The Political Thought of Thomas Aquinas* (Chicago, 1958), 270.

[30] "Some Medieval Commentaries," 33. This recipe, a description of *salcitiae*, "assaturae qua condiuntur, et salsae sunt, ut delectabilius comedantur," occurs at the end of a discussion of despotism in the *Politics* commentary 7. 2. (*Opera omnia*, 8: 637). The text of Aristotle (7. 2. 1324b) is: "One does not hunt *men* to furnish a banquet or a festival . . . what is meant to be hunted for that purpose is any wild animal meant to be eaten" (p. 286 in the translation of Ernest Barker [Oxford, 1946], which will be used here in all English citations of the *Politics*).

[31] He railed against those who, like the liver in the body, "omnes alios convertunt in amaritudinem." These are the sort, he said, who drove Aristotle from Athens, and caused his remark about avoiding the fate of Socrates (*Opera omnia*, 8: 803–804). For a similar citation by Oresme, see the *Livre de Politiques* 3. 1. (fol. 73a, p. 114b in the edition of Albert Douglas Menut (Philadelphia, 1970).

[32] *In libros politicorum Aristotelis expositio*, ed. Raimondo M. Spiazzi (Rome, 1951). Aquinas's part in this commentary goes to 3. 6. (inclusive). When Peter of Auvergne completed the work, he began at the start of book 3. Thus the versions of the two men overlap for the first part of that book. Aquinas's version is printed in editions of his work; one can see the duplicated section of Peter of Auvergne in Gundisalvus M. Grech, *The Commentary of Peter of Auvergne on Aristotle's Politics. The Inedited Part* (Rome, 1967). On this section, see idem, "The Manuscript Tradition of Peter of Auvergne's Inedited Commentary on Aristotle's 'Politics,'" *Angelicum* 41 (1964): 438–449. See also the Hertling article cited above in n. 25, and Martin Grabmann, "Welchen Teil der aristotelischen Politik hat der hl. Thomas von Aquin selbst kommentiert?" *Philosophisches Jahrbuch der Görres-Gesellschaft* 28 (1915): 373–379; M.-D. Browne, "L'Authenticité du commentaire de S. Thomas sur la Politique d'Aristote," *Revue Thomiste* 25 (1920): 78–83; A. O'Rahilly, "Notes on St. Thomas: II. The Commentary on the Politics," *Irish Ecclesiastical Record* 30 (1927): 614–622; Werner Gebauer, "Die Aufnahme der Politik der Aristoteles und die naturrechtliche Begründung des Staates durch Thomas von Aquino," *Vierteljahrschrift für Sozial-und Wirtschaftsgeschichte* 29 (1936): 137–160; Conor Martin, "The Vulgate Text of Aquinas's Commentary on Aristotle's *Politics*," *Dominican Studies* 5 (1952): 35–64; and H.-F. Dondaine, "Le *Super Politicam* de Saint Thomas: tradition manuscrite et imprimée," *Revue des sciences philosophiques et théologiques* 48 (1964): 585–602.

the structure of every argument.[33] The spirit of this commentary is unlike that of Albertus. While Albertus no doubt intended to say nothing of his own opinions, he could not keep himself from digressing. Aquinas remained closer to the *intentio Aristotelis*. His style has been described as "self-effacing"[34] and "streamlined."[35]

We enter another generation of commentators with the work of the Englishman Walter Burley,[36] who was born around the time of Aquinas's death. Burley lived until at least 1344, and wrote his commentary between 1340–1345.[37] His technique, diagrammatical in the extreme, is unlike that of other writers discussed here. He divided his text into tractates, then *capitula*, then *partes principales*, and *particulares*.[38] He resembles an archaeologist squaring off his territory; indeed his book is a sort of excavation. In addition to this scheme of division, Burley provided for each book an apparatus, listing principal questions, notable propositions, and conclusions.[39] Burley's explication is as complex as his text-surveying. It involved, as Daly explains, three levels of explication: *ad litteram* (for words and phrases); *ad sensum* (a less restricted form allowing the expression of the author's opinion); and *ad sententiam* (a form of still greater length and depth, which allowed the author still more independence).[40] However strange Burley's methods may seem to a modern reader, the commentary he created was useful and popular.[41]

---

[33] The technique used by Aquinas was continued by Peter of Auvergne, but see Browne, "L'Authenticité du commentaire de S. Thomas," 82, for a difference in methods of dividing the text.

[34] Gilby, *The Political Thought of Thomas Aquinas*, 270.

[35] Martin, "Some Medieval Commentaries," p. 33. Thomas Renna, "Aristotle and the French Monarchy, 1260–1303," *Viator* 9 (1978): 315, n. 27, contrasts this style with that of Peter of Auvergne: "Whereas Aquinas's commentary is virtually a literal paraphrase of Aristotle's text, Peter's commentary sometimes interpolates quite freely-especially when the text concerns the topic of monarchy."

[36] There is no critical edition of this commentary. For a list of manuscripts, see S. Harrison Thomson, "Walter Burley's Commentary on the *Politics* of Aristotle," *Mélanges Auguste Pelzer* (Louvain, 1947), 564, or Lohr, "Medieval Latin Aristotle Commentaries," *Traditio* 24 (1968): 186–187. See also Anneliese Maier, "Zu Walter Burleys Politik-Kommentar," *Recherches de théologie ancienne et médiévale* 14 (1947): 332–336, or in *Ausgehendes Mittelalter*, 3 vols. (Rome, 1964–1977), 1: 93–99; Lowrie J. Daly, "Walter Burley and John Wyclif on some Aspects of Kingship," *Mélanges Eugène Tisserant*, 7 vols. (Vatican City, 1964), 4: 163–184; idem, "Some Notes on Walter Burley's Commentary on the *Politics*," *Essays in Medieval History Presented to Bertie Wilkinson*, eds. T. A. Sandquist and M. R. Powicke (Toronto, 1969): 270–281; idem, "The Conclusions of Walter Burley's Commentary on the *Politics*," *Manuscripta* 12 (1968): 79–92, for books 1–4; 13 (1969): 142–149, for books 5–6; and 15 (1971): 13–22, for books 7–8.

[37] The dedications of the commentary suggest this date. See Thomson, "Walter Burley's Commentary," 563, and Maier, "Zu Walter Burleys Politik-Kommentar," for details.

[38] See Daly, "The Conclusions of Walter Burley's Commentary" (*Manuscripta* 12), 81. Burley explained in a dedicatory letter to Clement VI that he wished to reduce the text of Aristotle to syllogisms more clear and artificial than those of his predecessors (see Daly, "Walter Burley and John Wyclif," 176, n. 32).

[39] See the series of articles by Daly, "The Conclusions of Walter Burley's Commentary."

[40] "The Conclusions of Walter Burley's Commentary" (*Manuscripta* 12), 81. See also his article "Some Notes on Walter Burley's Commentary." We shall see a similar, in fact a greater, range of explications in the glosses of Oresme.

[41] Thomson, "Walter Burley's Commentary," 563, n. 26, says that there are apparently more manuscripts of this commentary than there are of the *Defensor Pacis*. He adds that the com-

In the *Quaestiones super octo libros Politicorum* of Jean Buridan[42] we discover an example of the second general type of commentary. The question form is suited to a more advanced stage in the assimilation of a text than the exposition: comprehension of a text is needed for free-standing discussion of ideas.[43] Because the author of questions may choose his subjects he tells us what is important to him. The resemblance between commentary and text is destroyed. One could reconstruct much of the *Politics* by looking at a literal exposition. In Buridan's *Quaestiones*, on the other hand, what is incidental in the *Politics* becomes substantial, and what is substantial in the *Politics* becomes perfunctory.[44]

A typical Buridan *quaestio* is organized this way: the proposition to be discussed is introduced, followed by a series of brief arguments which either support or dispute the proposition. (These generally contradict the final conclusion of the quaestio.) Propositions *in oppositum* sometimes follow. Then we find *articules*, fairly specific queries suggested by the main proposition of the question. These are supplemented by *notabiles,* and sometimes countered by opposing statements, or *dubitationes.* Eventually, all the *articules* are resolved, and *conclusiones responsivae,* which answer the main proposition (and sometimes the *articules*) are given. The quaestio concludes with responses *ad rationes,* that is, to the brief arguments given at the beginning of the question.

The *Livre de Politiques* and the Earlier Commentary Tradition

Oresme's use of earlier commentaries, if reduced to a bare tabulation of citations, may appear strange or arbitrary. He mentioned Albertus Magnus over forty times, apparently preferring his commentary to that of Thomas Aquinas/Peter of Auvergne, even for the earlier section of the *Politics* where the explication was that of Aquinas. Oresme sometimes followed Albertus into errors which his own knowledge should have prevented. At the same time, however, he very often introduced an interpretation of Albertus merely to contradict it. Oresme made no citation and perhaps no use of the commentary of Walter Burley, although, as we have seen, this was a popular and much-copied guide to the *Politics.* Nor did Oresme mention

---

mentary was printed over twenty times before 1500, and seventeen times more after that date (ibid., 561).

[42] The *Quaestiones* exist in several manuscripts (see Lohr, "Medieval Latin Aristotle Commentaries" [*Traditio* 26 (1970): 181] for a list). There have also been several printings (Menut, *Le Livre de Politiques,* 26b). The Paris, 1513, edition, reprinted by Minerva in Frankfurt (1969) will be used here for reference. For information on the *Quaestiones,* see Edmond Faral, "Jean Buridan. Notes sur les manuscrits, les éditions et le contenu de ses ouvrages," *Archives d'histoire doctrinale et littéraire du moyen âge* 21 (1946): 1–53, esp. 48–52, and Mario Grignaschi, "Un commentaire nominaliste de la Politique d'Aristote: Jean Buridan," *Anciens pays et assemblées d'états* 19 (1960): 125–142.

[43] Grignaschi, "Un commentaire nominaliste," 126.

[44] As J. Barthélemy-Saint Hilaire has said: "Ill est évident qu'Aristote ici ne sert que de prétexte et de manteau" (*Politique d'Aristote traduite en français,* 2 vols. [Paris, 1837], 1: lxxxix, 19). Many of Buridan's questions could more properly be called ethical than political.

the *Quaestiones* of his presumed mentor Jean Buridan, though he probably knew of them.[45] It is difficult to discover the influence which medieval writers exerted upon each other because they did not cite as conscientiously as modern writers, but a closer examination of Oresme's references allows us to suggest explanations for his choices.

Another aspect of the relationship between the *Livre de Politiques* and its predecessors is progress in the understanding of the text. One might think that in the century after the appearance of Moerbeke's rather obscure translation, commentators advanced fairly steadily in the understanding and appreciation of the *Politics*. Oresme himself thought that he was making Aristotle more accessible by rejecting the misinterpretations of earlier writers: "And no one should marvel if I do not always follow the expositors, for I often find them at odds with each other, and at variance with the text."[46] He certainly did not hesitate to disagree with his predecessors, or to choose between them. His corrections, unfortunately, were not always improvements since in some cases his glosses were less accurate than those he rejected. After a century of study there was no consensus on the meaning of the text of the *Politics*, or on the identification of the words and names in the text.

Oresme's glosses may sometimes reveal a faulty understanding, but they also show progress in the independent use of the text. The earliest commentators were forced to work their way very slowly through the translation of Moerbeke, with little effort to spare for ideas.[47] Authors of quaestiones had more freedom. Jean Buridan, though confined as an expositor by the conventions of scholastic disputation, was able to choose his questions and move away from the social preoccupations of the *Politics* to consider the ethical problems of individuals. Those writers who used the *Politics* outside the commentary tradition, like John of Paris and Marsilius of Padua, were also free to apply the ideas (or supposed ideas) of Aristotle to a variety of subjects and situations.

Oresme returned to textual explication, explaining sentences and words and adapting his text to a new language as others had done a century before. At the same time, as his longer glosses prove, he discussed a variety of important contemporary issues while translating and defining. He had a good deal to say about the church, whereas earlier commentators had sel-

---

[45] According to Menut (*Le Livre de Politiques,* 14a), Oresme never mentioned Buridan. We have seen (chap. 1, no. 10) that Buridan mentioned Oresme at least once.

[46]*Le Livre de Politiques* 3. 19. (fol. 103d, p. 144a). He also said several times that his exposition accorded best with the text: "Saint Thomas expose ceste clause autrement, mes ceste translacion se acorde miex au texte et a raison" (2. 17. [fol. 60b, pp. 102b–103a]), and similarly in 2. 21. (fol. 66d, pp. 109b–110a): "Ceste chose est obscure et, paraventure, mal translatee ou mal escripte. Et sunt les expositeurs contraires. Et la translation que je ay ici mise s'acorde plus au texte que ne funt leur expositions, et est plus raisonnable" (5.29. [fol. 207b–c, p. 248b]), and similarly in 7. 25. (fol. 276a, p. 318b).

[47] Lowrie J. Daly, "Walter Burley and John Wyclif on some Aspects of Kingship," 169. We have noted that the voices of some strong personalities (for example Albertus Magnus) could not entirely be suppressed.

dom spoken of Christian institutions. The contemporary flavor which makes the *Livre de Politiques* seem attractive and lively to the modern reader undoubtedly had the same effect upon the fourteenth-century reader.

To understand Oresme's preferences among the earlier commentaries, it will be useful to see how the earlier commentators used each other's work.

First, it is a reasonable assumption that Thomas Aquinas used the commentary of his teacher Albertus Magnus. In fact it has been suggested that Albertus Magnus was influenced by the commentary of Aquinas. Charles Jourdain,[48] and, following him, Wilhelm Oncken,[49] have noted that in his *Politics* commentary Albertus produced an *expositio literalis* rather than his characteristic paraphrase in the manner of Avicenna. Because this exposition resembles that of Thomas, they reason, it was modeled on his. Another support for this argument concerns the statement made by Aquinas in his commentary that the *Problemata* of Aristotle was not yet available in the West. But Albertus Magnus cites this work in his commentary, which suggests that he was writing after the time of his pupil's study of the *Politics*. Against this Georg Hertling argues that Aquinas also cited the *Problemata*, and that his knowledge of this work may have come from Albertus Magnus.[50] Or the two may have cited the work independently. Hertling also notes that Albertus made errors which he could have avoided had he seen the Aquinas/Auvergne commentary.[51] Martin Grabmann, in support of Hertling's position, mentions other scholastics from whom Albertus might have borrowed the technique of expositio literalis.[52] Further support for Hertling's argument comes from Mario Grignaschi, who thinks that many passages in the exposition of Peter of Auvergne cannot be explained without reference to the commentary of Albertus Magnus.[53] In finishing with this first generation of commentaries, we may note that, according to F. Edward Cranz, no scholastic writers are mentioned in the *Quaestiones* of Peter of Auvergne.[54]

---

[48] *La Philosophie de saint Thomas d'Aquin,* 2 vols. (Paris, 1858), 1: 400, cited in Georg von Hertling, "Zur Geschichte der Aristotelischen Politik im Mittelalter," 449.

[49] *Die Staatslehre des Aristoteles in historisch-politischen Umrissen,* 2 vols. in one (Leipzig, 1870–1875), 1: 70, cited in Hertling, "Zur Geschichte," p. 449.

[50] In Hertling, "Zur Geschichte," 451–453.

[51] Ibid., 452–453. Émile Bridrey, *La théorie de la monnaie au XIVe siècle. Nicole Oresme. Étude d'histoire des doctrines et des faits économiques* (Paris, 1906), says that Aquinas "rectifie couramment les leçons fautives ou des explications invraisemblables d'Albert" (370). Oresme in turn, as we have said and will see in more detail, sometimes rejected correct interpretations of Albertus Magnus in order to propose incorrect interpretations of his own.

[52] "Die mittelalterlichen Kommentare zur Politik des Aristoteles," *SBAW* 1941, 2, pt. 10, p. 13, with reference to his article "Methoden und Hilfsmittel des Aristotelesstudiums im Mittelalter," ibid., 1939, pt. 5, 30 ff. The authors he mentions include Adam of Bocfield, Johannes Pagus, and Nicholas of Paris.

[53] "Nicole Oresme et son commentaire à la 'Politique' d'Aristote," 104. On the other hand, he notes that in the sections of the commentary done by Aquinas, the echo of the commentary of Albertus is "à peine perceptible" (ibid., 105).

[54] "Aristotelianism in Medieval Political Theory," 300.

The commentary of Burley owes more to its predecessors than is apparent from a superficial inspection. According to S. Harrison Thomson, "Any references to Christian writers are notable by their absence, as indeed any reference to Christian doctrine."[55] Thomson also says that it is not possible to know whether Burley used the commentary of Albertus Magnus.[56] One citation of Peter of Auvergne comes from the *Commentarius in Meteora*, not from his commentary or quaestiones on the *Politics*.[57] If Burley did not mention Christian writers by name, however, Lowrie J. Daly feels that there is no doubt he used the Aquinas/Auvergne commentary, and that his dependence on the earlier works is "at times almost word for word."[58] Elsewhere Daly speaks of the "sometime[s] slavish way in which Burley follows the commentary [of?] Aquinas-Auvergne,"[59] adding that "in some instances his text is almost a series of quotations from Peter of Auvergne's commentary."[60]

Jean Buridan mentioned scholastic writers far more often than did Burley, but one must not draw hasty conclusions from this fact. Buridan cited Aquinas thirteen times, for example, but none of these citations mention the *Politics* or a commentary on the *Politics*, and few of them have any apparent connection with this text. Two of the citations refer specifically to the *Summa Theologica*. Perhaps he made so little use of the Aquinas/Auvergne commentary because it was largely written not by Thomas Aquinas but by Peter of Auvergne (who is not mentioned at all by Buridan). However, the section commented by Aquinas contains Aristotle's discussion of the development of human communities, and other important material which one would expect to arouse interest. Similarly, there are about thirty-four references to Albertus Magnus, but less than one-fourth of these contain a phrase like "secundo huius" to show that they refer to a commentary on the *Politics*. Some may refer to Albertus's *Ethics* commentary. Walter Burley is not mentioned. There are thirteen references to an *expositor* (or something like this designation), of which only three refer to the *Politics*. At least two of these seem to refer to commentaries on the *Ethics*, and some others may refer to commentaries on the pseudo-Aristotelian *Economics*. There is one reference to "multas glosas" and there are four to a *commentator* (Averroës?), of which three concern the *Ethics* and one, apparently, the *Metaphysics*.[61]

---

[55] "Walter Burley's Commentary on the *Politics* of Aristotle," 576.

[56] Ibid., 570.

[57] Ibid., 577.

[58] "Some Notes on Walter Burley's Commentary on the *Politics*," 279.

[59] "The Conclusions of Walter Burley's Commentary on the *Politics*," 15.

[60] "Walter Burley and John Wyclif on some Aspects of Kingship," p. 179. Daly also presents parallel segments from the two commentaries (179–183). Similarly, Bridrey (*Nicole Oresme*, 369) says: "Une remarque générale qui s'impose, c'est que tous ces commentateurs se connaissent et se copient successivement sans, semble-t-il, la moindre pudeur. . . . on trouve chez Burleigh des passages de saint Thomas textuellement reproduits."

[61] This enumeration comes from the author's examination of the *Quaestiones* (in the Paris, 1513, edition, reprinted by Minerva in Frankfurt [1969]).

Oresme's use of these early commentaries is extensive. More precisely, he cites Albertus Magnus forty-five times, Thomas Aquinas twice, and Peter of Auvergne once.[62] Walter Burley and Jean Buridan are not mentioned at all.[63] Menut says that Oresme made "numerous borrowings" from the version of Aquinas, and suggests that he may have adapted from the Burley commentary aspects of his table of contents, chapter analyses and division of books.[64] Grignaschi thinks that some of Oresme's citations of an *expositio* may refer to the commentary of Burley,[65] and that it may have been through Burley that Oresme learned of the collection of descriptions of constitutions which, according to Diogenes Laertius, had been compiled by Aristotle.[66]

It would be impossible to explain with certainty why Oresme made these choices, but one can make suggestions. The most puzzling problem is surely Oresme's treatment of Albertus Magnus, his frequent citation, frequent disagreement, and occasional incautious agreement. Menut has suggested that the source of Oresme's criticism may have been Albertus Magnus's support of the mendicant orders, for whom Oresme had little enthusiasm.[67] If this were true, it would seem that Oresme mentioned the Dominican a great many times merely to contradict him. It is possible that Oresme was spiteful enough to do this, but the points of disagreement between the two commentators have virtually nothing to do with apostolic poverty. And Oresme did not mention Albertus Magnus in his lengthy criticisms of mendicancy. Besides, Thomas Aquinas was also a Dominican and a defender of the mendicant orders, and he received no such treatment in the *Livre de Politiques*. At any rate, it was the Franciscans who were the particular objects of Oresme's scorn and sarcasm. Even so, we do not see a flaying of

---

[62] "Maistre Pierre d'Auvergne" is cited as the continuator of the Aquinas commentary, not as the author of his *Quaestiones* (*Le Livre de Politiques* 5. 1. [fol. 164d–165a, p. 203b]).

[63] The notes of Menut to his edition of the *Livre de Ethiques* (New York, 1940) allow us to compare Oresme's use of the work of his fellow *Ethics* commentators with the use he made of earlier *Politics* commentaries. In glossing the *Ethics* Oresme made even fewer name references to his predecessors than he did in the glosses for the *Politics*. According to Menut's Index of Proper Names (83–84) Eustathius is mentioned eleven times, Albertus Magnus four times, and Aquinas, Burley and Buridan not at all. There are several references to "les Docteurs" or "aucuns docteurs" or simply "aucuns." In his notes, however, Menut suggests who these figures might be. Here Buridan appears as "un expositeur" (3. 14. [fol. 53d, p. 205]), and in seven groups of authorities. We shall see that one reason why Buridan might have been an unsatisfactory source of *Politics* commentary was that he concentrated on questions which might more properly be considered ethical than political. This characteristic would not interfere with his usefulness as a source of *Ethics* commentary. In the *Livre de Ethiques* Aquinas is identified by Menut as Oresme's source in three places, Albertus Magnus is identified six times, and Burley appears seven times.

[64] *Le Livre de Politiques*, introduction, 26a.

[65] "Nicole Oresme et son commentaire," 106.

[66] Ibid., 125, with reference to Grabmann, "Die mittelalterlichen Kommentare," 54–55. The work of Burley's which is in question here, however, is not his *Politics* commentary but his popular *De vita et moribus philosophrum*. The text of Oresme, from 4. 3. (fol. 129d, p. 168a) is: ". . . il est escript ou livre de la vie Aristote que en alant oveques le roy Alexandre contre ceulz de Perse il composa les hystoires de .cc. et .1. policies. Item, illeques meisme est dit que il escripst au roy Alexandre un livre de royalme." (Grignaschi notes that Peter of Auvergne was also aware of this legend [125].)

[67] Introduction to *Le Livre de Politiques* 26a, n. 23.

Franciscan authors in his commentary. And even if one were to accept the explanation that Oresme was acting here as a partisan, there would still remain the question why he sometimes followed Albertus Magnus into error. A closer look at the purpose and style of the commentaries may provide an answer.

The *Livre de Politiques* was meant, like the early commentaries, to serve as an introduction to a text, to be a guidebook for a new audience. That is why Oresme used a flexible commentary/gloss form, which allowed him to interrupt himself whenever he saw a need to explain, identify, or expostulate. The structure of his commentary, which was still broadly based upon that of Aristotle's text, affected his use of the work of his predecessors.

A series of quaestiones like those of Jean Buridan would not be very useful to Oresme, for such a series is not closely tied to its text. Many of the details explained by Oresme were not mentioned at all by Buridan. Furthermore, Buridan used his independence of the text to choose many subjects of ethical rather than political interest. He did treat many of the essential controversies raised in the *Politics*, such as the questions of the proper form of government and the nature of good laws, but many of his discussions have only an incidental connection with the text he was ostensibly expounding. Buridan's commentary is further distinguished from that of Oresme by an almost complete lack of attention to contemporary affairs. The bits of local color which lend a certain animation to the glosses of Oresme are absent from the disputations of Buridan. Nor did Buridan occupy himself with the details of Greek history presented by Aristotle. His interest in questions for the sake of questions did not oblige him to do so. Thus Oresme's failure to mention his old colleague can be understood.

The form of the Aquinas/Auvergne commentary is much closer to that of the *Livre de Politiques* than that of Buridan's *Quaestiones*, but its style, which has been described as "ruthlessly and austerely to the point,"[68] made it useful for the interpretation of the text rather than for the sort of digressions we find in the glosses of Oresme. Similarly, Walter Burley has been described as "a rather laconic writer."[69] Burley explained to his readers that he did not consider himself qualified to identify the historical examples found in his text.[70] Furthermore, these two commentators seldom applied their texts to the medieval world.

Albertus Magnus, on the other hand, was a commentator congenial to Oresme. We see him described as "chatty,"[71] and the same writer says that

---

[68] Conor Martin, "Some Medieval Commentaries on Aristotle's *Politics*," *History* 36 (1951): 33. See above, however (n. 35), for the difference in style between Aquinas and his continuator Peter of Auvergne.

[69] Daly, "The Conclusions of Walter Burley's Commentary" (*Manuscripta* 12), 81.

[70] Martin, "Some Medieval Commentaries," 38. See also Daly, "Walter Burley and John Wyclif," 178. The text of Burley's disclaimer is cited in Grabmann, "Die mittelalterlichen Kommentare," p. 32 (from Clm. 8402, fol. 135ᵛ): ". . . non sermones grecos interpretabor nec exponam, quia illius lingue totaliter sum ignarus."

[71] See above, n. 30, from Martin, "Some Medieval Commentaries," 33.

Albertus discusses unfamiliar references "with a freedom and confidence unembarrassed by any sense of privation."[72] Oresme in his etymologies is often similarly uninformed and unabashed. Perhaps his caution was overcome by his desire to be helpful. Moreover, Albertus, like Oresme but with less frequency and breadth, brought bits of his century into his commentary.[73] Thus there is a compatibility of range and style between Albertus Magnus and Oresme, which may have led Oresme to cite this predecessor so frequently. Perhaps Albertus was simply considered a good authority; Buridan mentioned him over thirty times.[74] It will be easier to see why Oresme, hostile or not, rejected so many of Albertus Magnus's explications, when we examine in detail how the *Livre de Politiques* reflects progress in the understanding of Aristotle's text.

To compare the commentary of Oresme with that of his predecessors, we must concentrate on the work of Albertus Magnus and Aquinas/Auvergne. *Quaestiones* like those of Buridan were not, like these works, designed primarily to explain the text of Aristotle. Burley's commentary was, but since he declined to explain Greek words and historical references (and since Oresme, by either not using him or simply not mentioning him, makes it hard to speak of his contribution to the *Livre de Politiques*), he has little place in this comparison. In speaking of Oresme's explication of the *Politics* we must also mention, as a background, his numerous complaints about the Latin text.[75] He excused some of the errors (or imagined errors) of Albertus Magnus on the grounds of defect in the Latin version.[76]

---

[72] Ibid., 37.

[73] Grignaschi, "Nicole Oresme et son commentaire," 103.

[74] Grignaschi, ibid., 103, also remarks that Buridan shared the preference for Albertus Magnus. But to him this preference is hard to explain, given "la supériorité manifeste du commentaire Thomiste."

[75] See above, chap. 1, n. 63. In one case Oresme suggested that the translator used the rather inaccurate word *pretor* to describe the members of the Greek popular courts because of ignorance of the proper Greek word (3. 1. [fol. 74b, p. 115b], and see Menut's note; this text is found on p. 153, line 2 of Susemihl's edition of Moerbeke [Leipzig, 1872]). In 5. 21. (fol. 195d, p. 236b) Oresme said: "Le texte est corrumpu où fu mal translaté." At another point he said "Ceste chose est obscure et, paraventure, mal translatee ou mal escripte" (5. 29. [fol. 207b, p. 248b]). In 8. 12. he said that his texts were "pas bien corrigiés" (fol. 308d, p. 356a). He complained of lacunae: "Mes si comme dit un expositeur, celui qui translata cest livre de grec en latin dit que en l'exemplaire de grec apres ces moz *Adhuc autem* estoit une espace et y failloit texte. Et aussi une autre espace apres ces moz *compatientes et sine;* et par ce appert que cest texte est imparfaict" (8. 8. [fol. 303b, p. 349a]; p. 353, line 1 in Susemihl's Moerbeke).

[76] In 3. 4. (fol. 80d, p. 121b) he said "Albert expose ceste clause au contraire pour une negation qui ne est pas en son texte. . . ." Aristotle spoke here of Jason of Pherae, a tyrant who could not live in private station and hungered when he could not tyrannize (*Politics* 3. 4. 1277a; Barker, 103). Oresme understood this, but Albertus, according to Oresme, said that Jason was a poet who said that the people hungered for a good prince. What Albertus said was somewhat different (*Opera omnia* [Paris, 1890–], 8 [1891]: 220).

In 3.9., Oresme said: "Et est assavoir que le texte que Albert expose en cest pas est faulx, car en lieu de *tirannis*, il met *terminus*" (fol. 88c, p. 129a). Actually Albertus (8: 235) does have "tyrannis." As Menut's note suggests, it was probably Oresme's manuscript of the commentary which was incorrect. In 4. 3., Oresme said: "Mes Albert l'expose au contraire, et je cuide qu'il failloit en son texte une negation" (fol. 129c, p. 168a). Here (*Politics* 4. 3. 1289b; Barker, p. 160) Aristotle spoke of the notables who were wealthy enough to raise horses. Albertus's text does seem to have the negative: "*Hoc enim non facile non divites facere*" (8: 327).

Most of the identifications and definitions given by Oresme are correct and useful, but sometimes he errs where he should confess ignorance.[77] Occasionally Albertus Magnus leads him into error: Oresme describes Mitylene by repeating Albertus's statement that it is "an island near Sicily."[78] He describes it again, on the authority of Albertus, as an island between Greece and Apulia.[79] Following Albertus, he places Miletus in the apparently crowded environs of Sicily,[80] and "la policie laconique" in "the region now called Apulia and Calabria."[81]

Sometimes Oresme made his own blunders. In one outstanding case he was misled by the word *xenelasias*, one of the transliterated Greek words from the first, incomplete Latin translation of the *Politics*. In trying to explain this term, which is the equivalent of "ab expulsione" in the complete translation, Oresme created a new historical figure: Zenesalias, the founder of the state of Crete.[82] In one case he chided Albertus Magnus for lacking a

---

Once again, in 5. 25., Oresme cited an alleged difference between the text exposed by Albertus and that of others: "Aucuns textes ont *ad moderatius*, mes Albert dit *ad modum artius*" (fol. 200b, p. 241b). But Albertus (8: 532) does have *"ad moderatius."*

[77] Sometimes he did confess ignorance, as in identifying Thrasybulus: "Je treuve au quint livre de Justin un ainsi nommé, et fu de Athenes et est bien recommendé. Je ne say se ce fu cestuy" (5. 23. [fol. 198c, p. 239b]; *Politics* 5. 10. 1312b [Barker, p. 240]). In 8. 11. (fol. 307a, p. 354a), in trying to explain the "septigona et trigona et iambi" mentioned by Aristotle in 8. 6. 1341a (Susemihl, p. 362, lines 7–8) and translated by Barker as "heptagons," "triangles," and "sackbuts" (p. 348), Oresme said "Un expositeur dit que *septigone* estoit un instrument qui avoit .vii. angles ou .vii. cordes; et *trigone* .iii. et *jambus* .ii. cordes. *Nescio.*" Oresme's source is most likely Peter of Auvergne (ed. Spiazzi, p. 432, #1325).
For some examples of extraordinary medieval distortions of ancient history, see C. W. C. Oman, "Some Mediaeval Conceptions of Ancient History," *Transactions of the Royal Historical Society*, 4th ser. 4 (1921): 1–22; Ernst Robert Curtius, *Europäische Literatur und lateinisches Mittelalter* (Berlin and Munich, 1948), 407–409 (pp. 405–406 in the English translation by Willard R. Trask, *European Literature and the Latin Middle Ages* [New York, 1953]) contains examples of distorted mythology, including the transformation of Venus into a man. Oresme knew better: *Le Livre de Ethiques* 7. 10. (fol. 143b, p. 384); *Le Livre de Politiques* 2. 16. (fols. 57d–58a, p. 100b).

[78] "Albert dit que ce est une isle pres de Sicile" (3. 20. [fols. 106d–107a, p. 147a]). Albertus had said: *"Qualem elegerunt quandoque Mitylenaei* (et est Mitylaenia insula juxta Siciliam posita in mari) *Pittacum adversus profugas . . ."* (*Opera omnia* [Paris, 1890], 8: 288).

[79] "Albert dit que ce est une isle entre Grece et Apulle" (5. 6. [fol. 173c, p. 213a]). Albertus's text is: "Et inducit aliud exemplum, ibi, *Et circa Mitylenam autem* (Mitylenam enim insula est inter Graeciam et Apuliam in mari sita) *ex haereditatibus dissentione facta, multorum fuit principium malorum . . ."* (8: 448).

[80] ". . . il avint a Milet. Albert dit que ce est une isle pres de Sicile qui est encor ainsi nommee . . ." (5. 9. [fol. 176d, p. 216b]). Albertus had said: "Et dat examplum, ibi, *Sicut in Mileto* (insula quaedem est juxta Siciliam, quae usque hodie vocatur Miletum insula) *ex Prytania . . ."* (8: 457).

[81] *Le Livre de Politiques* 7. 21. (fol. 270c, p. 312a). For the text of Albertus, see *Opera omnia* as cited, 8: 286. (He says "magna Graecia.")

[82] "Et l'autre translacion dit que Zenasalius la fist loing, ce est a dire que il funda Crete loing des autres terres" (2. 20. [fol. 65a, p. 108a]). See Albertus, *Opera omnia*, 8: 183, and the *Livre de Politiques*, introd., 25a–26a.
For another such creation, see Jean Seznec, *La survivance des dieux antiques* (London, 1940), who shows how the god Demogorgon was created out of a grammatical error (pp. 189 n. 5, 195, 202 n. 3, 203 n. 5, 248 n. 1, 272, 279, and 289, as well as C. Landi, *Demogorgone, con saggi di nuova ed delle "Geneologia deorum gentilium"* [Palermo, 1930]). For Albertus's creation of Rhetor, the writer on jurisprudence, see Gilby, *The Political Thought of Thomas Aquinas* (Chicago, 1958), 270. See also A. Mansion, "Disparition graduelle des mots grecs dans les traduc-

proper historical background when his own gloss was incorrect.[83] Oresme also had his own store of geographical misinformation.[84]

Some of Oresme's glosses are superior to those of his voluble predecessor. Albertus misunderstands Aristotle's reference (*Politics* 3. 4. 1277) to Jason of Pherae, who "was a hungry man except when he was tyrant."[85] Oresme did better, but he excused the other on the grounds of faulty text. Similarly, Albertus misunderstood a reference to the Sacred War of Phocis while Oresme got it right.[86] Oresme was also, according to Grignaschi, the first commentator correctly to understand the role of the popular court judges mentioned in *Politics* 3. 1. 1275a. Albertus seemed to think that these were like the Roman praetors, while Oresme understood that the office of which Aristotle spoke was of less importance.[87]

In his etymologies as in his identifications, Oresme sometimes tried to do more than his knowledge allowed. Here again he followed not the modest

---

tions médiévales d'Aristote," *Mélanges Joseph de Ghellinck,* 2 vols. (Gembloux, 1951), 2: 631 – 645.

Oresme made another startling transformation (if not a new creation) in the *Livre de Ethiques* 5. 15. (fol. 104a, p. 304) where the Spartan general Brasidas became "Braside . . . une dame qui fist pluseurs biens en une cité appellee Amphipoli. . . ." Similarly, Alcibiades, as mentioned in *Consolatio Philosophiae* 3. pr. 8, became a beautiful woman in Chaucer's version of Boethius, and in Villon's "Ballade des dames du temps jadis."

[83] In 5. 1. 1301b, Aristotle spoke of the Spartan regent Pausanias, the victor at Platea, traitor and plotter against the ephorate. Oresme identified him as the later Spartan king Pausanias, who opposed the thirty tyrants of Athens (5.1. [fol. 166d, p. 205b]). In *Epitoma* 5. 10., Justin said: "Dum haec aguntur, nuntiatur Lacedaemone in bellum Athenienses exarsisse; ad quod comprimendum Pausanias rex mittitur" (ed. Franz Rühl [Leipzig, 1886], p. 50). Albertus has: "Et dat exemplum in Lacedaemonia, ubi Lysander conatus fuit dissolvere regnum, et Pausanias Rex conatus fuit dissolvere ephoriam, et in Epidamno transmutata fuit politia secundum partem principatus pro *philarchis,* id est, principatum ambientibus et amantibus" (*Opera omnia,* 8: 427). Thus it was Albertus who was right.

[84] In *Politics* 2. 10. 1271b, where Aristotle speaks of Minos, who "carried his attacks as far as Sicily, where he died near Camicus . . ." (Barker 81), Oresme said that Minos had died near the mountain called *Cheminee* and added this gloss: "C'est le Mont Ethna, duquel il ist perpetuelment feu et fumee. Mez selon une autre translation, il mourut en une cité appellee Cammeon . . ." (2. 19. [fol. 63a, pp. 105b–106a]). Menut says this interpretation "defies explanation" (p. 106a, n. 3) but see Aquinas (ed. R. Spiazzi [Turin, 1951], p. 108, #323): ". . . Camerinam, idest circa montem Vulcani vel Ethnae ex quibus ignis eructat."

[85] Barker, 103. For the texts involved, see above, n. 76.

[86] Aristotle mentioned this war in 5. 4. 1304a. The gloss of Oresme is: "Albert dit que ce est a dire forte guerre, et que *sacrum,* ce est fort. Mes je ne treuve pas ceste signification es aucteurs de grammaire. Mes par aventure que celle guerre fu appellee *sainte* ou *sacree* pource que l'eritage de quoy la dissention fu meue appartenoit as temples des diex, ou que la guerre estoit du commandement des diex . . ." (5. 6. [fol. 173d, p. 213a]). Albertus's text is: ". . . *seditio haec principium fuit sacri belli Phoceis,* id est, fortissimi belli: quia *sacrum* idem est quod forte" (*Opera omnia,* 8: 449). Nicholas G. L. Hammond, in *A History of Greece to 322 B. C.* (Oxford, 1967), 512–513, says that a sacred war such as the Third Sacred War of Phocis was a war "on behalf of the god of Delphi in which no prisoners were to be taken and no mercy shown to the vanquished. Such conditions meant war to the death." So in a way the war was "fortissim[um] bell[um]."

[87] What Moerbeke (ed. Susemihl, 153, line 2) translated as *praetor* is "the office of judge in the popular courts" in Aristotle (Barker, 94). This is clearly a less powerful office than that of the praetor in Rome. Albertus and Aquinas, although speaking vaguely, attributed too much power to this office, Albertus saying "*Velut praetor et concionator,* supple, qui principantur ad vitam. Praetor enim est, qui in praetorio audit et judicat causas et leges condit" (*Opera omnia,* 8: 209), and Aquinas saying ". . . praetor, qui scilicet habet potestatem iudicandi de aliquibus causis . . ." (3. 1. 353. [ed. Spiazzi, p. 122]). Oresme's gloss came closer to the truth: "Et me

example of Walter Burley, who admitted his ignorance, but rather the enthusiastic example of Albertus Magnus. Oresme was sometimes close to the truth, if unoriginal, as in his explanation of the word for monarchy.[88] Sometimes, as Menut says in one of his notes, his attempts are "approximately correct," as in his derivation of *astinomie* or *astynomos* (city-superintendant).[89] Occasionally, he managed to understand a passage in spite of his incorrect etymology, as in the case of *obeliscolycnia*.[90] In other cases, however, his success may be gauged by the comments of Menut: "completely ridiculous";[91] "untenable";[92] "fantastic";[93] "wholly incorrect";[94] "hardly approximate";[95] and "another false etymology."[96]

semble que Aristote ne entent pas par *preteur* tele chose comme estoient les preteurs de quoy les lays romaines parlent es *Digestes;* car telz preteurs avoient tres grant auctorité et estoient princes. Mes le preteur de quoy il parle ici avoit petite office, si comme l'en peut entendre par le texte. Et peut estre que la translateur mist *pretor* pour le nom grec, qui estoit ignoré; car des maintenant ne fussent aucunes lays escriptes, l'en ne sceut quel povoir ou quel office les preteurs de Rome avoient" (3. 1. [fol. 74b, p. 115b]). The "nom grec" from Aristotle's text was δικαστὴς or juryman (see Susemihl, 153, line 2 of the Greek). See Mario Grignaschi, "La Définition du 'civis' dans la scolastique," *Anciens pays et assemblées d'états* 35 (1966), 80.

[88] "Il entent par monarchie le princey la ou un seul a souveraine seigneurie. Et est dit de *monos*, que est un, et de *archos*, que est prince ou princey. Et donques monarchie est princey de un seul" (3. 8. [fol. 87d, p. 128a]). This is not from Albertus (8: 237) or Aquinas (p. 139).

[89] "Il est dit de *asti* en grec, qui signifie le corps de la cité quant as edifices; et de *gnomos* ou *nomos*, que est regle" (6. 10. [fol. 229b, p. 271b]). Oresme came closer to Albertus (8: 609) whose editor remarks, speaking of his etymology for this word: ". . . nam, ut patet ex pluribus etymologiis quas dat Albertus noster, linguam graecam non optime callebat."

[90] This is the Latin form of the Greek word ὀβελισκολύχνια (pl.). It refers, as Barker says (p. 196, n. 1) to spits which can serve as lampholders. They are meant by Aristotle (*Politics* 4. 15. 1299b) to represent, like the Delphic knife of 1. 2. 1252b, objects with more than one function. Oresme produced what Menut calls a "much distorted transcription" (p. 197a, n. 4), *obelicos klisma*, from Moerbeke's *obeliscolychnia* (ed. Susemihl, p. 443, line 4). Oresme also failed to give a correct definition of this word, but he did grasp the meaning of the passage: "En grec *obelisco*, ce est haste ou broche, si comme dit Saint Jerome; et *klisma*, ce est un petit vaissel, si comme une cuiller ou un saucier. Et celui estoit appellé *obeliscoklisma* qui faisoit toutes ces choses. Et semblablement en une petite cité ou communité un seul peut bien faire pluseurs offices compassibles, et seroit peu occupé en une" (4. 21. [fol. 158a, p. 197b]). For the reference to Jerome, from Menut's notes, see *Patrologia latina*, ed. J. P. Migne, 22: 928: ". . . virgulae, id est obeli sunt. . . ." This is closer to Peter of Auvergne (p. 236) than to Albertus (8: 407).

[91] *Le Livre de Politiques* 4. 7. (fol. 135b, p. 174a), where Oresme explained the word demagogue: "Sunt aucuns qui meinent le peuple a leur volenté et ne sunt pas princes. Et est cest mot dit de *demos* en grec, que est peuple; et de *dogos*, qui est duction ou menement." Albertus comes close to this (8: 345).

[92] Ibid., 4. 17. (fol. 151c, p. 190b), where Oresme tried to explain the word *dyatetes* (διαιτητής in the Greek, *diaetetes* in Moerbeke [ed. Susemihl, p. 427, line 7], and "neutral arbitrator" in Barker, p. 186, *Politics* 4. 12. 1297a). Oresme's gloss is: "Et est dit de *dya* qu'est .ii. et *thesis* que est position; car il est posé et mis entre .ii., ce est assavoir entre le povre et les tres riche." This seems to be from Albertus (8: 387).

[93] Ibid., 4. 21. (fol. 157b, p. 196b). Here Oresme transformed Moerbeke's correct transcription of γυναικονόμος as *gynaeconomus* (Susemihl, p. 441, line 3), which is translated by Barker as "inspecto[r] of women" (p. 195, *Politics* 4. 15. 1299a), into *germothonomos*, "ce est a dire mestre de mestiers ou d'un mestier," and supplied this gloss: "En grec *germos* ce est labeur, et *gomos* ou *nomos*, ce est regle. Et donques *germothonomos* est celui qui regule les laboureurs. Et *tho-* en grec, ce ne est fors un article prepositif, aussi comme quant l'en dit *le maistre, maistre* est nom et *le* est un article prepositif." (See Albertus, 8: 406.) Similarly, in 6. 13. (fol. 233b, p. 275b), Oresme had a bit more luck with his explanation of *gynoconomie*, but ended his etymology with a reference to "*pto*, qui est une preposition greque," which, according to Menut (n. 4), "defies explanation." (But see Albertus, 8: 406.)

[94] Ibid., 5. 26. (fol. 204d, pp. 245b–246a). Aristotle spoke in 5. 11. 1313b of the "lavish offerings to temples made by the family of Cypselus" (Barker, 245). Moerbeke has "anathe-

In interpreting the text of the *Politics* Oresme had much the same success as he had with the allusions and foreign words contained in it. He had trouble with both his Latin text and his predecessors' versions of it. In one case noted by Menut, he chose to translate the verb *dictari*, which he defined as "sentencier," instead of *ditari*, the quite different verb from Moerbeke. This inevitably caused confusion in his explication of the text.[97] In another case, as Menut remarks, when faced with a choice between texts reading *lenioribus* and *leonibus moribus*, Oresme chose the former, which he translated as "more gentle and more domesticable." In fact Aristotle's reference was to the habits of lions, and Moerbeke's translation of *leonibus moribus* had been correct.[98] Another problem emerged when Oresme thought he saw a difference between the text of the complete Latin translation of Moerbeke and that of the dangerous "autre translacion." In fact, as Menut points out, the two texts scarcely differ in wording or meaning.[99] In a similar case, Oresme found a disagreement between the explications of Albertus Magnus and Peter of Auvergne, though the latter was probably derived from the former,[100] and elsewhere, he accepted an interpretation of Peter instead of the correct interpretation of Albertus.[101]

---

mata Cypselidorum" (Susemihl, p. 575, line 8), and Oresme translated this as "les anathemes des Kipsellides," saying in his gloss "Et firent faire au peuple uns haus edifices appellés *anathemes. Et est ce mot en *ana* en grec, qui est haut; et *thesis,* qui est mise; car il estoient mis haut." This is from neither Albertus (8: 534) nor Peter (p. 295).

[95] Ibid., 8. 10. (fol. 305b, pp. 351b–352a). Oresme was trying to explain what Barker has as the "rattle of Archytas" (p. 346, *Politics* 8. 6. 1340b). Oresme said that perhaps this was like a psaltery, and offered this derivation of the word *platagen* (Susemihl, p. 358, lines 1–2): "Et est dit de *platon* qu'est *latum* en latin, ce est lay; et de ce est dit *plat* en françoys." He was wrong, as Menut says, not only about the derivation of *plat* from *latum*, but also about the origin of the word itself, which comes from a Greek word meaning to clap hands, crack or clash. (This is not from Albertus [8: 787] or Peter [p. 430].)

[96] Ibid., 5. 29. (fol. 207b, p. 248b). Here Oresme says "Et selon ce fu dit tirant de *tyro*, qui signifie fort." (This is neither Albertus [8: 539] nor Peter [300].)

[97] Ibid., 4. 5. (fol. 133b–c, p. 172a). Aristotle had said (4. 4. 1291a; p. 166 in Barker) that sometimes men who serve as heavily armed soldiers (and must therefore be rich; hence *ditari*) also are farmers. Moerbeke correctly used the verb *ditari* in translating this passage (Susemihl, p. 391, line 1), but Oresme said in his gloss: "Les offices sunt distinctees quant est de soi, mes peut estre que un en fait pluseurs; mes je cuide que la ou il dit 'dictari' il doit avoir 'dictare,' ce est a dire 'sentencier'; car les cultiveurs des champs souloient tenir les jugemens, si comme dit Ovide. . . ." (This is not from Albertus [8: 337] or Peter [p. 199].)

[98] Ibid., 8. 5. (fol. 299a, p. 344a). Aristotle thought that ferocious and ill-disciplined youths might, like wolves, prove unequal to danger, whereas noble youths, like lions, would prove themselves (*Politics* 8. 4. 1338b; 338–339 in Barker, whose translation does not, however, mention lions). The reference for Susemihl's edition of Moerbeke is p. 343, line 4. Oresme's gloss shows that he understood the meaning of the text even if he chose the wrong translation: "Es textes qui me semblent les plus vrays il a *lenioribus*, es plus soueves et plus domestiques ou domesques; mes les autres textes ont *leoninis moribus*, ce est a dire es gens ou bestes qui ont meurs de lyon, et que en elles est plus fortitude. . . ." Oresme follows neither Albertus (8: 768) nor Peter (p. 419).

[99] Ibid., 2. 17. (fols. 60d–61a, p. 103b), from *Politics* 2. 9. 1271a. Menut prints the pertinent sections of the two commentaries in his note.

[100] Ibid., 3. 20. (fols. 107d–108a, p. 148a), from *Politics* 3. 14. 1285b. Grignaschi describes this misunderstanding and provides the Latin texts, in his article "Nicole Oresme et son commentaire," 104–105, n. 1.

[101] *Le Livre de Politiques* 6. 3. (fol. 219a, p. 260a), from *Politics* 3. 3. 1318a. Here in describing a rather complex scheme of representation Oresme chose an interpretation which "renversait de

Grignaschi has described occasions when Oresme was able to improve upon the interpretations of his predecessors. In one case, according to Grignaschi, he apparently went beyond the Latin of Moerbeke to come near to the Greek original, without dependence upon Albertus Magnus or Peter of Auvergne.[102] In discussing the power of the popular assembly in a democracy, Oresme followed Peter rather than Albertus: this time it was the right choice.[103] Oresme showed his independence by rejecting the interpretations of both these commentaries for his own (correct) interpretation of "the military kind of excellence" which "shows itself in a mass,"[104] and by taking up and bettering a gloss of Albertus on equality in democracies, thus bringing it closer to the meaning of Aristotle.[105]

If the purpose of a commentary is held to be that of a modern edition, that is, the establishment of a correct and carefully annotated text, with infallible notes and an up-to-date bibliography, the *Livre de Politiques* is no more than a qualified success. It does not reflect absolute progress in the understanding of Aristotle's text nor does it reconcile the interpretations of Oresme's predecessors. Only part of their work was put to evident use, and that part not always to its best use. But if we assume that Oresme's purpose was to explicate and animate his text for a new audience, he may be credited for his contribution to the tradition of the *Politics*. He also deserves praise and attention for the unprecedented breadth of his adaptation and application of the text, a breadth which encompasses much of political life as he knew it.

---

fond en comble l'enseignement d'Aristote" (Grignaschi, "Nicole Oresme et son commentaire," 143, n. 1). Albertus, Grignaschi notes (ibid.)," avait compris assez exactement ce passage." For Albertus, see 8: 569; for Peter, 316–317.

[102] "Nicole Oresme et son commentaire," 131, n. 1, with reference to *Le Livre de Politiques* 6. 1. (fol. 216d, p. 257b).

[103] *Le Livre de Politiques* 6. 2. (fol. 218a, p. 258b), from *Politics* 6. 2. 1317b. Grignaschi (138 and n. 1) says: "Le texte a été traduit en tenant compte de l'interprétation de Pierre. Albert qui lisait 'aut paucissimorum aut maximorum' n'était pas parvenu à en comprendre le sens" (Albertus, 8: 565; Peter, p. 314).

[104] *Le Livre de Politiques* 3. 8. (fol. 88a, p. 128b), from *Politics* 3. 7. 1279a–b (Barker, p. 114). Oresme said: "Et sunt ceulz qui ont la vertu de fortitude appellee *fortitude politique* ou *fortitude civile*, de laquelle il fu determiné ou .xvii.ᵉ chapitre du tiers d'*Ethiques*." Grignaschi (100, n. 2) says: ". . . il ne se laissa pas dérouter par les gloses de Saint Albert et de Saint Thomas sur la 'politie' et il déclara sans hésitation qu'Aristote attribuait aux citoyens des 'polities' la vertu militaire" (Albertus, 8: 238; Aquinas, 139).

[105] *Le Livre de Politiques* 6. 3. (fol. 219a–b, p. 260a), from *Politics* 6. 3. 1318a. Aristotle had asked whether a constitution based on property or one based on numbers was more in accordance with justice. Oresme's text and gloss were "[A constitution based on property] Est tres juste selon le juste ou droit democratique . . ." and "Apres il met l'autre membre par maniere de solution et de response; car il dit: Aut quod est nota solucionis," and, returning again to the text "Ou se celle est plus juste qui est selon la multitude." Grignaschi (144, n. 7) says: "L'interprétation d'Oresme semble bien correspondre à la glose d'Albert. Cependant c'est Oresme et non pas Albert qui a vu dans ce *aut* la preuve qu'Aristote inclinait vers la solution la plus démocratique." For the *aut*, see Susemihl's edition of Moerbeke, p. 464, line 1. For Albertus, see 8: 570.

INTRODUCTORY REMARKS: THE FRANCE OF CHARLES V AND THE *LIVRE DE POLITIQUES*

A discussion of the *Politics* and political life, unlike a discussion of the *Politics* and political thought, requires justification. The fourteenth century is a fascinating but slippery period for the historian of political life. At that time notions of the state had unquestionably advanced beyond the feudal and private, and royal governments, in France and England at least, were acquiring preeminence and becoming the center of growing loyalty. It is not possible to speak of a fully sovereign state in fourteenth-century theory or practice: for the majority, political life was a local phenomenon and loyalty immediate and particular. Even among the educated and articulate there was no unity of ideas about where allegiance should lie.

It would be risky to generalize about such a century, or to fix upon one person or one work as its epitome. A modest design carries a more solid promise of success. It is not too ambitious to ask, for example, whether there was present in the fourteenth century the notion that the nation-state had a preeminence surpassing that of the other levels of government, whether there was expressed during this century the idea that the elements of the state were joined by something more than a mass of private arrangements, and that each king was to be seen as a representative of the crown rather than as the owner of his kingdom. One can ask how the church was affected by centralization, and finally what its role should be as against the nation-state. The translation project of Charles allows us to see how these matters were illuminated by the *Politics*, and how this text was understood and used by a king trying to build a national monarchy.

Charles V might have been invented for the historian ambitious to find a meeting-point between classical political thought and medieval political life. Unsuited both in mind and spirit to be a warrior king after the old pattern, he possessed sufficient wisdom and wit to glorify himself, the monarchy and France. His reign, marked as it was by the protracted struggle with England, provides an excellent field for the study of political practice and ideas. The war provided both imperative and pretext for the assumption of new prerogatives by the royal administration. At the same time the growth and articulation of the government was paralleled by that of the church, so that the need for a reasonable accommodation of jurisdictions became obvious.

It is clear from the glosses of Oresme that he had his eyes open. Much of what he could see in his position at the court in Paris is reflected in his commentary, which is informed by a belief that Aristotle could do some service to Valois France.

III. NATIONAL SOVEREIGNTY AND THE HIERARCHY OF COMMUNITIES

Determination of the location of sovereignty is the foundation of order in political life[1] as in political thought. Incoherence and confusion are its opposites. If a ruler is to stand at the head of anything resembling a nation,

---

[1] For political development and ideology, see Noël Valois, *La France et le grand schisme d'occident*, 4 vols. (Paris, 1896–1902); Jean Rivière, *Le problème de l'église et de l'état au temps de Philippe le Bel: étude de théologie positive* (Paris, 1926); Heinrich Mitteis, *Der Staat des hohen Mittelalters* (Weimar, 1940, with an English translation by H. F. Orton, *The State in the Middle Ages* [Amsterdam and New York, 1975]); Walter Ullmann, "The Development of the Medieval Idea of Sovereignty," *English Historical Review* 64 (1949): 1–33; Robert Folz, *L'Idée d'empire en occident du Ve au XIVe siècle* (Paris, 1953); Marcel David, *La souveraineté et les limites juridiques du pouvoir monarchique du IXe au XVe siècle* (Paris, 1954); Peter N. Riesenberg, *Inalienability of Sovereignty in Medieval Political Thought* (New York, 1956); Ernst Kantorowicz, *The King's Two Bodies* (Princeton, 1957); Michael Wilks, *The Problem of Sovereignty in the Later Middle Ages* (Cambridge, 1963); Gaines Post, *Studies in Medieval Legal Thought* (Princeton, 1964); Joseph R. Strayer, *On the Medieval Origins of the Modern State* (Princeton, 1970); Michael Altschul, "Kingship, Government, and Politics in the Middle Ages. Some Recent Studies," *Medievalia et Humanistica*, n. s. 2 (1971): 133–152; Bernard Guenée, "Y a-t-il un État des XIVe et XVe siècles?" *Annales* 26 (1971): 399–406; and J. A. Wahl, "Baldus de Ubaldis and the Foundations of the Nation-State," *Manuscripta* 21 (1977): 80–96.

For material more closely related to the reign of Charles V, see: Léopold Delisle, *Mandements et actes divers de Charles V (1364–1380), recueillis dans les collections de la Bibliothèque Nationale* (Paris, 1874); Ernest Lavisse, "Étude sur le pouvoir royal au temps de Charles V," *Revue historique* 26 (1884): 233–280; Charles Benoist, *La Politique du roi Charles V* (Paris, 1886); Siméon Luce, *La France pendant la guerre de cent ans: épisodes historiques et vie privée au XIVe et XVe siècles*, 2 vols. (Paris, 1890–1893); Edward S. Dewick, ed., *The Coronation Book of Charles V of France* (London, 1899, Bradshaw Society 16); Roland Delachenal, *Histoire de Charles V*, 5 vols. (Paris, 1909–1931); idem, ed., *Chroniques des règnes de Jean II et de Charles V*, 4 vols. (Paris, 1910–1920); Gaston Dodu, "Les idées de Charles V en matière de gouvernement," *Revue des questions historiques*, 3rd ser. 14 (1929): 5–46; Gaston Zeller, "Les rois de France candidats à l'empire. Essai sur l'idéologie impériale," *Revue historique* 173 (1934): 273–311; S. Solente, editor of Christine de Pisan's *Le Livre des fais et bonnes meurs du sage roy Charles V*, 2 vols. (Paris, 1936–1940); Joseph L. Calmette, *Charles V* (Paris, 1945); Pierre Pradel, "Art et politique sous Charles V," *La Revue des arts* 1 (1951): 88–93.

More recent work includes André Bossuat, "La formule 'Le roi est empereur en son royaume' et son emploi au XVe siècle devant le parlement de Paris," *Revue historique de droit français et étranger*, 4th ser. 39 (1961): 371–381; Pierre Chaplais, "La souveraineté du roi de France et le pouvoir législatif en Guyenne au début du XIVe siècle," *Le moyen âge* 69 (1963): 449–469; Bernard Guenée, "État et nation en France au moyen âge," *Revue historique* 237 (1967): 17–30; Charles T. Wood, "Regnum Francie: A Problem in Capetian Administrative Usage," *Traditio* 23 (1967): 117–147; Peter S. Lewis, *Later Medieval France* (London, 1968); Joseph R. Strayer, "France: The Holy Land, the Chosen People, and the Most Christian King," in T. K. Rabb and J. E. Seigal, eds., *Action and Conviction in Early Modern Europe* (Princeton, 1969): 3–16, also in Strayer's *Medieval Statecraft and the Perspectives of History* (Princeton, 1971): 300–314; and Donal Byrne, "Rex imago Dei: Charles V of France and the *Livre des propriétés des choses*," *Journal of Medieval History* 7. 1. (March 1981): 97–113. René Fedou, *L'État au Moyen Age* (Paris, 1971), which chiefly concerns France, is a useful introduction to the secondary literature.

For an unusually gloomy assessment of the reign of Charles V, see Raymond Cazelles, *Société politique, noblesse et couronne sous Jean le Bon et Charles V* (Geneva, 1982), especially 570.

his government must be recognized as the supreme power within the borders of his country. Two things must be determined in order to establish sovereignty: the nature and boundaries of the state itself, and the nature of the preeminence enjoyed by its government.

We are speaking here of a territorial sovereignty, a sovereignty exercised by one level of government with regard to other levels of government, not with regard to custom or to natural law. It is not concerned with the division of power among the parts of the central government but with the right of ultimate authority within a given area, and with the exclusive control, direct or indirect, of the most essential functions of government, including law, justice, and war-making.

It is true that this falls short of the *puissance souveraine* of Bodin. It is equally true that legal sovereignty is an important matter. Nevertheless, the achievement of territorial sovereignty is a great accomplishment for a central government. It is an accomplishment which was brought about in the Middle Ages, and was essential to the creation of the modern state. By the fourteenth century the French royal government had acquired a preeminence which deserves to be called sovereignty or national sovereignty.[2] We shall see an awareness of this preeminence in the glosses of Oresme. Thus the use of this expression is justified. It is also helpful to speak of sovereignty because it allows us to refer both to independence from international bodies and to superiority over mere local powers. These two goals of national governments paralleled each other, and involved the same prerogatives.[3]

These common prerogatives were those of *imperium*, that is, the powers of an emperor or *princeps*.[4] They included hearing final appeals, making universally binding legislation, creating notaries, waging the just war, levying general taxation, and controlling coinage and the military.[5] These functions could no more be allowed to subjects than they could be reserved to the emperor, so that the king like Janus must show the same face in two directions. Similarly, the concept of high treason must be extended to crimes against the king, but not to crimes against barons.[6]

---

[2] As Joseph Strayer says in "The Promise of the Fourteenth Century" (in *Medieval Statecraft*), 319: "The idea [of the sovereign state] appears in almost complete form in the reign of Philip the Fair (1285–1314). . . ." See also *Medieval Origins*, 53.

[3] As David says, sovereignty involves "le refus de toute ingérence, tant interne qu'externe" (*La souveraineté*, p. 46).

[4] Ibid., 22. Jurists in the fifteenth century used these two titles together (Bossuat, "La formule 'Le roi est empereur,'" 377).

[5] For discussions of the prerogatives of empire, see Ullmann, "The Development of the Medieval Idea," 3, and Folz, *L'Idée d'empire*, 172, n. 27. Riesenberg, *Inalienability of Sovereignty*, 6, says that by the end of the Middle Ages, estimates of these prerogatives had gone up into the hundreds, with 408 on the list of Antonius de Petra.

[6] See Maxime Lemosse, "La lèse-majesté dans la monarchie franque," *Revue du moyen âge latin* 2 (1946): 5–24, who shows how the notion of high treason was replaced during the early Middle Ages by the feudal conception of *infidelitas*, which was "plutôt un manquement à la foi qui lie un sujet envers son maître par un lien particulier relatif et presque contractuel" (p. 7), and then revived with the recovery of Roman law. See the *Livre de Ethiques* 5. 10. (fol. 98c, p. 292).

Freedom from the interference of supranational powers was sought first.[7]
By the time of Charles V the practical independence of kingdoms was
accepted and the empire was not regarded as a serious threat.[8] The distinction between the titles of king or prince and that of emperor was weakened
as civilians and canonists asserted that a king was like an emperor within his
kingdom and could perform the functions of an emperor, or as these writers
used the terms *rex* and *imperator* interchangeably.[9] Theorists recognized the
de facto independence of kingdoms, and, increasingly, their *de jure* independence as well.[10]

---

[7] Strayer, "The Historical Experience of Nation-Building in Europe" (from *Medieval State-craft*), 345.

[8] In *Studies in Political Thought from Gerson to Grotius 1414-1625* (Cambridge, 1931), 24, J. N. Figgis quotes (without reference) the remark of Bryce that Dante's *De monarchia* was "not a prophecy but a dream." Beryl Smalley, in her introduction to *Trends in Medieval Political Thought* (Oxford, 1965), xi, mentions Étienne Gilson's comment that Dante "proved that the empire was [dead] by taking it seriously." In "Two Notes on Nationalism in the Middle Ages" (*Traditio* 9 [1953]): 320, Gaines Post says that by the mid-thirteenth century, "The kingdom, independent of the Empire . . . was now a Nation in fact if not yet in name."
For theories of national independence see Ullmann, "The Development of the Medieval Idea"; Rivière, "Sur une création juridique des publicistes français" (Appendix 4, pp. 424–430 of *Le problème de l'église et de l'état*); Sergio Mochi Onory, *Fonti canonistiche dell'idea moderna dello stato* (*imperium spirituale-iurisdictio divisa-sovranità*) (Milan, 1951), 271–288; Riesenberg, *Inalienability of Sovereignty*, 82–94; Gaines Post, "Public Law, the State, and Nationalism," in *Studies in Medieval Legal Thought*, 434–493; and, for French writers, Zeller, "Les rois de France candidats à l'empire." References in the following notes will be to these works.

[9] Among the civilians were: Andreas de Isernia (Rivière, *Le Problème de l'église*, 427; Ullmann, "The Development of the Medieval Idea," 22; Riesenberg, *Inalienability of Sovereignty*, 89); Marinus de Caramanico, who allowed the king of Sicily prerogatives similar to those of the emperor (Ullmann, 18–19; Riesenberg, 89); Lucas de Penna (Riesenberg, 89); Cynus of Pistoia (Rivière, 427); Oldradus da Ponte (Rivière, 427; Riesenberg, 90); Bartolus of Sassoferrato (Rivière, 425; Riesenberg, 82); and Baldus de Ubaldis (Rivière, 425). On Baldus, see J. A. Wahl, "Baldus de Ubaldis and the Foundations of the Nation-State," *Manuscripta* 21 (1977): 80–96.
Among the canonists to use the formula *rex est imperator* were: Huguccio (Mochi Onory, *Fonti canonistiche*, 162–177; Riesenberg, 83); Alanus Anglicus (Rivière, 428; Post, 464–466); Guido de Baysio "Archidiaconus" (Ullmann, 9; Mochi Onory, 165); and Laurentius Hispanus (Post, "Public Law, the State," 481). Post (455) gives a sketch of the controversy surrounding the use of the phrase *rex imperator*. It was the opinion of C. N. S. Woolf (*Bartolus of Sassoferrato* [Cambridge, 1913], p. 379) that the use of this phrase, which could be said to imply no more than *de facto* independence, made it possible to "shelve the problem" of whether *de jure* independence was involved as well.

[10] Baldus and Bartolus maintained a distinction between fact and theory (Ullmann, "The Development of the Medieval Idea," 5–6). The same is true of Oldradus da Ponte (Riesenberg, 90; Rivière, 427), and the canonists Bernardus Compostellanus (Ullmann, 4); Tancred of Bologna (Riesenberg, 85–86; Mochi Onory, 284); Johannes Teutonicus (Ullmann, 3; Mochi Onory, 279; Riesenberg, 84); Laurentius Hispanus (Mochi Onory, 276; Riesenberg, 85); and Panormitanus (Riesenberg, 87). Innocent III's dictum, ". . . rex [the king of France] ipse superiorem in temporalibus minime recognoscat . . .," could be taken as a denial of legal independence (*Decretales* 4. 17. 13., with Ullmann's reference [p. 4] to Carl Mirbt, *Quellen zur Geschichte des Papsttums und des römischen Katholizismus*, 4th ed. [Tübingen, 1924], p. 183). The *Glossa Ordinaria* adopted this interpretation (John Watt, "The *Quaestio in utramque partem* reconsidered," *Studia Gratiana* 13 [1967], 428–429). William of Ockham was among the imperialists who used this decretal to show that national kingdoms had no true independence from the empire (Riesenberg, 94, from *Dialogus* 3. 2. 2. 7. [ed. Melchior Goldast, *Monarchia s. Romani Imperii*, 3 vols. (Hanover, 1611), 2: 908]). This was not true of the *Pastoralis cura* of Clement V, who denied that nations were in any way dependent upon the empire (Ullmann, 1–2).

French writers were naturally sympathetic to the independence of king-doms.[11] John of Paris claimed national independence on Aristotelian grounds, saying that man's natural desire to live in a community would not best be fulfilled in a universal association.[12] The polemicists of Philip IV defended France from the empire as well as from the papacy.[13] During the reign of Charles V, the author of the *Songe du Vergier* placed the title of king above that of emperor,[14] and called the French king emperor in his own realm.[15]

---

[11] Stephen of Tournai (Mochi Onory, 97; Riesenberg, 83–84) and Durand of Mende the Elder (Riesenberg, 86; Folz, *L'idée d'empire*, 172) were among French canonists who attributed to the French king the powers of an emperor. Jean de Blanot (Johannes de Blanosco), writing in the middle of the thirteenth century, declared that the prince recognized no superior *in temporalibus* (Post, 471, and see Robert Feenstra, "Jean de Blanot et la formule 'Rex Francie in regno suo princeps est,'" *Études d'Histoire du droit canonique dediées à Gabriel Le Bras*, 2 vols. [Paris, 1965] 2: 885–895), and claimed that rebellion against the king was high treason, for the king is *princeps* in his own realm (Ullmann, 11). Jacques de Révigny, writing a few decades later, had the same opinion on high treason, though he seemed to think that the king became the object of this crime not as a prince but as a magistrate of a prince (Rivière, 425; Post, 473). Post also notes that, though Révigny "on the whole expresses the theory of independence" (472) he failed to assert the *de jure* independence of France (ibid.). A French jurist of the very end of the thirteenth century ("probably Thomas of Pouilly") said that the French king like the emperor has all the laws "in eius pectore" (Ernst Kantorowicz, "Kingship under the Impact of Scientific Jurisprudence," from Marshall Clagett, Gaines Post, and Robert Reynolds, eds., *Twelfth-Century Europe and the Foundations of Modern Society* [Madison, Wis., 1961], 104, 110).

Pierre de Belleperche made high claims for the empire (Post, 474–476) but it is possible that he was thinking of a French empire, like that of Pierre Dubois (Zeller, "Les rois de France candidats à l'empire," 296; Post, 448) and John of Jandun (Zeller, 300; Post, 475–476, 480), who said that the French deserved an empire because of their natural inclination toward perfection (from Antoine Le Roux de Lincey, *Paris et ses historiens aux XIVᵉ et XVᵉ siècles, documents et écrits originaux* . . . [Paris, 1867], 61). The memory of Charlemagne's empire encouraged French writers to dream of more than independence: see Gabrielle M. Spiegel, "The *Reditus Regni ad Stirpem Karoli Magni*: A New Look," *French Historical Studies* 7 (1971): 145–174.

[12] Ullmann, 17, from *De regia potestate et papali* 3. See also chapter 21 and chapter 18: ". . . quilibet rex est in hoc caput regni, et imperator monarcha si fuerit est caput mundi" (164–165 in the edition of Bleienstein, as cited above in chap. 2, n. 19).

[13] The author of *Rex pacificus* asserted the independence of the French kingdom from the Roman empire, and placed the king on a level with the emperor (Ullmann, 14; Rivière, 426), while the author of the *Quaestio in utramque partem* denied that France, with its *rex imperator* and its Trojan origins, had ever been subject to anyone (Ullmann, 14–15; Zeller, 295). On the other hand, the author of the *Disputatio inter clericum et militem* described France as a detached part of the empire, with all the rights and privileges of the empire (Rivière, 426). Among the jurists of the time, Jean Faure (Johannes Faber), like the author of the *Disputatio*, used more or less historical arguments, defending French independence as a right acquired by prescription (Ullmann, 12; Riesenberg, 91–92), and Pierre Jame (Petrus Jacobi) said that the French were *foederati* rather than subjects of the empire (Ullmann, 12, and see also p. 29 for a similar argument used by Oldradus da Ponte; Post, 477–480). Guillaume de Plaisian claimed that "dominus Rex sit imperator in regno suo et imperare possit terre et mari" (cited in Kantorowicz, "Kingship under the Impact of Scientific Jurisprudence," 104, 111, with a reference to the "Mémoire relatif au paréage de 1307," edited by A. Maisonobe in the *Bulletin de la société d'agriculture, industrie, sciences et arts du Département de la Lozère* [Mende, 1896], 521).

[14] Zeller, 305–306; Folz, *L'Idée d'empire*, 173.

[15] Ed. Jean Louis Brunet, in vol. 2 of Pierre Dupuy, *Traitez des droits et libertez de l'église gallicane*, 4 vols. (Paris, 1731–1751), chap. 1. 36, p. 36. See also the Latin version, the *Somnium viridarii*, 36 (1: 70 of Goldast, *Monarchia*). The *Songe* in the Brunet edition has been reproduced in *Revue du moyen âge latin* 13 (1957) and 14 (1958), while the *Somnium* is reproduced ibid. 22

The kings also spoke out. Louis VII called himself emperor.[16] Louis IX claimed to hold his kingdom from no one but God, and to observe Roman law by choice alone.[17] Philip IV was no more friendly to the emperor than to the papacy.[18] The same attitude may be seen in the legislation of Charles V, whose ordinance on the majority of the royal heirs describes the French king as the inheritor of the Caesars, and cites the maxim that the virtue of the Caesars does not wait upon their years.[19] Charles made his position especially clear during the visit of the emperor Charles IV, in 1378. The king obliged his imperial uncle to spend Christmas at Cambrai, a town of the empire, rather than at the royal town of Saint-Quentin, lest the latter indulge "ses magnificences et estas impériaulx."[20] So anxious was Charles V to avoid "aucun signe de dominacion"[21] that a black horse was sent to Charles IV for his entry into Paris, rather than a white horse such as the emperor would have used when surveying his own lands.[22]

Freeing France from external interference was essential to the making of a nation. It was a negative achievement, however, and a useless one without a

---

(1966). See also: Georges de Lagarde, "Le 'Songe du Verger' et les origines du gallicanisme," *Revue des sciences religieuses* 14 (1934): 1–33, 219–237; Friedrich Merzbacher, "Das Somnium viridarii von 1376 als Spiegel des gallikanischen Staatskirchenrechts," *Zeitschrift der Savigny-Stiftung für Rechtsgeschichte, kan. Abt.* 42 (1956): 55–72; Marion Lièvre, "Note sur les sources du *Somnium Viridarii* et du *Songe du Vergier*," *Romania* 81 (1960): 483–491; Jean-Pierre Royer, *L'Église et le royaume de France au XIVe siècle d'après le "Songe du Vergier" et la jurisprudence du Parlement* (Paris, 1969), and Quillet as cited above in chap. 1, n. 56.

[16] Ullmann, 11, from Alexandre Teulet, *Layettes du trésor des chartes (Inventaires et documents)*, 5 vols. (Paris, 1863–1909), 1 (1863): 75, #141: "Ludovicus Dei ordinante providentia Francorum imperator augustus."

[17] Paul Marie Viollet, ed., *Les Établissements de Saint Louis, accompagnés des textes primitifs et de textes derivés*, 4 vols. (Paris, 1881–1886), 2: 135, lines 6–7: ". . . li rois ne tient de nului fors de Dieu et de luy." (The "luy" is the monastery of St. Denis [see Spiegel, "*Reditus Regni,*" 160]). For Roman law, see Ullmann, 11, from François André Isambert, *Recueil général des anciennes lois françaises, depuis l'an 420 jusqu'à la révolution de 1789*, 29 vols. (Paris, 1821–1833), 1: 264, #169 (July 1254). Independence from Roman law seemed naturally to accompany independence from the (formerly or originally) Roman empire. (See Post, "Two Notes on Nationalism," *Traditio* 9 [1953]: p. 302, for restrictions on the teaching of Roman law in France, and for a listing by Hostiensis of countries which by not observing Roman law placed themselves outside the empire.)

[18] In 1312 he informed Henry VII that France had never recognized a temporal superior (*Monumenta Germaniae historica inde ab anno Christi quingentesimo usque ad annum millesimum et quingentesimum. Legum sectio IV: Constitutiones et acta publica imperatorum et regum* [Hanover and Leipzig, 1909–1911], 4, pt. 2: 812–814, #811).

[19] For the description "héritier des Cesars" and the use of Ovid's maxim, "Caesaribus virtus contigit ante diem . . .," see the "Édit, Loi ou Constitution qui fixe la majorité des Rois à quatorze ans commencés," from August of 1374, in Isambert, *Recueil général des anciennes lois* 5: 415–423, #546, at pp. 415, 419. See below, chap. 4, nn. 81–88, for Oresme's opinions on private and public succession. Charles was sickly and likely to leave a young heir. Oresme, perhaps mindful of this, said in a gloss on succession that the manners, not the numerical age of a king, determine fitness (*Le Livre de Politiques* 3. 23. [fol. 115a–b, p. 155a]).

[20] Dodu, "Les idées de Charles V," 43–44, from Delachenal, *Chroniques des règnes de Jean II et de Charles V*, 2: 199.

[21] Zeller, "Les rois de France candidats à l'empire," 308, from Delachenal, *Chroniques des règnes*, 2: 211.

[22] Dodu, "Les idées de Charles V," 43–44, from Christine de Pisan, *Le Livre des fais et bonnes meurs* 3. 35. (Solente 2: 97). See also Delachenal, 2: 211, and see also the illustrations in vol. 4, especially 36, which shows Charles IV on his black horse and Charles V on his white horse.

positive conception of France. We have seen that national ideas were current among legal writers; can we speak also of national sentiment?[23]

It is necessary for national sentiment that a group of people settled in a definite area feel a sense of loyalty and common purpose with those, even distant or unknown, who share their language and way of life, and that beyond this they feel an attachment to their land and give their highest allegiance not merely to the ruler at the head of the central administration but to the system of government he represents. This allegiance must transcend local political loyalties, and imply a willingness to sacrifice for the good of the nation as a whole. This definition is of course artificial and unrealistic. It would probably be safe to say that such a definition could have been formed inside only a few fourteenth-century heads, and that it represents a sentiment very seldom found in its pure and perfect form in any century. It may be that most of the people living in what is now France participated in this sentiment only to the extent that they honored the king and loathed the English. But as the war with England continued and as the monarchy broadened its prerogatives, a combination of practical necessity and inherited notions, largely classical, of loyalty to the *patria*, gave rise to popular expressions (and public exactions) which would scarcely have been possible a few centuries before, and which make it possible to speak, not of nationalism perhaps, but surely of sentiment for, and even obligation toward, the nation.

In France broad notions of patriotism[24] were joined by religious exaltation of the French monarchy and people,[25] and by traditions which included heroes like Charlemagne and legends like the descent of the French from the Trojans.[26] (Here as in the use of the *Politics* in political thought, classical elements helped the Middle Ages to free itself from classical political config-

---

[23] See Ch.-V. Langlois, "Les Anglais du moyen âge d'après les sources françaises," *Revue historique* 52 (1893): 298–315; Georges Ascoli, *La Grande-Bretagne devant l'opinion française depuis la guerre de cent ans jusqu'à la fin du XVIe siècle* (Paris, 1927); Dorothy Kirkland, "The Growth of National Sentiment in France before the Fifteenth Century," *History*, n.s. 23 (June 1938): 12–24; Halvdan Koht, "The Dawn of Nationalism in Europe," *American Historical Review* 52 (1946–1947): 265–280; Ernst Kantorowicz, "Pro Patria Mori" in Medieval Political Thought," *AHR* 56 (1950–1951): 472–492; Gaines Post, "Two Notes on Nationalism in the Middle Ages," *Traditio* 9 (1953): 281–320, which consists of two parts, "Pugna pro patria" (281–296) and "Rex imperator" (296–320); P. S. Lewis, "War-propaganda and Historiography in Fifteenth-Century France and England," *Transactions of the Royal Historical Society,* 5th ser. 15 (1965): 1–21; idem, *Later Medieval France*, pp. 59–77; Joseph R. Strayer, "France: The Holy Land, the Chosen People, and the Most Christian King," as cited above in n. 1; Karl Ferdinand Werner, "Les nations et le sentiment national dans l'Europe médiévale," *Revue historique* 244 (1970): 285–304, and Josette Wisman, "L'éveil du sentiment national au Moyen Age: la pensée politique de Christine de Pisan," ibid., 257 (1977): 289–297.

[24] See Kantorowicz, "Pro Patria Mori," and Post, "Pugna pro patria," from "Two Notes on Nationalism," 281–296.

[25] See Strayer, "France: The Holy Land, the Chosen People, and the Most Christian King," and see below, the discussion of the royal religion, in the chapter on church and state.

[26] See Wisman, "L'éveil du sentiment national," 293, and for a comment by Oresme on the French descent from Hector, see below, n. 173. For examples of the persistent tendency of medieval nationalists to seek a classical ancestry for their people, see Koht, "The Dawn of Nationalism."

urations.) Pride in the French language was shown in the translations commissioned by Jean II and Charles V, which have, at least in the latter case, been considered a form of royal propaganda.[27] The negative side of national feeling was reflected in vilification of the English enemy,[28] and defense of the French position in the Hundred Years War.[29] Among the people of France, despite considerable unpatriotic brigandage, there arose stereotypical views of the English, who were taxed with faithlessness, cruelty, and regicide, along with the repulsive vices of beer-drinking and speaking bad French.[30]

Along with national sentiment came national boundaries.[31] France was increasingly described as a territorial unit rather than as a people recognizing a ruler.[32] During the thirteenth century the title of the French king was changing from *rex Francorum* to *rex Francie*.[33] The expression *regnum Francie* had appeared around the beginning of the century.[34] This century also saw

---

[27] See Lewis, "War-propaganda and Historiography," 9, and *Later Medieval France*, 65–66.

[28] See Langlois, "Les Anglais du moyen âge"; Ascoli, *La Grande-Bretagne*; Kirkland, "The Growth of National Sentiment," 13–17; Koht, "The Dawn of Nationalism," for a criss-crossing of prejudices all over Europe; Lewis, "War-propaganda and Historiography," and *Later Medieval France*, 63–64.

[29] Lewis, *Later Medieval France*, 66, and Wisman, "L'éveil du sentiment national," 294, for the views of Christine de Pisan. We shall see (below, n. 175) that Oresme's glosses on the succession of women could be applied to the provisions of the Salic Law and thus to the succession dispute between France and England. For the similar interest of Raoul de Presles in the *lex Voconia* against inheritance by women, as shown in his translation of *The City of God*, see Shulamith Shahar, "Traduction et commentaire de la 'Cité de Dieu' par un penseur politique sous Charles V," *L'Information Historique* 39. 1. (January–February 1977), 48–49.

[30] See Lewis, *Later Medieval France*, 74, for the example of Bernard Georges, who preferred a life of outlawry in France to a life of beer-drinking in England. (One must add that this irresistible example dates from 1454.)

[31] Bernard Guenée has described the appearance of geographical notions of the French state ("État et nation en France au moyen âge"). John B. Freed, "The Friars and the Delineation of State Boundaries in the Thirteenth Century," in William C. Jordan, Bruce McNab, and Teofilo Ruiz, eds., *Order and Innovation in the Middle Ages* (Princeton, 1976): 31–40, shows how the organization of the mendicant orders into provinces aided in the definition of national boundaries.

Subjection to the French king was the usual standard for imposing interdicts ("État et nation en France," p. 24). See also Margaret Lügge, "'Gallia' und 'Francia' im Mittelalter," *Bonner historische Forschungen* 15 (1960): 173, where examples of this usage are given. Gerhart B. Ladner, "Aspects of Mediaeval Thought on Church and State," *Review of Politics* 9 (1947): 410, n. 27, notes that even as early as Gregory VII many papal documents spoke of people and countries rather than of rulers.

[32] Strayer, in *Medieval Origins*, 17.

[33] Kantorowicz, "Pro Patria Mori," 487, n. 52, with a reference to Percy Ernst Schramm, *Der König von Frankreich. Das Wesen der Monarchie vom 9. zum 16. Jahrhundert*, 2 vols. in one (Weimar, 1939), 1: 111, n. 1. See also Gabrielle M. Spiegel, "'Defense of the realm': evolution of a Capetian propaganda slogan," *Journal of Medieval History* 3 (1977), p. 131, n. 15, for use of *Francie rex*.

[34] Guenée, "État et nation en France," 24, with references to Teulet, *Layettes du trésor des chartes* 1: 159a (#571, from July of 1190, featuring the expressions "regis Francie" and "rege Francie"); 187b (#443, from February 1195–1196, with the expression "rege Francorum," and #445, from March 1195–1196, with "Francie regnum"); 254b (#720, from June of 1204, with "Franciae rex"); and 291b (#762, from June of 1205, with "barones regni Francie" and "rege Francie"). See also Spiegel, "Defense of the realm," 119, 123. In 1318 we see the expression *natione gallicus* in use; thereafter it appears frequently in Latin and French forms. See Guenée,

the use of a variety of terms to describe natives and foreigners, terms which had originally applied to seigneuries rather than to kingdoms as a whole.[35] The fourteenth century brought the notion of the frontier.[36] Loyalties assumed a territorial aspect. One Frenchman, when offered a choice between Plantagenet and Valois kings, each descended from Saint Louis, decided in favor of the Valois king, who had been born on French soil.[37]

The struggle of the king to establish sovereignty within his kingdom was the counterpart of his assertion of independence from the empire and papacy. He had to fight one extreme of medieval political organization, impractical universalism; then the other, inefficient particularism. The motto "imperator in regno suo" was used first against competition from abroad and then against competition at home.[38]

The characteristics of the king's sovereignty distinguish it from the power of administrators on other levels. It is not, like feudal government, contractual or conditional.[39] It affects its objects equally and directly.[40] It must

"État et nation," 21, from Gustave Dupont-Ferrier, "De quelques synonymes du terme 'province' dans le langage administratif de la France," *Revue historique* 161 (1929), 301, and Louise R. Loomis, "Nationality at the Council of Constance," *American Historical Review* 44 (1938–1939), 525, for *natio gallicana*. (For *nacion de France*, see Dupont-Ferrier, 301.)

[35] Guenée, "État et nation en France," 25. A document from the end of the century distinguishes between those born within and without the kingdom (ibid., with a reference to Henri Regnault, *La condition juridique du bâtard au moyen âge* [Pont-Audemer, 1922], 133–134, and to Marguerite Boulet-Sautel, "L'Aubain dans la France coutumière du Moyen Age," *Recueils de la Société Jean Bodin* 10 [1958]: 65–100).

[36] Guenée, "État et nation en France," 25. See also, idem, "Les limites [de la France]," in Michel François, ed., *La France et les Français* (Paris, 1972), 54–60.

[37] Guenée, "État et nation en France," 27, from the *Salachronica*: "Phelipe de Valois fu couronné pur ceo qu'il estoit nee du realme," in turn cited from Eugène Déprez, *Les préliminaires de la guerre de Cent Ans. La papauté, la France, et l'Angleterre (1328–1342)* (Paris, 1902, *Bibliothèque des Écoles françaises d'Athènes et de Rome*, 86), 34.

[38] Bossuat, "La formule 'le roi est empereur,' " 371, with reference to Olivier-Martin, *Histoire du droit français des origines à la Révolution* (Paris, 1948): 302, #235.

[39] Bossuat, "La formule 'Le roi est empereur,' " 380.

[40] See Dodu, "Les idées de Charles V," 24, for a reference to Charles V's ordinance on the regency: "l'office des rois est de gouverner et administrer sagement la chose publique, non une partie d'icelle mettre en ordonnance, et l'autre laissier sans provision convenable . . ." (Isambert, *Recueil général des anciennes lois*, 5: 424). Philip IV, in order to defend his kingdom, "had to assert that all people living within certain boundaries were 'in regno et de regno' (in the kingdom and part of the kingdom) . . ." (Strayer, "France: The Holy Land, the Chosen People, and the Most Christian King," 305, from *Medieval Statecraft*; see ibid., p. 259, from "The Laicization of French and English Society . . .").

We also find this idea among theorists. Riesenberg (*Inalienability of Sovereignty*, 86–87) mentions Durand of Mende, who claimed that the king in his realm is greater than the emperor in his, because the king alone does not recognize the emperor as his liege, while all men of his realm have a direct relationship with the king (citing his *Speculum iuris* [Venice, 1585], *De feudis*, § quoniam). See also Post, "Public Law, the State, and Nationalism," 445, for the opinion of Jean de Blanot that "the vassals of the king's vassals are directly subject to the king not by reason of homage but by reason of this jurisdiction" (from *Tractatus super feudis et homagiis*, ed. J. Acher, in *Nouvelle revue historique de droit français et étranger* 30 [1906]: 125–178). Jacques de Révigny (Post, 473–474) held the same opinion (see *Les oeuvres de Jacques de Révigny . . . d'après deux manuscrits de la Bibliothèque Nationale* [Paris, 1899], ed. Pierre de Tourtoulon, pp. 48–50).

exceed feudal *suzeraineté* or *superioritas*,[41] though it could be built up by using feudal prerogatives.[42] For example, under Philip IV taxation was based on payments given in place of military service.[43]

A king emerging from a hierarchy had to seek relative, before absolute, superiority.[44] Even the word "sovereign" seemed at times to admit of degree: the king could be described as "more sovereign" than his barons. Beaumanoir said that each baron is sovereign in his own barony, while the king is sovereign over all.[45] At the same time, he showed the qualitative superiority of royal power by saying that barons cannot contradict royal legislation.[46] Barons were peers to each other, not to the king.[47]

By the time of Charles V the consolidation of royal authority had gone so far that, as Lavisse says, it was exercised "without dispute, though not without caution, in the feudal domains in matters of justice, war and fi-

---

[41] See David, *La souveraineté*, 71, n. 11, on the views of Calasso, who thinks that *superioritas* has a feudal significance, and Mochi Onory, who thinks that it refers to a "prééminence monarchique." David himself has adopted the sensible position that the word was used in both senses, and points out that different usages can sometimes be found within one work. We shall soon see how Oresme used such terms in the *Livre de Politiques*.

Lemarignier ("Autour de la royauté," 23–24) gives some examples of the distinction between feudal homage and allegiance owed to the king (e.g., *Li Livres de jostice et de plat* [*ca.* 1260], ed. P.-N. Rapetti [Paris, 1850], p. 67). Lemarignier further notes that Jean de Blanot and Guillaume Durand distinguished two sorts of homage, of which one, influenced by Roman law, goes to a *suprema et generalis jurisdictio.* (His reference is to W. Kienast, *Untertaneid und Treuvorbehalt in Frankreich und England* [Weimar, 1952], p. 78, n. 2, and p. 79, n. 1.) Louis Halphen, "La place de la royauté dans le système féodale," in *A travers l'histoire du moyen âge* (Paris, 1950): 266–274, shows how kings from Louis VI to Louis X avoided doing homage for lands apparently held from others, in effect reviving the conceptions of royal sovereignty and the abstract state against the opposing feudal conception of royalty.

[42] Philip Augustus for example was able greatly to strengthen his position on a feudal basis. Charles E. Petit-Dutaillis (*La monarchie féodale en France et en Angleterre, X^e–XIIIe siècle* [Paris, 1933], 203–204), says that he derived as much profit from his status as supreme suzerain and culmination of the feudal hierarchy, as he did from his status as a consecrated king. See also Thomas Bisson, "The Problem of Feudal Monarchy: Aragon, Catalonia, and France," *Speculum* 53 (1978): 473.

[43] See Bisson, "The Problem of Feudal Monarchy," 478, and Strayer, "The Development of Feudal Institutions" (in *Medieval Statecraft*), 82.

[44] Strayer, "The Historical Experience of Nation-Building," 345. Strayer (p. 345, n. 6) cites an example from the "Mémoire relatif au paréage de 1307" (see n. 13 above) in which Philip the Fair and the bishop of Mende quarreled over who was *major dominus* and had *major jurisdictio* or *superioritas.*

[45] Philippe de Remi, Sire de Beaumanoir, *Coutumes de Beauvaisis,* ed. Amédée Salmon, 2 vols. (Paris, 1899–1900), 2: 23, #1403: ". . . en tous les lieus la ou li rois n'est pas nommés, nous entendons de ceus qui tienent en baronie, car chascuns barons est souverains en sa baronie." See also David, *La souveraineté,* pp. 68, 70; Chaplais, "La souveraineté du roi de France," 452; and Strayer, "Laicization," 260 (in *Medieval Statecraft*).

[46] *Coutumes de Beauvaisis* 1. 51. (ed. Salmon, 2: 23–24, #1043): "Voirs est que li rois est souverains par dessus tous et a de son droit la general garde de tout son roiaume par quoi il puet fere teus establissemens comme il li plest pour le commun pourfit, et ce qu'il establist doit estre tenu." It should be noted that, as Chaplais ("La souveraineté du roi de France," 455) points out, the authority to make laws was for Beaumanoir the primary aspect of sovereignty. See the long citation from Beaumanoir #1510, n. 61 below.

[47] Lewis, *Later Medieval France,* 85, and Chaplais, "La souveraineté du roi de France," 450–451, n. 5.

nance."[48] Warfare was becoming the monopoly of a national army.[49] The necessities of war in turn provided justification for taxation. Writers of the mid-fourteenth century followed Philip IV in supporting extraordinary demands for money on the basis of necessity and defense,[50] a prerogative reserved for the king alone.[51] The enormous ransom set for Jean II at Brétigny in 1360[52] was a legitimate feudal aid; the tax for the defense of the kingdom, established three years later, was not. Neither the *fouages* for defense nor the *aides* for ransom proved to be temporary or exceptional.[53]

Royal jurisdiction was exercised even in the territories conceded to the English. Charles took an appeal from Gascon nobles against the Black Prince, on the grounds that "we can and should give all justice in cases of sovereignty and final jurisdiction [*ressort*]."[54] In an act of 28 November 1368 Charles declared that he was sovereign lord of Guyenne in cases of appeal.[55]

The king extended his control beyond the order of lords and vassals,

---

[48] "Le pouvoir royal au temps de Charles V," 235.

[49] Ibid., 249, and see Raymond Cazelles, "La Réglementation royale de la guerre privée de Saint Louis à Charles V et la precarité des ordonnances," *Revue historique de droit français et étranger,* 4th ser. 38 (1960): 530–548.

[50] For Philip, see Lewis, *Later Medieval France,* 104. One of his counselors, Guillaume de Plaisian, went so far as to declare that ". . . omnia que sunt infra fines regni sui sint domini Regis . . . [and can be taken and used] ex causa publice utilitatis et deffensionis regni sui . . ." (from "Mémoire relatif au paréage de 1307" [as cited above, n. 13], 521, from Strayer, "The Laicization of French and English Society in the Thirteenth Century," *Medieval Statecraft,* 261, n. 16). See also Post, "Public Law, the State, and Nationalism," 448, and Gabrielle M. Spiegel, " 'Defense of the realm': evolution of a Capetian propaganda slogan," *Journal of Medieval History* 3 (1977): 115–133, who argues that "the chroniclers' persistent focus on the image of the king as royal defender facilitated the interior evolution of the meaning of 'defense of the realm' from that of feudal *tuitio* to the public concept of Roman jurisprudence" (p. 115). Oresme was not one of the writers of this period who favored taxation, as we shall see in chap. 4.

[51] Post, "Public Law, the State, and Nationalism," 448 and n. 47, for Jean Faure, who said: "Argumentum, quod villa vel collegium non possit indicere collectas, nec barones ob necessitatem patriae. . . . Et hoc tenet Hostiensis, videlicet, quod nullus possit indicere, nisi princeps. . . . Item dic, quod nec princeps potest indicere, nisi ob necessitatem vel utilitatem publicam, quin peccet . . ." (from *Summa Codicis* [Lyons, 1594] to C. 4, 62, 1). Post adds that this opinion "was common among the legists of the thirteenth century and earlier." For Pierre Jame on the right of kings to impose extraordinary taxes "pro defensione regni," see Post as cited, 478. Beryl Smalley cites the contemporary (ca. 1334–1336) English example of Robert Holcot, who also thought that taxes could be taken only by princes, and then only for public necessity (from Holcot's commentary on Wisdom, lectio 23 C, fol. 38va from manuscript 27 = C of Balliol College, Oxford; cited in *English Friars and Antiquity in the Early Fourteenth Century* [New York, 1960], 196–197).

[52] The sum was 3,000,000 *écus d'or* (Lewis, *Later Medieval France,* 105).

[53] Ibid., 107. Charles did abolish the *fouages* (on his deathbed) but this had little lasting effect.

[54] ". . . nous pouvons et devons faire toute justice, en cas de souveraineté et ressort" (cited in Delachenal, *Histoire de Charles V,* 4: 103). See Pierre Chaplais, "Some Documents regarding the Fulfilment and Interpretation of the Treaty of Brétigny (1361–1369)," *Camden Miscellany* 19 (1952): 1–84. On p. 51, n. 1, he defines *ressort* as "the right to give judical decisions which could not be challenged before a higher court."

[55] Lavisse, "Le pouvoir royal au temps de Charles V," 236, from Delisle, *Mandements et actes divers,* 241, #478: ". . . nous, qui sommes seigneur souverain du pais de Guienne. . . ." The author of the *Songe du Vergier* supported such claims: "Doncques la souveraineté et le ressort demourerent au roy de France comme à celuy qui estoit vray et souverain seigneur naturel de tant de temps qu'il n'est memoire du contraire" (1. 146. [ed. Brunet, as cited in n. 15, 2: 172]).

creating the consulates of communes and suppressing them.[56] In the case of Tournai suppression was justified by the superiority of royal government, rather than as a response to a breach of contract.

The most detailed and striking evidence of the position attained by the king appears in the ordinance of 8 May 1372, for the conservation of the king's rights in Montpellier.[57] Here we see the practice of royal sovereignty in a city being ceded to another authority. A royal governor, with a royal seal, a procurator and an advocate were to be sent to protect the rights of the king of France, and to disable the government of the king of Navarre.[58] The ordinance speaks of "Souverainetez et Ressors" at least eight times, and makes nearly as many references to "souverainetez" alone. We are told at least nine times that the king exercises his prerogatives "seul et pour le tout." At least three times, we are told that these prerogatives apply to the whole kingdom. In addition, the preamble to the ordinance says that these rights always pertain to the king.

What were the rights so strongly asserted? These included several of the old prerogatives of imperium, such as the creation of public notaries, the legitimation of bastards, and the restriction of high treason to crimes against the king.[59] It cannot be doubted that certain functions were considered to be monopolies of the royal government by the time of Charles V. The prerogatives to be guaranteed to him included several which had been exercised by the duke of Guyenne up to the start of the war.[60] This is not sovereignty in the sense given by Bodin, but as a list of rights held by one king in lands ceded to another it is impressive.

A few words should be said, however, about sovereignty in that other, more modern sense, the sense which involves limitation by the law and in lawmaking. Even here the royal government was not as restricted as it is sometimes made to appear. Political theorists were able to use the ideas of Aristotle, of Roman law, and of Christian sources with the usual kaleidoscopic effect. The result was a wide range of theory, some of which was far from the idea of a state bound by law. Nor was political practice likely to

---

[56] For the creation of the consulate of Angoulême (from Charles's regency) see Lavisse, "Le pouvoir royal au temps de Charles V," p. 260, from Denis François Secousse, *Ordonnances des roys de France de la troisième race*, 21 vols. (Paris, 1723–1849), 3: 305. For the suppression of the commune of Tournai, see Lavisse, "Le pouvoir royal," 265.

[57] "Instruction pour la conservation des droits de Souveraineté, de Ressort et autres droits Royaux, dans la Ville et Baronnie de Montpellier, cédées au Roy de Navarre" (*Ordonnances . . . de la troisième race*, ed. Secousse, 5: 477–480). As Lavisse says ("Le pouvoir royal," 258), ". . . le document prouve qu'il existait au XIVᵉ siècle une théorie complète des droits du pouvoir royal et que ces droits étaient fort étendus. . . ." As Royer (*L'Église et le royaume de France*, as cited above in n. 15; 207–208) says, this document is reproduced in the *Songe du Vergier* 2. 251. On the same subject, see Shulamith Shahar, "Une source encore inconnue du Songe du Vergier: l'Ordonnance de 1372," *Le Moyen Age* 76 (1970): 285–291.

[58] Lavisse, "Le pouvoir royal," 244.

[59] They also included the right of royal officials to hear appeals, to control coinage, to establish impositions, to recall the banished, to make remission for crimes, and to give letters of amortization.

[60] Chaplais, "La souveraineté du roi de France," 466.

allow absolute limitation. By the end of the thirteenth century, the observance of law by the king seemed to be voluntary and selective. Good custom could not be altered, but bad custom could be,[61] especially in times of war or to serve the common good. The ordinances of Charles V, who was partial to the exalted terminology of the later emperors,[62] speak of the king as *legibus solutus*, not bound by law.[63]

Nor was Charles disposed to share his authority, for he considered himself the sole judge of public necessity.[64] He was not averse to taking counsel;[65] indeed, his request for translations of works of political theory would have made no sense had he cared only for his own opinion. This habit, however, because it was voluntary, strengthened him. After having trouble with the Estates-General during his regency, he called no general assemblies of the kingdom during the last decade of his reign.[66] The last meeting of the Estates-General under Charles in 1369 was more like a gathering of notables than a body with governing authority.[67]

Of course Charles did not wish to style himself a tyrant.[68] He favored voluntary observance of the law, and regular and rational procedure in government. At the same time he intended to regulate the fragmented power of feudal administrations with the centralized power of a sovereign,

---

[61] Ibid., 463. See also F. Olivier-Martin, "Le roi de France et les mauvaises coutumes au moyen âge," *Zeitschrift der Savigny-Stiftung für Rechtsgeschichte, Germ. Abt.* 58 (1938): 108–137. David (*La souveraineté*, 240–241) is not impressed by the respect paid to the law in the thirteenth to fifteenth centuries. For Oresme's views on law-changing and the fate of laws "indiscretement mises," see below, chap. 4, n. 120. Beaumanoir spoke of the lawmaking powers of the prince in time of war (*Les coutumes de Beauvaisis* #1510 [Salmon 2: 261–262]): "Mes ou tans de guerre et ou tans que l'en se doute de guerre, il convient fere as rois et as princes, as barons, et as autres seigneurs, mout de choses que, s'il les fesoit ou tans de pes, il feroient tort a leur sougiès. . . ." Pierre Dubois, speaking of the king's right to take the goods of the church in time of necessity, said: ". . . tunc in casu necessitatis defensionis regni, que legem non habet . . ." (*De recuperatione Terrae Sanctae* 123, ed. Charles V. Langlois [Paris, 1891], 116).

[62] Dodu, "Les idées de Charles V," 26.

[63] Lewis, *Later Medieval France*, 85, from *Ordonnances . . . de la troisième race*, ed. Secousse, 6: 29. Charles's law on the majority of the royal heirs (see n. 19 above) explains that "les lois qui exigent un certain âge pour la majorité *disposent seulement pour ceux qui leur sont soumis*" (Dodu, "Les idées de Charles V," 26).

[64] Dodu, "Les idées de Charles V," 27.

[65] Lavisse, "Le pouvoir royal au temps de Charles V," 277, from the ordinance on guardianship (Isambert, *Recueil général des anciennes lois*, 5: 434): "De temps comme les granz faiz et les granz besoignes sont faites par conseil de plusieurs sages hommes, de tant sont-elles plus seures et plus certaines . . ." (from an enactment of October 1374). See also Dodu, "Les idées de Charles V," p. 31, n. 4, for a list of ordinances acknowledging the help of counsel.

[66] Lewis, *Later Medieval France*, 337.

[67] Dodu, "Les idées de Charles V," 27.

[68] Dodu, "Les idées de Charles V," pp. 30–31: "Ennemi de la tyrannie autant qu'Oresme, Mézières ou Aristote, Charles préfère que les choses se passent selon des règles, de façon légale. . . . 'Le tyran,' précise Oresme, 'est comme ung monstre à nature, ci comme ung corps duquel la teste est si grosse que le résidu d'icelui est si faible qu'il ne la peut soutenir.'"
The citation from Oresme is from chapter 25 of his treatise on currency (edited by Charles Johnson, *The De moneta of Nicholas Oresme . . .* [London, 1956], p. 44): ". . . [the tyrant] est sicut unum monstrum, sicut unus homo cuius caput est tam magnum, tam grossum, quod non potest a reliquo debili corpore sustentari."

the personal government of amateur administrators with a professional group of public officials. His reign is described as a triumph of reason over violence, disorder and arbitrariness.[69] How might these processes be illuminated by a reading of Aristotle?

National Sovereignty: The Contribution of Aristotle

To support national sovereignty using the *Politics*, we begin with the first sentences of the *Politics*, which form the foundation of all that follows: Aristotle's description of the hierarchy of increasingly self-sufficient human communities, which culminates in the political community, the "most sovereign and inclusive" of associations.[70] For Aristotle the end of government is the good life, and it is the political association which best supports the good life, smaller and larger groups being equally unsuited to this purpose. Aristotle emphasized this by characterizing the difference between the political association and the smaller or lower communities as qualitative rather than merely quantitative,[71] and by describing his ideal city as "surveyable."[72] The special superiority of this perfected organization gives it sovereignty over less complete organizations, as Aristotle's definition implies, and saves it from being incorporated into, or replaced by, associations too large to promote the good life.

This hierarchy of communities must have been very attractive to medieval writers, who received the *Politics* at a time when feudal and imperial models of political life were becoming obsolete. Virtually all adopted the hierarchy and its self-sufficient culmination, which they called the *communitas perfecta*.[73] This conception of political organization was particularly

---

[69] Benoist, *La Politique du roi Charles V*, xvi–xvii.

[70] *Politics* 1. 1. 1252a (Barker, p. 1). For the use of Aristotle, see the citations in n. 1. above, especially Ullmann's "The Development of the Medieval Idea of Sovereignty," and Wilks's *The Problem of Sovereignty*. See also such general works as Otto von Gierke, *Political Theories of the Middle Age* (Cambridge, 1900); C. H. McIlwain, *The Growth of Political Thought in the West* (New York, 1932); Helene Wieruszowski, *Vom Imperium zum nationalen Königtum* (Munich and Berlin, 1933); Friedrich August Freiherr von der Heydte, *Die Geburtsstunde des souveränen Staates* (Regensburg, 1952); and Ewart Lewis, *Medieval Political Ideas*, 2 vols. (New York, 1954), esp. 2: 430–505. Although Quentin Skinner, in his conclusion to *The foundations of modern political thought*, 2 vols. (Cambridge, 1978), 2: 349, says that "any attempt to excavate the foundations of modern political thought needs to begin with the recovery and translation of Aristotle's *Politics*," it is his intention to emphasize other contributions (1: xiv).

[71] *Politics* 1. 1. 1252a.

[72] Ibid., 7. 4. 1326b, where he says that "the citizens of a state must know one another's characters" (Barker, 292), and 7. 5. 1327a, where he says that the territory of the ideal city should be "such as to be surveyable" (Barker, 293).

[73] This is after the "communitas perfecta civitas" of Moerbeke (in the edition of Franz Susemihl, *Aristotelis Politicorum libri octo* . . . [Leipzig, 1872], p. 6, lines 9–10) which in Barker's translation is "the final and perfect association" (p. 4, from *Politics* 1. 2. 1252b).

For medieval writers, see Thomas Aquinas, *De Regimine Principum* 1. 1. (edited by Joseph Mathis [Turin, 1924], p. 3): ". . . in uno autem dico [lege: vico], quantum ad ea quae ad unum artificium pertinent; in civitate vero, quae est perfecta communitas, quantum ad omnia necessaria vitae; sed adhuc magis in provincia una . . ."; John of Paris, *De reg. pot. et pap.* 1 (ed. Bleienstein, p. 76): ". . . [the self-sufficient community] non est communitas domus vel vici sed civitatis vel regni"; Giles of Rome, *De regimine principum* 3. 1. 1. (p. 238 in the Rome 1556

useful because it provided a respectable alternative to the empire,[74] and could at the same time be used against the localism of political practice.[75]

The medieval writers who took up the hierarchy of communities and recognized the necessity of the communitas perfecta in achieving the good life[76] did not always use this idea according to the understanding of Aristotle. The ideal of surveyability could be realized in a medieval city-state, but not in the nation-state. Nevertheless, some writers tried to ignore the essential intimacy of the true *polis* in order to make the kingdom seem to be the perfect culmination of political organization. The regnum was frequently added to the hierarchy of communities, with the implication that it was superior to smaller communities as a location of the good life.[77]

---

edition): ". . . communitas civitatis, quae est principalissima communitas respectu vici, et domus, maxime ordinatur ad bonum"; Engelbert of Admont, *De ortu et fine Romani imperii* 15. (in Goldast, *Politica Imperialia* [Frankfurt, 1614], p. 764): ". . . sicut multae domus ordinantur ad unam civitatem, et ad bonum ipsius: et multae civitates, et populi civitatum ad unam gentem et regnum, et ad bonum ipsius, . . . sic etiam multa regna mundi, et bonum ipsorum, ordinantur ad unum naturale regnum et imperium . . ."; James of Viterbo, *De regimine christiano* 1. 1. (ed. H.-X. Arquillière, as *Le plus ancien traité de l'église. Jacques de Viterbe De regimine christiano* [Paris, 1926], 92): ". . . Quanto autem plures sunt sibi invicem sociati, magis possunt sibi ad vitam sufficere. . . . Est igitur civitas domo perfectior et regnum civitate . . ."; Dante, *De Monarchia* 1. 3. (ed. L. Bertalot [Florence and Rome, 1920], 12): ". . . sic alius est finis ad quem singularem hominem, alius ad quem ordinat domesticam communitatem, alius ad quem viciniam, et alius ad quem civitatem, et alius ad quem regnum, et denique optimus ad quem universaliter genus humanum. . . ."

[74] Moromichi Watanabe, *The Political Ideas of Nicholas of Cusa, with Special Reference to his De Concordantia Catholica. Travaux d'humanisme et renaissance* 58 (Geneva, 1963), 116. Lagarde ("Une adaptation de la Politique" [see chap. 2, n. 16], p. 262) has said that Aristotle could be used to support the notion that "la communauté parfaite n'était pas forcément universelle. . . ." See also Alessandro Passerin d'Entrèves, *The Notion of the State* (Oxford, 1967), p. 30, and Wilks, *The Problem of Sovereignty*, 431. See also Helmut G. Walther, *Imperiales Königtum, Konziliarismus und Volkssouveränität. Studien zu den Grenzen des mittelalterlichen Souveränitätsgedankens* (Munich, 1976), 222.

[75] Gierke, *Political Theories of the Middle Age*, 96. See also his *Johannes Althusius und die Entwicklung der naturrechtlichen Staatstheorien* (Breslau, 1913), 231.

[76] For Thomas Aquinas, John of Paris, and James of Viterbo, see the citations in n. 73 above. See also Giles of Rome, *De Regimine Principum* 3. 1. 1. (p. 238 in the Rome, 1556, edition): ". . . Nam civitas sicut complectitur domum et vicum; et est principalior communitatibus illis, et magis sufficiens in vita . . ."; Ptolemy of Lucca (in his continuation of Aquinas's *De Regimine Principum* 4. 2. [ed. Mathis, p. 82]): ". . . civitatem [est] necessariam homini constituendam propter communitatem multitudinis, sine qua homo vivere decenter non potest . . ."; Engelbert of Admont, *De ortu et fine* 13. (Goldast, *Politica Imperialia*, p. 761): ". . . felicitas regni est finis intentus in constitutione et administratione, sive regimine regum et regnorum . . ."; Dante, *De Monarchia* 1. 5. (ed. Bertalot, p. 17): ". . . civitatem, cuius finis est bene sufficienterque vivere . . ."; Marsilius of Padua, *Defensor Pacis*, 1. 4. 1. (ed. Richard Scholz [Hanover, 1932], p. 16): "Quod autem dixit Aristoteles: *vivendi gracia facta, existens autem gracia bene vivendi*, significat causam finalem ipsius [communitatem] perfectam . . ."; Augustinus Triumphus, *Summa de ecclesiastica potestate* 1. 6. (p. 82 of the Rome, 1479, edition): ". . . [communitas civitatis] est communitas perfecta secundum philosophum: quia si civitas bene ordinata est in ea debet invenire quicquid necessarium est ad vitam humanam."

[77] "Now Aristotle's 'State' is the πόλις, but the πόλις entered medieval thought both as the Regnum or Provincia and as the Civitas" (C. N. S. Woolf, *Bartolus of Sassoferrato* [Cambridge, 1913], 274 [see also ibid., n. 2]).

See the citation from Aquinas, *De Regimine Principum*, above in n. 73, and his *In decem libros Ethicorum Aristotelis ad Nicomachum expositio* 1. 2., ed. R. Spiazzi (Turin, 1949), p. 8: ". . . aliquando amabile quidem est, quod hoc [i.e., amor] exhibeatur uni soli civitati, sed multo divinius est, quod exhibeatur toti genti, in qua multae civitates continentur. Dicitur autem hoc esse

Dante thought the kingdom to be more perfect than the city. He did not stop here, however. Like some other medieval thinkers, who had perhaps before their eyes the vision of Rome with its extended territory and citizenship, he added the empire to the hierarchy.[78] As a supporter of the empire Dante abandoned Aristotle's insistence upon the balanced qualities of the polis in favor of a general principle that bigger is better.[79] If the family is

---

divinius, eo quod magis pertinet ad Dei similitudinem. . . ." The continuator of Aquinas's *De Regimine Principum,* Ptolemy of Lucca, spoke of contemporary kingdoms, including France, as equivalent to the *civitas* (4. 16.). See also Giles of Rome, *De Reg. Princ.* 3. 1. 5. (p. 244 in the Rome 1556 edition): ". . . regnum sit quasi quaedam confoederatio plurium civitatem, eo quod uniantur sub uno rege . . ."; John of Paris, *De reg. pot. et pap.* 4. (ed. Bleienstein, p. 84): ". . . nominat regimen non solum domus vel vici vel civitatis sed provinciae in qua invenitur maxima sufficientia eorum quae pertinent ad totam vitam . . ." (see also the citation in n. 73); James of Viterbo, *De reg. christ.* 1. 1. (ed. Arquillière, p. 92): "Bonum autem tanto maius quanto communius . . . ideo civitas domo perfectior est et regnum perfectius civitate"; Dante, *De mon.* 1. 5. (ed. Bertalot, p. 17): ". . . civitatem, cuius finis est bene sufficienterque vivere . . ." (see also the citation from *De mon.* in n. 73 above); idem, *Convivio* 4. 4., for a text with a similar import; William of Ockham, *Dialogus* 3. 1. 2. 5. (in Goldast, *Monarchia,* 2: 794): ". . . *Regnum* vel *Ducatus* . . . potest communitas appellari . . . et multa, quae dicuntur de civitate, proportionaliter intelligenda sunt de regno et quacunque communitate, quae plures complectitur civitates"; Marsilius of Padua, *Defensor Pacis* 1. 2. 2. (ed. Scholz, 10–11): ". . . pluralitatem civitatum seu provinciarum sub uno regimine contentarum: secundum quam accepcionem, non differt regnum a civitate in policie specie, sed magis secundum quantitatem."

[78] For Engelbert of Admont and Dante, see the citations above, in n. 73, After speaking of the *communitas perfecta* (see n. 76) Augustinus Triumphus turns to the "communitas totius orbis qui constituitur ex omnibus regnis." In the *De mon.* 1. 3. (ed. Bertalot, 12–13) Dante said: "Est ergo aliqua propria operatio humane universitatis . . . ad quam quidem operationem nec homo unus, nec domus una, nec una vicinia, nec una civitas, nec regnum particulare pertingere potest." Although Passerin d'Entrèves says that Aquinas makes no open mention of the notion of universal empire (*The Medieval Contribution to Political Thought* [London, 1939], 36), Aquinas did allude to the subject in *Summa Theologica,* suppl. qu. 40, a. 6 (*Opera omnia* [Rome, 1882–], 12 [1906]: 77): "*Bonum* autem *commune* est *divinius quam bonum speciale* . . . cum tota Ecclesia sit *unum corpus,* oportet, si ista unitas debet conservari, quod sit aliqua potestas regitiva respectu totius Ecclesiae, supra potestatem episcopalem. . . ." (This is clearly limited to the church.) Aquinas was said to have mentioned the empire in an exposition of the Second Letter to the Thessalonians, according to notes by Reginald of Piperno. (See Gerhart B. Ladner, "Aspects of Mediaeval Thought on Church and State," *Review of Politics* 9 [1947]: 419, who notes that this work is probably not authentic.) William of Ockham recognized that Aristotle did not speak of these larger units of government (*Dial.* 3. 1. 2. 30. [Goldast, 2: 819]): ". . . Aristotele[s], qui solummodo loquitur de politiis, quae in civitatibus custodiuntur. . . ." Remigio da Girolami carried this principle to the universal church rather than to the universal empire. In *De bono communi* (fol. 97ʳ of the Florence MS., Bibl. Naz. Cod. Conv. Soppr. C. 4. 940, from Lorenzo Minio-Palluelo, "Remigio Girolami's *De bono communi:* Florence at the Time of Dante's Banishment and the Philosopher's Answer to the Crisis," *Italian Studies* 11 [1956]: 62), he said: ". . . quanto bonum est communius, tanto est magis amandum . . . bonum universalis ecclesie magis quam bonum unius regni." See n. 111 for Oresme.

[79] Gierke has called this a "grossly illogical device" (*Political Theories of the Middle Age,* 96). For expressions of this principle by Aquinas and James of Viterbo, see n. 77, and n. 78 for Remigio da Girolami. Aquinas also expressed this principle (but not, it should be remembered, for a universal *secular* government) in *ST* 2ᵃ 2ᵃᵉ, qu. 50, art. 1 (*Opera omnia* [Rome, 1882–], 8 [1895]: 374). Engelbert of Admont, in *De ortu et fine* (Goldast, *Politica Imperialia,* 762) said: ". . . magnitudo regni secundum quantitatem virtutis, semper facit ad augmentum felicitatis ipsius." After this, however (762), he denied that a larger kingdom is necessarily better than a smaller one. Graziolo Bambagliolo said in his *Tractato de le volgar sententie sopra le virtù morali* (ed. Ludovico Frati, in *Rimatori bolognesi del Trecento* [Bologna, 1915], 19), in *rubrica* 27: "Quanto è perfecto il ben, tanto più vale/Quant'egl' è piu comune e generale;/Perchè ciascun contenta e satisface,/E nascene unïone e dolce pace."

more self-sufficient than the individual, the village more self-sufficient than the family, and the city-state a communitas perfecta, then the kingdom must be *perfectior* and the empire the best of all, the most complete state and the one best able to provide the good life. Instead of speaking of the good life, Dante, like an Averroist,[80] spoke of the development of the human intellect. He believed that the intellectual development of the world and the creation of a rational life for mankind could not be accomplished without the peace which only a universal government could guarantee. Dante used Aristotle's metaphysical principles, like the *ordinatio ad unum,* to support this theory.[81] His extreme extension of the hierarchy of communities is in spirit very distant from the glosses of Oresme, and provides a good parting contrast to the *Livre de Politiques.*

Oresme and National Sovereignty

Oresme, although presumably sympathetic toward the regnum or nation-state, did not express this sympathy in his commentary on the first chapters of the *Politics.* In his glosses on Aristotle's description of the hierarchy of communities Oresme attempts nothing more than an explication of the text. When he introduces the "most sovereign and inclusive" association, his comments are simple and unambitious:

And thus as it contains all the other communities which are a part of it and are below it, as was said in the twelfth chapter of *Ethics* 8, it seems that the good and end for which it is ordained embraces the ends of the others. And consequently, it is most principal and most divine[82] because, as was said in the first chapter of the *Ethics,* the more general a good is, the more it is divine and the more it is to be honored. After this [Aristotle] makes a comparison between the city and the other [lower] communities, and first he rectifies an error.[83]

---

[80] See Martin Grabmann, "Studien über den Einfluss der aristotelischen Philosophie auf die mittelalterlichen Theorien über das Verhältnis von Kirche und Staat," *Sitzungsberichte der Bayerischen Akademie der Wissenschaften zu München. Philosophisch-Historische Abteilung,* 1934, part 2, 85–87; Heydte, *Die Geburtsstunde,* 184; Kantorowicz, *The King's Two Bodies,* 471–472, 475; Alan Gewirth, *Marsilius of Padua. The Defender of Peace,* 2 vols. (New York, 1951–1956), 1: 41, n. 40, for a summary of opinions.

[81] *De mon.* 1. 5. (ed. Bertalot, p. 16); *Convivio* 4. 4. (in *Opere di Dante,* eds. G. Busnelli, G. Vandelli [Florence, 1954], 5: 33). This principle appears in the *Politics* 1. 3. 1254a (in Susemihl's edition of Moerbeke, 17, lines 9–11): ". . . quaecunque enim ex pluribus constituta sunt et fit unum aliquod commune, sive ex coniunctus sive ex divisis, in omnibus videtur principans et subiectum." It is not certain that Dante read the *Politics* itself; see Allan H. Gilbert, "Had Dante Read the *Politics* of Aristotle?" *Publications of the Modern Language Association* 43, no. 3 (1928): 602–613.

That Dante's use of Aristotle to support the empire was a misuse is not doubted. There is some disagreement, however, about whether Dante merely made an illegitimate extension of the *polis* of Aristotle, or actually changed it into something quite different. For an introduction to this controversy, see Peterman as cited above in chap. 2, n. 21, who says (p. 23): ". . . Dante's 'universal civil order of mankind' (*universalis civilitatis humani generis*) does not merely expand Aristotle's πόλις (*polis*)—which virtually all commentators recognize—it transforms it."

[82] For Thomas Aquinas and the divinity of the common good, see above, nn. 77, 78.

[83] *Le Livre de Politiques* 1. 1. (fol. 5a, p. 45b). For his citation of the *Ethics,* see 8. 9. 1160a (p. 489 in the translation of Harris Rackham [London and New York, 1926]): "But all these [lower]

The error to which Oresme refers is one which Aristotle ascribes to Plato. According to Aristotle, Plato considers the differences between the master of slaves, the father, the king, and the statesman to be those of degree rather than of kind, thus denying the special nature and purpose of the political association. Oresme does not take up this controversy; the first part of his gloss suggests that he did not grasp the distinction between qualitative and quantitative differences, for he merely suggests that there are differences of some kind between the sorts of power or government mentioned by Aristotle:

Political and royal government pertain to a large multitude or community. They differ in that royal government is sovereign and political government is under royal government, over a city or country, and is regulated by the customs and laws of the region. But the household management of a father over his wife and children is paternal government, and his power over slaves is called despotic. And all together, that is to say the government which a father or one in a similar position exercises over his wife and children and slaves, this is called economic government.[84]

After following Aristotle through his description of the evolution of human associations, Oresme arrives at the "communité parfeite."[85] Here he embarks upon a comparison between the elements of this community and the elements of an oration, a comparison which fails to show how the complete association differs essentially from the incomplete association.

. . . the husband and wife make up one sort of community, and the master and slave another, and so on, in the same way that letters make up syllables. Furthermore, a household is made up of the communities mentioned above, just as syllables make up a phrase. Finally, a city is made up of several streets, just as a complete and rhetorically perfect oration is made up of several short orations.[86]

Thus in the commentary on the crucial first chapters of the *Politics* Oresme does not seem to have linked the idea of the communitas perfecta with the idea of a sovereign nation-state. In his glosses on the *Ethics*, however,

---

associations seem to be subordinate to the association of the State, which aims not at a temporary advantage but at one covering the whole of life"; 1. 2. 1094b (Rackham, 7): "To secure the good of one person only is better than nothing; but to secure the good of a nation or a state is a nobler and more divine achievement."

[84] *Le Livre de Politiques* 1. 1. (fol. 5a–b, p. 45b). Oresme did refer here to "princey royal" as sovereign, but he contrasted this with the more restricted "princey politique" as though comparing two forms of political association, rather than contrasting it with the less perfect associations of the household.

[85] Ibid., 1. 2. (fol. 7b, p. 48a). This is Oresme's translation of Moerbeke's "communitas perfecta civitas" (ed. Susemihl, 6, lines 9–10).

[86] *Le Livre de Politiques* 1. 2. (fol. 7b, p. 48a). A similar comparison occurs in 1. 1. (fol. 5b–c, p. 46a), and in the *Livre de Ethiques* 8. 17. (fol. 173a, p. 443).

Oresme did appreciate the practical advantages of the city, as he showed in a gloss from 3. 1. (fol. 75b, p. 116b), but this gloss speaks only of a practical, not a qualitative, advantage, and speaks of that rather doubtfully: ". . . ce est impossible en ceste mortel vie de avoir toute souffisance. Et aussi convient il que aucunes choses viennent de païs estranges, comme sunt aucunes espices et pierres precieuses, etc. Mes nulle communité ne est tant pres de par soy souffisante comme est cité, si comme il fu dit ou secunt chapitre du premier."

such a connection was made. In *Ethics* 8. 9. 1160a Aristotle said that the community called the state encompasses all the other communities in the hierarchy, for it serves the whole of man's life.[87] Here is Oresme's gloss: "And for this reason, the political community orders all the other, partial communities, because it is sovereign, and universal, and has domination over all the others."[88]

If we look for evidence of Oresme's support of the nation-state in his treatment of the communitas perfecta, we shall not get far, despite the connection he made in the *Livre de Ethiques*. What did he mean, in any case, when he spoke of the "communication politique"? His glosses on the relationship between the polis of Aristotle and larger communities are not very useful, for they seem inconsistent. While discussing the ideal city of the *Politics*, Oresme made glosses which suggest that he accepted Aristotle's objections to unsurveyable political units. For example, he made this neat summary of Aristotle's opinions on the proper size of the city: "And therefore self-sufficiency determines the minimum size of a city, and governability the maximum size."[89] Other glosses from this chapter give the same impression. Where Aristotle said that the increase in the size of a state cannot continue indefinitely, Oresme added this gloss: "For above the original, very small city there may be another, larger, city, and again another, even larger. But it would be possible for a multitude to become so large that it would no longer be a city, but an ill-defined sort of thing."[90] Where Aristotle said that justice and the distribution of offices would suffer in a state in which the governors cannot know the characters of the citizens,[91] Oresme enlarged upon this theme and applied it to an institution he knew well:

For the prince cannot have sufficient knowledge of so many cases. And thus he will necessarily make bad appointments and distributions of honors and of the goods of

---

[87] For the text from the *Ethics*, see above, n. 83.

[88] *Le Livre de Ethiques* 8. 13. (fol. 168c, p. 433), in Menut's edition. See also ibid.: ". . . toute communicacion est contenue souz politique."

[89] *Le Livre de Politiques* 7. 10. (fol. 247c, p. 289b). Aristotle said that the best population for a state is "the greatest surveyable number required for achieving a life of self-sufficiency" (*Politics* 7. 4. 1326b; Barker, 292). Oresme's translation of this is: "assoufisance de vivre, laquele puisse estre de legier resgardee et ordenee" (7. 10. [fol. 247c, p. 289b]).

[90] *Le Livre de Politiques* 7. 10. (fol. 247a, p. 289a). In glossing Aristotle's statement that "The less the area of [the king's] prerogative, the longer will the authority of a king last unimpaired" (*Politics* 5. 11. 1313a; 243 in Barker), Oresme understood that Aristotle was not speaking of the geographical extent of power, but invoked self-sufficiency all the same: "Il ne entent pas que leur seigneurie soit appeticee quant a extension ou largesce de païz; car royalme doit estre souffisanment grant et a mesure, si comme il sera declaré ou .vii.ᵉ livre. Mes il entent quant a la domination ou puissance que les roys ont en leur royalmes et sus leur subgiés" (5. 25. [fol. 200c, p. 241b]).

The idea that "the wider [the] territories [of the emperor], the less will his *imperium* be" ("sacius esset, imperium minui in dimensione terrarum") was offered by another learned counselor (Gervase of Tillbury) to his patron (Otto IV): see "Gervase of Tillbury," by H. G. Richardson, in Sylvia Thrupp, ed., *Change in Medieval Society* (New York, 1964), 97, with a reference to *M. G. H. Scriptores*, 27: 376.

[91] *Politics* 7. 4. 1326b.

office. . . . if the government of the pope were not ordained by the special grace of the Holy Spirit, it would not be good to attribute to him the power to distribute all the benefices in Christendom.[92]

In other places his attitude seems to be different. Aristotle's discussion of the identity of the state provoked Oresme to write a fairly long gloss.[93] This gloss focuses more on the question of what is the proper notion of the city than on Aristotle's conclusion that the identity of the state is determined by its constitution. Oresme introduced several meanings for the word *cité*, including "any town where there is a bishop" (which he rejected as irrelevant to the discussion),[94] and "a great multitude of dwelling-places or houses" (which he rejected as "improper, as though one were to speak of the chamber of the Parlement as the Parlement").[95] He decided that the name of city is given most properly to men, as Aristotle had said when he called a city a self-sufficient multitude of citizens.[96] Oresme added a qualification which brought his definition closer to that of Aristotle: "Moreover, each multitude of citizens which is governed as one political unit and by the same ruler or rulers may be called a city; because the government gives the form to the city and gives it unity, as it is said."[97] Then he extended the definition, using this criterion, to units larger than cities. In this way he could speak not only of units larger than the city but also of units defined by territory as well as by citizenry and by common government, of the rex Francie as well as the rex Francorum.

In this way, a whole kingdom or country is a great city, which contains several partial cities. And in accordance with this, in the past many people living far from the city or location of Rome were called Roman citizens, as was said in the second chapter of Saint Paul and of his father, who was from Tarsus. And therefore the kingdom or empire of Rome was a city of which the principal center was Rome.[98]

Here the distinction between the city as a surveyable ideal and the city as a larger, unsurveyable (and therefore unsatisfactory) unit is obscured. In one place, Oresme underlined the particular qualities of the intimate polis, as Aristotle had done, and accepted its limitations of size and population; in another, he seemed to put the polis on a level with kingdoms and even empires. In the first case, he seemed to understand and appreciate the ideas

---

[92] *Le Livre de Politiques* 7. 10. (fol. 247b, p. 289b).
[93] *Politics* 3. 3. 1276b; *Le Livre de Politiques* 3. 3. (fols. 78a–79a, pp. 119b–120a).
[94] Fol. 78a–b, p. 119b. He called this a vulgar description, "qui ne est point a propos."
[95] Fol. 78b, p. 119b.
[96] "Item, cité est dicte plus proprement des hommes, et pour ce, il fu dit ou premier chapitre que cité est une multitude de citoiens par soy souffisante" (ibid.).
[97] Fol. 78c, p. 119b.
[98] Fol. 78c, pp. 119b–120a. In the "Table des expositions des fors mos de *Politiques*" (fol. 328a, p. 372b), Oresme defined "Monarche" as "cellui qu'un seul tient le souverain princey sus une cité ou sus un païz." (Cf. the similar definition for "Monarchie" in the "Table des moz divers et estranges" in the *Livre de Ethiques*, fol. 223c, p. 545a). In the prologue to the *Livre de Ethiques* he called "politiques" the art of governing "royaumes et citéz et toutes communitéz" (fol. 1a, p. 97). See also fol. 1b, p. 98, for a nearly identical expression.

of Aristotle; in the second, he made questionable additions to his hierarchy of communities. In the first case, Oresme seems a detached commentator. In the second, he seems to adapt his text to political circumstances which had arisen since the time of Aristotle, reminding us of the enormous change in ideas of citizenship which occurred between that time and the era of the Roman empire, and of the powerful impression made by this empire upon later generations. Yet even in the first, apparently detached, example, he made a pointed reference to the fourteenth-century church. Perhaps a better way to explain the inconsistency is to assume that Oresme was taking into account the difference between the ideal and the real. At one point he was discussing a plan for the best city, a city which must be properly constituted in all its respects, especially size and population. But when considering the identity of the polis, or the meaning of the word cité, he was speaking of real states. Aristotle himself said that "Babylon (which, it is said, had been captured for three whole days before some of its inhabitants knew of the fact) may perhaps be counted a polis of dubious nature. . . ."[99] Earlier in this chapter he had said that "the issue which it [the division of territory and population] raises can easily be met if we remember that the word 'polis' or state is used in different senses."[100] Oresme's translation of Aristotle's remark on Babylon seems to miss Aristotle's point, however: "Babylon . . . should more properly be called a people or a region than a city. . . . One part of the city did not know or was not aware of its capture until the third day. . . . But we will have a better opportunity to consider this doubt or question at another time."[101]

In any case, these statements of Aristotle left Oresme free to concentrate on the identity of actual states. If he accepted Aristotle's conclusion that it is the constitution more than any other characteristic which determines the identity of the state, he could legitimately carry that conclusion to an extreme, and include even an empire under the definition of a polis. This would be done, as it was done by Aristotle, for the purposes of discussion, not, as it was apparently done by Dante, as a hopeful suggestion for political practice. (We shall see very soon that Oresme was no proponent of universal

---

[99] *Politics* 3. 3. 1276a; p. 98 in Barker. Barker's note (p. 99, n. 1) is useful here: "Aristotle accordingly considers the size of the polis as a *practical* question for statesmanship when he comes to construct an ideal state. . . . He thus leaves unsolved, in this passage, the problem of the connection of the size of the polis with the *theoretical* question of the identity of the state–though he seems to incline to the view that a very large polis cannot possess a real identity."

[100] Ibid., 98.

[101] *Le Livre de Politiques* 3. 3. (fol. 77a, p. 118a–b). His glosses on this section merely add historical details and do not take up the question of the identity of the *polis*. It must be said that Moerbeke's translation was not much closer to Aristotle than was that of Oresme: ". . . talis autem forte est et Babylon et omnis quae habet circumscriptionem magis gentis quam civitatis: qua quidem capta aiunt tertio die non sensisse quandam partem civitatis. sed de hac quidem dubitatione in aliud tempus opportuna speculatio . . ." (Susemihl, p. 159, lines 9–12). The "doubte" of Oresme and the "dubitatione" of Moerbeke seem to be the equivalents of "a doubtful nature" in Aristotle. Oresme had nothing of present interest to say in his gloss on Aristotle's remark that the word *polis* or state can be used in different senses.

government.) If we accept this interpretation of the glosses, they do not really contradict each other; nor do they contradict Aristotle. It should be noted, however, that they do not offer very much support for the exclusive sovereignty of the nation-state, or even for its legitimacy as a political organization.

Perhaps we can get a better idea of what Oresme thought about territorial sovereignty if we consider the problem of the empire.

We have seen that the Aristotelian predecessors of Oresme freely adapted the hierarchy of communities to suit their own circumstances and preferences. Some spoke of the preeminence of the kingdom; others, of the empire. We have also seen that some jurists and publicists claimed that the French king possessed the prerogatives of an emperor within his own kingdom. This was an imperialism without universality, one which denied the necessity of a general temporal sovereign while remaining attached to notions of authority from the Roman empire.

There was also a more aggressive French imperialism in the fourteenth century. If the domination of the West had passed from nation to nation, and had already come to the French under Charlemagne, as some believed, it seemed reasonable to hope for a new French empire.[102] At the start of the century the Norman lawyer Pierre Dubois had championed such an empire in his *De recuperatione Terrae Sanctae*.[103] According to his plan, the French king was to become a peace-making emperor in the West, with his brother performing the same function in the East. The church was to be reformed and placed under the control of the French monarchy. This treatise, despite the best efforts of Dubois, was not well known in the fourteenth century.[104] Thus Oresme, who might have shared some of the attitudes of his fellow Norman (though probably not his grandiose schemes) shows no acquaintance with him. Oresme did not mention a French empire.[105]

He did not, however, neglect the question of universal government: it is the subject of his longest gloss.[106] The gloss arose from the above-mentioned discussion of Aristotle on the size and population of the ideal city. Oresme said that he wanted to treat a subject "which I do not find argued elsewhere. And that is to say whether, since a city may become too large and

---

[102] See Edmund E. Stengel, "Kaisertitel und Souveränitätsidee. Studien zur Vorgeschichte des modernen Staatsbegriff," *Deutsches Archiv für Geschichte des Mittelalters* 3 (1939): 1–56. See also Spiegel, *"Reditus Regni"* (as cited above in n. 11), 165. She describes the aspirations of Philip Augustus, who "judged one man sufficient for the government of the whole world."

[103] Ed. Charles V. Langlois (Paris, 1891). There is also an English translation by Walther I. Brandt, *The Recovery of the Holy Land, Columbia University Records of Civilization* 51 (New York, 1956).

[104] Rivière, *Le problème de l'église et de l'état*, 126, 343.

[105] He did, however, speak of the translation of "le plus grant princey, la plus grande prosperité mondaine," from people to people and of its present lodging in France (see below, n. 172). It does not seem that he is speaking of the domination of other nations by France; at the beginning of this gloss (*Le Livre de Politiques* 7. 13. [fol. 255c, p. 297a]) he says "Mes si comme il appert ou .x.ᵉ chapitre, monarchie universele ne est pas bonnement possible et seroit injuste."

[106] Ibid., 7. 10. (fols. 247c–253b, pp. 289b–294b).

since there are many cities in the world, a kingdom can become too large and whether there should be several kingdoms in the world and no one power to which they are subject."[107] This gloss is organized precisely, like a quaestio. Oresme presents arguments in favor of universal monarchy, then opposing arguments, and then (after excepting the domination of the pope from his discussion),[108] a response to the arguments in favor of universal monarchy.

Oresme began the arguments in favor of the empire with a bit of metaphysics from Aristotle, saying (rather as Dante had said) that all things prefer to be well-disposed, and that unity is preferred to plurality by all things.[109] He then introduced several arguments by analogy: if there is one God, one human race like a "little world,"[110] one sun governing the heavens, one pope, one church, and one species of animal which governs all the rest, there should be a single secular ruler. He mentioned Aristotle's belief that superior peoples and individuals have a duty to rule. He spoke of the need to secure peace through a universal government, and praised the empires of the past as bearers of peace and prosperity. He used a notion similar to the expanded hierarchy of communities or "bigger is better" principle used by Dante and other supporters of the empire.[111] This was taken from the Bible; by a curious misinterpretation of a verse from Proverbs he made an argument for the empire on the grounds that a multiplicity of rulers is the result of sin.[112]

When opposing universal government, Oresme preferred common sense and practical observation to analogy and metaphysics. He did compare the overgrown nation to a giant which can be maintained only with difficulty, but this is an analogy with practical implications.[113] He also compared the

---

[107] Fol. 247c–d, pp. 289b–290a.

[108] ". . . je di que la policie esperituele de Saincte Eglise quant a ce ne est pas subjecte a ceste science. Car celle monarchie esperituele vient de Dieu par grace especial. . . . Et donques a ceste policie ne est pas semblable la policie temporele, laquelle vient de Dieu par autre influence et par autre maniere" (fol. 251c, p. 293a).

[109] *Metaphysics* 12. 10. 1075b–1076a (translated by Hugh Tredennick [Cambridge, Mass. and London, 1935: Loeb Classical Library], 175): ". . . the world must not be governed badly: 'The rule of many is not good; let one be the ruler.'" Aristotle's citation is from the *Iliad* 2. 204. (But see *Politics* 4. 4. 1292a). Dante used this in *De mon.* 1. 10. (ed. Bertalot, p. 21). See also the references above in n. 81.

[110] Fol. 247d, p. 290a.

[111] ". . . aussi comme pluseurs personnes funt une maison, et pluseurs maisons funt une rue, et pluseurs rues une cité, et pluseurs cités un royalme, il semble que pluseurs royalmes et tous ensemble doivent faire un empire universel et total" (fol. 249a, p. 291a).

[112] The verse, Proverbs 28: 2: "Propter peccata terrae multi principes eius . . ." seems to mean that a rapid succession of rulers within a single country is the result of the transgressions of the people, for the conclusion of the verse says that a wise man can bring stability to the land. Earlier, Oresme used this flexible verse to refer to a multiplicity of rulers within one state (*Le Livre de Politiques* 4. 7. [fol. 135c, p. 174b]). Several interpretations of the verse are given when this argument is refuted (fol. 252c, p. 294a).

[113] "Et la chose publique selon ce que dit Plautarcus est aussi comme un corps humain. Et donques se un royalme ou une chose publique se estendoit par toutes terres, ce seroit . . . comme les corps des geans . . ." (fol. 249b, p. 291a). The reference to Plutarch is the same ascription made by John of Salisbury in *Policraticus* 5. 2. See chap. 4, nn. 135–136, for other organic analogies in the *Livre de Politiques*. Oresme also cited Augustine, *De Civitate Dei* 3. 10. on the inconveniences of an overgrown body or state.

political life of men to the organization of bees, saying that even among bees there is a leader for every group, not one leader for all the bees in the world.[114] This was merely a reply to an argument from the opposing side. Oresme's only *a priori* argument concerns the causes of the growth of kingdoms. If they increase due to the iniquity of the conquered peoples, he said, then a universal monarchy would presuppose universal wickedness, "which is not conformable to human nature."[115] If, on the other hand, kingdoms increase through the iniquity of the conquerors (Oresme recalled the question of Augustine, whether kingdoms are anything but *magna latrocinia*),[116] then they exist without justice. Oresme made one appeal to authority, mentioning Old Testament warnings against, and threats of, the establishment of foreign kings.[117]

The rest of his arguments are more practical or empirical. He reminded proponents of the empire that the monarchies of the "Golden Age" were not really very large.[118] He argued that an extensive and heterogeneous political unit is not likely to endure. He added to Aristotle's remarks on the difficulty of governing large numbers of people (remarks which had prompted this gloss) a complaint of Solomon about the magnitude of his task as ruler.[119] He emphasized the problems of governing several peoples at once.[120] As Augustine had said, a man and his dog, or two mute beasts of

---

[114] "Or est il certain qu'une tele mosche ne est pas mestresse sus toutes celles du monde, mes sunt pluseurs telez" (*Le Livre de Politiques* 7. 10. [fol. 250a–b, p. 292a]). The author of the *Songe du Vergier* made a similar argument (in 1. 36, p. 34 in the edition of Brunet): ". . . ainsi comme toutes les mousches du monde n'ont pas ung seul roy ou prince, mais les mousches d'ung lieu en ont ung et celles de ung aultre lieu en ont ung aultre." The author of this treatise made extensive borrowings from Oresme: see Robert Bossuat, "Nicole Oresme et le Songe du Verger," *Le moyen âge* 53 (1947): 99–101, and in general Jeannine Quillet, *La Philosophie politique du songe du vergier (1378). Sources doctrinals* (Paris, 1977).

[115] *Le Livre de Politiques* 7. 10. (fol. 250c, p. 292a). Augustine, as Oresme remarks, had proposed just such a cause for the increase of the Roman empire (*De civ. Dei* 4. 15.).

[116] "Remota itaque iustitia quid sunt regna nisi magna latrocinia? Quia et latrocinia quid sunt nisi parva regna?" (*De civ. Dei* 4. 4. [in the Loeb edition of 7 vols. (Cambridge, Mass. and London, 1957–1972), 2 (this vol. [1963] with a translation by W. M. Green): 16]).

[117] He made reference to Deuteronomy 17: 15: "Eum constitues, quem Dominus Deus tuus elegerit de numero fratrum tuorum. Non poteris alterius gentis hominem regem facere, qui non sit frater tuus" (*Le Livre de Politiques* 7. 10. [fol. 250a, p. 291b]), and Jeremiah 5:15: "Ecce ego adducam super vos gentem de longinquo domus Israel, ait Dominus: gentem robustam, gentem antiquam, gentem, cuius ignorabis linguam, nec intelliges quid loquatur" (ibid., fol. 250a, p. 292a).

[118] "Item, es temps anciens que l'en appelloit les bons temps heroiques et les poëtes les nomment les siecles dorés, les royalmes ne estoient pas grans, si comme il peut assés apparoir par le premier chapitre du premier et par le .xx.ᵉ chapitre du tiers, et par les hystoires" (fol. 250c, p. 292a). The ".xx.ᵉ chapitre du tiers" (3. 14. in the *Politics*) discusses, among other things, the "kings of the Heroic Age," of whom we shall see much more in the chapter on church and state.

[119] This was taken from 3 Kings 3: 9: "Dabis ergo servo tuo cor docile, ut populum tuum iudicare possit, et discernere inter bonum et malum. quis enim poterat iudicare populum istum, populum tuum hunc multum?" (*Le Livre de Politiques* 7. 10. [fol. 249c, p. 291b]).

[120] "Mes une policie est espediente a une gent et autre a autre, si comme il appert ou .xvii.ᵉ chapitre du quart. Car selon la diversité des regions, des complexions, des inclinations et des meurs des gens, il convient que leur droiz positifs et leur gouvernemens soient differens" (fol. 249d, p. 291b). See above, n. 12, for a similar argument in John of Paris. The anonymous author of the "Lamentatio Ecclesie" written during the last years of Oresme's life put this attitude into

different species, are better able to understand each other than two men who do not speak each other's language.[121] It is unnatural, Oresme added, for a ruler to govern those who speak another language.[122] God and nature have shown their disapproval of universal monarchy by setting up natural boundaries, prohibiting the contact necessary among fellow citizens. No earthly kingdom can extend everywhere, just as no empire can last forever. Virgil's *imperium sine fine,* said Oresme, was merely a poetic fiction, and was contradicted by experience.[123] Finally, he warned, again arguing from experience and history, that a kingdom which has prospered while of moderate size will likely decline or be destroyed if it becomes excessively large.

The responses of Oresme to his own arguments in favor of universal monarchy differ as greatly in kind as do the arguments themselves. He made specific replies to the analogies, but also attacked them generally:

And such reasons, taken in a mystical or figurative sense, do not provide us with certainty, according to what Saint Augustine says. For he said of such an argument, in *Contra Donatistas:* "And it is not proper that we make use of such arguments while seeking the truth." And in a letter *Ad Vincentium,* he said that no one should introduce such allegories into his case if he has other means of proof.[124]

---

verse: "Qu'un homme ait gouvernance raisonable et paisible / Sur tous les gens du monde, c'est chose impossible. / En monde ha regions de si tres grant distance, / Que, se le pape estoit ou à Rome ou en France, / En .xx. ans ne pourroit par tout faire ordenance: / Tant dis pluseurs pourroient cheoir en desesperance." (This poem was published by N. Valois in *La France et le grande schisme d'occident,* 4 vols. [Paris, 1896–1902], 1: 389–394; cited from V. Martin, *Les origines du Gallicanisme,* 2 vols. in one [Paris, 1939], 2: 69.)

[121] "Nam si duo sibimet invicem fiant obviam neque praeterire, sed simul esse aliqua necessitate cogantur, quorum neuter linguam novit alterius, facilius sibi muta animalia, etiam diversi generis, quam illi, cum sint homines ambo, sociantur" (*De civ. Dei* 19. 7. [ed. cit. 6 (1960, trans. W. M. Green): 148]), from *Le Livre de Politiques* 7. 10. (fol. 250a, p. 291b). Thus, as Oresme implies, nature's gift of speech has both encouraged "communication civile" and set limits upon it (fols. 249d–250a, p. 291b).

[122] In his definition of "Monarchie" in the "Table des moz divers et estranges" in the *Livre de Ethiques* (fol. 223c, p. 545a in the edition of Menut), Oresme had said that the monarch, though he may have lordship over a "grant communité," cannot rule "toutes les gens du monde; car ce seroit contre raison et chose desnaturele que .i. homme mortel eüst tele seigneurie, si comme il appert ou .vii.ᵉ de *Politiques.*" See also the *Livre de Politiques* 1. 15. (fol. 28d, p. 72a); 7. 6. (fol. 241c, p. 284a).

[123] "Mes Virgile . . . dit comme Jupiter parloit des Romains: His ego nec metas rerum nec tempora pono. Imperium sine fine dedi. . . . Mes ce est une fiction poëtique. . . . Et experience de fait monstre le contraire" (*Le Livre de Politiques* 7. 10. [fol. 250b, p. 292a]). The Virgil reference is to *Aeneid* 1. 278–279.

The "fiction poëtique" of which Oresme speaks is not his own invention, but rather a standard device which was used to rationalize myths through historical, physical, or moral interpretations. For this and other treatments of myths in the Middle Ages, see Jean Seznec, *La survivance des dieux antiques* (London, 1940); available in English translation by Barbara F. Sessions, *The Survival of the Pagan Gods* (New York, 1953).

[124] *Le Livre de Politiques* 7. 10. (fol. 251c–d, p. 293a). I have been unable to find the reference in *Contra Donatistas:* Menut's reference is to Migne, *PL,* 43: 110. The closest I have been able to come to the reference to the letter to Vincent is this from *PL,* 33: 334: "Quis autem non impudentissime nitatur aliquid in allegoria positum pro se interpretari, nisi habeat et manifesta testimonia, quorum lumine illustrentur obscura?" (Menut cites *PL,* 33: 321). Compare to John of Paris, *De reg. pot. et pap.* 18, also citing the letter to Vincent.

We find here another sort of argument distrusted by Oresme (see n. 123 above). Earlier in this gloss he refers to analogical arguments as being "trop loing de raison pratique" and as being

Oresme denied that the entire human race is a "little world" or microcosm to be ruled by one man, saying rather that each man, or more to the point, each kingdom, is a microcosm. The "universal multitude of mankind," on the other hand, cannot be considered as one body, because it is divided by barriers which inhibit communication.[125] Oresme also denied the argument from the duty of the superior to rule. Like Guido Vernani, the opponent of Dante, he said that if the universal ruler must be superior to all mankind, only God would be qualified.[126] But the response which is most important for this discussion brought Oresme back to the hierarchy of communities and the communitas perfecta. Contending that a single monarchy is not needed to replace the evils of separation with the benefits of unity, he said:

But the end and limitation of [unification] comes when the multitude and the region have self-sufficiency, as it appears in the second chapter of book one [of the *Politics*]. And for this reason, it is not necessary to continue with unification beyond this point, or to combine several kingdoms under one sovereign. . . . And Saint Augustine in the nineteenth book of the *City of God* presents this argument and shows that the process of unification will be hindered by diversity in language, as was mentioned before in the eighth argument presented for the right side in this question.[127]

This gloss presents a variety of arguments, but it does not mention one important aspect of the imperial question. Although he mentioned the

---

"comme celle que Aristote appelle *sophismes de policie*" (fol. 251c, p. 293a). In 5. 25. (fol. 203a, p. 244a), speaking of the notion that the prince is a fountain of justice and thus above the law and possessed of unlimited power, he said "Et concluent par teles poësies et similitudes imparfaictes ou impropres et impertinens, si comme il sera monstré ou .vii.ᵉ livre. Et teles choses appelleroit Aristote *sophismes de policie*." Distrust of analogical argument was a prominent feature of fourteenth-century thought, as we see in an article about Oresme's old colleague: "John Buridan on the Habitability of the Earth," by Ernest A. Moody (*Speculum* 16[1941]), 420.

[125] ". . . chescun homme est un petit munde . . . la multitude universele des hommes . . . ne peut estre dit un corps ne un royalme ne un petit munde. Mes est pluseurs petis mundes, ce est assavoir pluseurs personnes, pluseurs royalmes et cités qui sunt parties du grant munde" (*Le Livre de Politiques* 7. 10. [fol. 251a–b, p. 292b]). The idea of man as a "little world" also appears in the *Songe du Vergier* 1. 38. (ed. Brunet, p. 38).

[126] ". . . tel homme [i.e., the one exceeding others in virtue and power] devroit estre pris pour prince en sa cité ou en son païz, mes non pas sus tout le munde. Car il en pourroit tout gouverner comme dit est, se il ne estoit Dieu, comme fu Jhesu Crist" (*Le Livre de Politiques* 7. 10. [fol. 252a, p. 293b]). For Vernani, see *De Reprobatione monarchie composite a Dante Alighiero florentina* (ed. Thomas Käpelli, in *Quellen und Forschungen aus italienischen Archiven und Bibliotheken* 28 [1937–1938], p. 128): "Monarcha ergo totius humani generis debet excedere in virtutibus et in prudentia totum genus humanum . . . solus dominus Iesus Christus et nullus alius fuit verus monarcha." Engelbert of Admont mentions this argument in *De ortu . . . et fine imperii Romani* 16.

Aristotle himself said something like this (*Politics* 7. 4. 1326a; 291 in Barker): "The creation of order for an infinite number is a task for the divine power which holds together [and reduces to order] the whole of this universe, where beauty [which goes with order] is usually found attending on number and magnitude [Barker's brackets]." In glossing these sentences Oresme refers the reader to the long gloss now under discussion: "Mes nulle cognoissance ne puissance humaine ne souffist pour ordener de tous les hommes du monde, si comme il sera apres declaré plus a plain" (*Le Livre de Politiques* 7. 9. [fol. 246a, p. 288a]).

[127] Fol. 252c–d, p. 294a. For the reference to Augustine, see above, n. 121.

papacy several times, Oresme said nothing of the medieval empire.[128] He
cited no writer later than Boethius, except when dealing with the problem of
spiritual and temporal authority.[129] Yet in the fourteenth century there were
many writers who dealt with the empire as a contemporary problem. Engelbert of Admont, Lupold of Bebenburg, and Conrad of Megenberg had
written for the imperialist side.[130] We have already encountered some of the
French opponents of imperial pretensions, for example the authors of the
Rex pacificus, the *Quaestio in utramque partem*, and the *Songe du Vergier*, and,
of course, Pierre Dubois. Oresme did not avoid contemporary questions, but
here he did not follow these writers. His discussion seems detached and
academic, though its length shows the importance of its subject and we are
not left in doubt as to which is the "right side in this question."

Oresme did not neglect earlier discussions of the imperial question; many
of his arguments had appeared in earlier works. He cited Augustine, and he
echoed (if only by chance) Guido Vernani. The analogies and historical
examples he used were commonplaces. There are also similarities between
the gloss of Oresme and the quaestio on universal government written by
Buridan.[131] Among the pro-imperial arguments presented by Buridan are
the unity of ecclesiastical government and of the government of God, and
the need for peace and concord. Among those *contra* are the divine imposition of a multiplicity of kings as punishment for Israel,[132] the difficulty of

---

[128] But see his remarks on the authority of Roman law (below, n. 136), and on the translation
of empire (above, n. 105, and below, n. 136). He did mention German electors of the empire in
Le Livre de Politiques 5. 1. (fol. 166c, p. 205a–b), speaking of cases in which the form of
government remains unchanged while the governors change: "Quant la policie se continue et
les lays et ordenances sunt unes meismes excepté que les princes qui estoient esleus ou prins
indifferentement de tous, il ordenent qu'il succedent d'un lignage ou d'un païz, si comme par
aventure quant il fu ordené que l'emperiere de Rome et les electeurs seroient Almans. Et
semblablement quant le princey demeure un meisme et il est translaté d'une gente en
autre. . . ."
  Oresme had more to say in the *Livre de Ethiques* (8. 13. [fol. 168d, p. 434]). Speaking of the
distinction between the king who thinks of the welfare of his subjects and the tyrant who cares
only for himself (*Ethics* 8. 10. 1160b) Oresme said: ". . . se aucuns appellent *monarchie* celui
qui seroit seigneur sur tous universelment, c'est une chose impossible selon raison . . . et
donques dire que l'empereur de Romme selon droit doie estre seigneur sus tous et par tout, c'est
une derision; car nul n'est tel seigneur fors Dieu." Menut notes (p. 434, n. 5) that this gloss must
have "delighted and flattered" Charles V.
  [129] Oresme cited Innocent III for the sun and moon analogy of spiritual and temporal powers
(fol. 248b, p. 290a) and mentioned the coronation service for the kings of France (fol. 250a,
p. 291b), but he did not mention the controversial writers of his own century.
  [130] Engelbert of Admont, *De ortu, progressu et fine imperii Romani* (ed. Melchior Goldast, in
Politica Imperialia [Frankfurt, 1614]: 754–773), written about 1307–1310; Lupold of Bebenburg, *De iure regni et imperii Romani* (ed. Simon Schardius, *De Iurisdictione, autoritate et prae-
minentia imperiali* . . . [Basel, 1566]: 328–409), written around 1340, and Conrad of Megenberg, *De translatione Romani imperii* (ed. Richard Scholz, *Unbekannte kirchenpolitische
Streitschriften aus der Zeit Ludwigs des Bayern*, 2 vols. [Rome, 1911–1914], 2: 249–345), from
about 1354. For an introduction to medieval thought on the empire, and for selections from the
first two of these writers, see E. Lewis, *Medieval Political Ideas*, 2: 430–505. See also Folz, *L'Idée
d'empire*, 173–178.
  [131] *Quaestiones super octo libros Politicorum* 8. 5.: "Utrum universitati mortalium expediat
quod universo sit unus solus secularis princeps" (fols. 113–114 in the Paris, 1513, edition).
  [132] Buridan, like Oresme, cited Proverbs 28: 2 (see above, n. 112). Buridan countered this
argument by saying that the best government is the one which most closely approximates the

governing peoples of differing cultures, and the impossibility of efficient rule by one man. Buridan, like Oresme, denied that one could make conclusive analogies between the universal authority of the pope and the authority of an emperor.[133]

Why did Oresme treat the problem of the empire in this way? Had he wished to write an entirely academic commentary, he need not have mentioned the papacy. Perhaps he felt that the prerogatives of the papacy were a greater danger to France than the pretensions of the empire. In the middle of the fourteenth century, as Folz has said, the problem for the empire was no longer whether it could exercise widespread power, but whether it could territorialize itself and thus enjoy an authority as complete as that of a king in his kingdom.[134]

Although Oresme made no direct comment upon the medieval empire, his attitude may be inferred from the thoroughgoing realism of these remarks in the last part of the gloss on universal monarchy:

. . . if everyone wished always to avoid war and to obey one sovereign who could always understand every matter, and judge it well, and properly order everything . . . it would be a splendid thing, as it seems. But in fact this is little more than a poetic fiction or a thought experiment ["ymagination mathematique"]. For as I have said earlier, the world is not run by hypothesis. It must be taken as it is. . . . and taking it as it is by nature, it scarcely seems possible that anyone could be a sovereign [universal] monarch and last for very long.[135]

---

conditions of equality existing before the Fall, and that is the government of many princes (fol. 113).

[133] "Nam presidentia spiritualis immediate ex divina ordinatione constituitur ergo nullus homo potest illam mutare. Sed presidentia in temporalibus non est ex iure divino nec immediate ex iure naturali sed ex iure humano et positivo. . ." (fol. 113). Compare to Oresme, above, n. 108.

[134] L'Idée d'empire, 173, 176. We may recall the remark of Bryce (n. 8 above) that Dante's Monarchia was "not a prophecy but an epilogue," and the rather withering remark of Oresme (cited above, n. 128) that to say the emperor of Rome should rule over all "c'est une derision."

[135] Le Livre de Politiques 7. 10. (fols. 252d–253a, p. 294a). (See n. 105 above, for another statement that such monarchy is not "bonnement possible" and would be unjust, and n. 128, for the remark that it would be impossible and a "derision," from the Livre de Éthiques.) Such a monarchy was called unreasonable and impossible in 3. 8. (fol. 87d, p. 128a).

Oresme showed a similar realism in discussing election, which would be a good means of succession if the laws regulating it were good and if they were kept (3. 23. [fol. 114d, p. 154b]). But Oresme said: "Mes la pollicie ne est pas gouvernee par si, et ne doit l'en supposer fors ce qui est de fait. Et convient prendre les choses teles comme elles sunt communement."

The ymagination is also mentioned in 2. 6. (fol. 42a, p. 84b) in relation to voluntary poverty, where Oresme speaks of "ymaginacions qui ne se pevent bonnement pratiquer." In 7. 27. (fol. 279b, p. 322a) when considering whether all the citizens in a state are likely to be virtuous (Politics 7. 13. 1332a) he said: "Et ce ne est pas chose possible naturelment ne onques ne avint que tous ceulz d'une grande multitude soient vertueus. Et donques tres bonne policie ne est pas chose possible. Et le philosophe ne doit pas bailler doctrine pratique pour instituer une policie feinte, ymaginee et aussi comme songee, laquele ne peut estre de fait." The ymaginacion joins the "fiction poëtique" (also mentioned in the citation above, and see above, n. 123) and the "sophisme de policie" (see above, n. 124) as a type of argument distrusted by Oresme.

The "mental experiment" was a quite specific sort of exercise to Oresme and to other fourteenth-century scientists. If referred to a sort of theoretical construct which could be used for illustration and speculation. These constructs (and hence universal government in this case)

The remarks in this gloss can be supplemented by scattered comments made by Oresme on the subject of Roman law. He was no more inclined than Louis IX to accept its authority:

And no matter how reasonable these laws may be, no one is obliged to obey them by the force or authority of the government of Rome, except those who belong to this state, if in fact it still exists. For each government and polity has its own positive laws, its own written and unwritten laws, and whether these laws are or are not conformable to those of Rome is of no importance. . . . And to say that all should be under the governance and the laws of Rome is simply foolish, and is an error against natural reason, as will be more clearly demonstrated in Book 7.[136]

As a *Politics* commentator Oresme has given us no coherent theory of national sovereignty, but his attitude toward external threats to the sovereignty of the nation-state is made clear in his discussions of the empire and Roman law. We can learn more about his attitude toward national sovereignty, especially sovereignty within the state and as against lesser powers,

---

were usually thought not to be possible and were "invented with the understanding that certain features of the real world were to be set aside" (Marshall Clagett, "Some Novel Trends in the Science of the Fourteenth Century," in *Art, Science, and History in the Renaissance*, ed. Charles S. Singleton [Baltimore, 1967], 276). Thus it is clear to what fictional realm Oresme was banishing the persistent dream of the empire, in favor of the French monarchy he served.

One might also note a possible cause of Oresme's annoyance at the "policie feinte" mentioned above, from 7. 13. Clearly one could imagine theoretical constructs as a scientist, but politics, as he says, is a practical art and not to be the subject of such dreams.

[136] *Le Livre de Politiques* 5. 25. (fol. 202d, p. 243b). It is interesting to see how often Oresme refers in his glosses to the ".vii.ᵉ livre" — that is, we can be sure, to the long gloss on universal government which is found there. It is also interesting to note in the "simply foolish" a sort of echo of his "derision" (see above, n. 128). A more direct echo of the "derision" of the *Livre de Ethiques* 8. 13. is found in the universal monarchy gloss of the *Livre de Politiques* 7. 10. (fols. 251d–252a, p. 293b). Speaking of Roman imperialist laws Oresme says: "Et teles choses sunt plus dignes de derision que de allegation ou d'autre response." Those who accept them are "simples." As Quillet remarks (*La Philosophie politique du songe du vergier*, p. 127), "Ce qui n'est nullement marsilien dans ce passage, c'est la critique des lois romaines." We may add that, as a philosopher and supporter of Aristotle's dictum that laws should be made to suit constitutions, and not constitutions to suit laws, Oresme expressed a general distaste for legists. In the gloss from 5. 25. he said that those who first learn law cannot afterwards learn philosophy, and continued: "Et je ay veu aucuns [legal scholars] si affichiés a leur opinion que il ne povoient oïr le contraire" (fol. 202d, p. 244a).

Oresme's "se il dure encore" ("if . . . it still exists") recalls the "imperator monarcha si fuerit" of John of Paris (see n. 12).

Oresme made similar remarks in the *Livre de Ethiques* 5. 15. (fol. 104a, p. 304): "Mais aucuns sont ignorans qui cuident que l'empire de Rome fust ou doie estre seigneur de tout le monde, et ce ne peut estre. Et dient que ce qui est contre les loys de Romme est contre droit absoluement et contre droit escript. Et ce n'est pas bien dit; car autres drois sont et ont esté en pluseurs regions, et escripz et non escripz; combien que ceulz de Rome fussent en aucun temps tenuz en grant pris, et que ilz fussent bien raisonnables et sont pour la plus grant partie."

In the gloss on universal government, in which it was argued in favor of the empire that Roman law calls Rome the "monarche du munde" (fol. 248c, p. 290b), Oresme responded that laws saying the Roman emperor is lord of the world are *apostudyamenos*, that is, "lay[s] indiscretement mise," about which we shall hear more, below, chap. 4, n. 120 (fol. 251d, p. 293a–b). In a gloss on moderation in kingship, Oresme took the occasion to attack the "malvese suggestion de telz adulateurs et flateurs" who made the law saying that the prince is "solutus legibus, et quia [quod, surely?] principi placuit, legis habet vigorem" (5. 25. [fol. 202a, p. 243a]).

by examining his use of words which describe public authority, particularly the word *souverain* and related expressions.

The first thing to be said about Oresme's usage is that it is not precise. The words souverain and souveraineté are used in association with other words like seigneurie, *princey*, and *domination*, so that the idea of sovereignty is expressed in several ways. The word souverain itself is sometimes used to mean nothing more than "extreme."[137]

Of the words princey and domination little need be said. Oresme gave a definition of princey in his "Table des expositions des fors mos de *Politiques*." This definition makes his meaning quite clear, and indicates the relationship between this term and the others:

Princey is the power and authority or domination and *seigneurie* of the prince. This is what is called *principatus* in Latin. And in the science of politics this word is used fairly loosely. For as it appears in the fourth book, in the twenty-first chapter, all offices are called *princeys* which are empowered to deal with matters of state or to make judgments or to command. And in fact commanding is the most proper and appropriate function of princes. And for this reason, sovereign princes are called emperors. For *imperare* means "to command."[138]

Thus the word was used to refer to public power, and was a fitting translation of Moerbeke's principatus. As such, it could refer to magistrates and magistracies,[139] as well as to a form of government, for example, "princey royal."[140] Both princey and *gouvernement* were used by Oresme to fill gaps in the text of Moerbeke, where a type of government is frequently designated by an adjective without a substantive equivalent to "government."[141]

Domination, a word sometimes modified by the adjective souverain, seems to refer specifically to "princey politique" or to what Aristotle would

---

[137] For example, Oresme provided "souveraine injustice" as a translation of Moerbeke's "iniustitiam . . . extremam" (*Le Livre de Politiques* 3. 12. [fol. 92d, p. 133a]; p. 189, lines 15–16 in Susemihl). Oresme also used the word in the sense of "extreme" or "greatest" in a gloss from 7. 14. (fol. 258a, p. 299b), in a gloss from 3. 23. (fol. 113d, p. 153b), and in the "Table des Notables" (fol. 321b–c, p. 366a). In the prologue to the *Livre de Ethiques* (fol. 1a, p. 97 in Menut's edition), Oresme called Aristotle the "souverain philosophe."

David, *La souveraineté*, 280, says that this was a common use of the word. In a note entitled "Recherche sémantique sur les mots souverain et souveraineté dans les traductions du Corpus," he examines French translations of Justinian from the thirteenth to the fifteenth centuries, and says that in them the word souverain "sert également à qualifier des notions abstraites sans rapport avec la politique." "Summa providentia," for example, becomes "souveraine porvéance." He also notes that the adjective souverain is seen more often than the substantive souveraineté, which has a more narrowly political meaning.

[138] *Le Livre de Politiques*, fol. 329a, p. 373a. This is the only one of the four terms mentioned in the table.

[139] See, for example, the text of the *Livre de Politiques* 2. 21. (fol. 67d, p. 111a), translated from *Politics* 2. 11. 1273b (p. 142, lines 9–10 in Susemihl's edition of Moerbeke).

[140] See, for example, the text of the *Livre de Politiques* 1. 1. (fol. 5b, p. 45b), translated from *Politics* 1. 1. 1252a (p. 2, line 6 in Susemihl's edition of Moerbeke).

[141] For example, Oresme has "princey ou gouvernement politique et royal" (*Le Livre de Politiques* 1. 1. [fol. 5a, p. 45b]), where Moerbeke has "politicum aut regale" (*Politics* 1. 1. 1252a; p. 2, line 4 in Susemihl; p. 1 in Barker, who has "statesman" and "monarch of a kingdom").

call the statesman's power exercised over fellow citizens.[142] It is contrasted with seigneurie, which indicates a more absolute sort of power, in this gloss from the *Livre de Politiques* 1. 15.:

And the reason [why the rule of the head of a household over his children is different from his rule over his wife] is that the father has full *seigneurie* over those of his children who are under age, just as the king has full *seigneurie* over his subjects. And the husband does not have full lordship over his wife, as was said in the fourteenth chapter of the eighth book of the *Ethics*; but he has *domination* over her according to the law of marriage. This is just as it is in a polity, where the one who is chosen must govern according to the statutes and laws and ordinances which have been established to guide him.[143]

When used in the text, domination is frequently a translation of Moerbeke's *dominativum*.[144]

The meanings attached by Oresme to the words seigneurie and souveraineté are more significant, and harder to determine. No definition is given for them. One is tempted to think that seigneurie implies a feudal or hierarchical domination, a power of relative aspect, while souveraineté carries with it notions of a public state, of a qualitatively superior power.[145]

Unfortunately Oresme does not make things so easy. In several cases the two words are used almost interchangeably. Both are used, for example, as equivalents of the Latin imperium.[146] In a gloss from 4. 21., Oresme com-

---

[142] *Politics* 1. 12. 1259b (Barker, 32).

[143] Fol. 28a, p. 71a. Here Aristotle (*Politics* 1. 12. 1259a–b; p. 32 in Barker) has been comparing marital authority to that of a statesman, paternal authority to that of a king, and the authority of a slaveowner to that of a despot. In another gloss (from 3. 17. [fol. 101c, p. 142a]), Oresme said that, while the multitude is not to have princey, which should belong to the souverain, it could have domination over certain things.

[144] See, for example, the text of the *Livre de Politiques* 3. 12. (fol. 92c, p. 133a), translated from *Politics* 3. 10. (p. 189, line 15 in Susemihl).

[145] The word seigneurie was often used with the idea of possession, which brings it closer to the feudal conception of power. The most obvious example is its use in the case of the ownership of slaves, a subject which appears frequently in the first book of the *Politics*. Slavery is certainly the prime example of what Oresme called "communication possessive" as it exists between "seigneur et . . . serf" (*Le Livre de Politiques* 3. 4. [fol. 80a, p. 121a]), from "possessio ex domino et servo" in Moerbeke (Susemihl, p. 164, lines 2–3, for which Barker has "property of master and slave" [*Politics* 3. 4. 1277a, p. 102]). See Quillet as cited above in n. 114; p. 149, n. 65.
Phrases like "seigneur des possessions" occur several times in a gloss from 7. 19. (fol. 265c–d, p. 307a) where he says that the citizens "doivent avoir richeces et estre seigneurs des possessions"; and in several places in the "Table des Notables": fol. 314d, p. 360a, and fol. 321d, p. 366b; fol. 315a, p. 360b; fol. 317a, p. 362a; fol. 320d, p. 365b, and see fol. 323c, p. 368a, for an example very similar to that from fol. 315a, p. 360b. Of course, the word seigneurie was used in several other ways; however, it is interesting that the words souveraineté and souverain do not seem to be used where power is a matter of possession, or of private possession. Souveraineté seems to indicate public power only.

[146] Of course it is worth asking about the Latin equivalents of these words. The case of seigneur is fairly clear. This is often a translation of Moerbeke's *dominus* (and thus seems to imply a sort of possessive lordship, as was said in the previous note). In 3. 9. (fol. 89a, p. 129b) "seigneurs de la policie" appears as an equivalent of Moerbeke's "domini politiae" (Susemihl, 180, line 11).
If we ask which word is translated as souverain or souveraineté, the answer may be "none." It is very hard to find examples of these words in the text, though they occur frequently in Oresme's glosses. We do see "[avoir] souverain presidence" in 1. 1. (fol. 5b, p. 45b) but this

mented on the role of the magistrate as commander: "And for this reason, sovereign princes are called emperors, for *imperare* means 'to command.' "[147] In his long gloss on universal monarchy, however, he explained the statement of (Virgil's) Jupiter, that the Roman imperium would be without limits, by saying that the Romans would be seigneurs everywhere and always.[148] Both words were also used to indicate dominance over foreign nations and peoples. In the gloss on universal monarchy, we see such phrases as "some laws which say that the emperor of Rome is *seigneur* of the whole world"; "*seigneurie* over the whole world"; and "*seigneurie* over all peoples."[149] Clearly, seigneurie represents something more than feudal lordship. In the same gloss, souverain is used in similar contexts: "A single mortal man should be king or sovereign emperor and hold sway over all"; "sovereign over all kings"; and "it scarcely seems possible that anyone could be a sovereign [universal] monarch and last for very long."[150]

Both words were used in discussions of the relationship between the ruler and the law. Seigneur and related expressions were used in several such discussions, and souveraineté and souverain in others.[151] In the translation of the first chapter of the *Politics* Oresme used the expression "souverain presidence" to describe the unrestricted power of the monarch.[152] In a gloss from 6. 12., he spoke of "sovereignty over positive laws," and in a gloss from 7. 21., of "the sovereignty of the keeping of [laws of succession?]."[153] On the other hand we find in his glosses: "There should be one or several sovereigns who hold governmental power and exercise it according to the laws"; "the law is like a sovereign prince"; and "the mortal sovereign prince [of the church] . . . should be under the law."[154]

---

phrase is a translation of Moerbeke's "praeest" (Susemihl, p. 2, line 6). Thus the word is used as an adjective and perhaps means no more than "greatest" (see n. 137 above). If we look at an example in which Aristotle seems clearly to be speaking of sovereignty, and see which words are used by Moerbeke and Oresme, we merely confuse the matter further. Where Barker gives us Aristotle's statement that "Rightly constituted laws should be the final sovereign" (*Politics* 3. 11. 1282b; p. 127), Moerbeke has "leges recte positas esse dominas" (p. 198, lines 2–3) and Oresme has "elles aient domination" (3. 14. [fol. 97b, p. 137b]).

[147] Fol. 157c, p. 196b. See above, n. 138.

[148] Fol. 250b, p. 292a. For the text, see n. 123.

[149] Fol. 251d, p. 293a; fol. 252b, p. 293b; fol. 252b, p. 293b.

[150] Fol. 247d, p. 290a; fol. 251b, p. 293a; fol. 253a, p. 294a.

[151] Oresme had "soient seigneurs tant seulement des choses de quoy les lays ne pevent dire ou determiner certainement" (*Le Livre de Politiques* 3. 14. [fol. 97d, p. 138a]), for Moerbeke's "de hiis esse dominos, de quibuscunque non possunt leges dicere certitudinaliter" (Susemihl, p. 198, lines 4–5). Barker's translation (*Politics* 3. 11. 1282b; p. 127) is: ". . . should be sovereign only in those matters on which the law is unable . . . to make an exact pronouncement." In a gloss from 1. 15. (see n. 143 above) Oresme said that one who lacks full seigneurie must follow the law, whether it be the law of marriage or the law of a state.

[152] See n. 146. Barker's translation is: "the latter [the monarch] has an uncontrolled and sole authority, while the former [the 'statesman'] exercises his authority in conformity with the rules imposed by the art of statesmanship and as one who rules and is ruled in turn" (*Politics* 1. 1. 1252a; pp. 1–2). See also n. 84 above, where Oresme says that sovereign royal government is above political government, which is regulated by law and custom.

[153] "Souvereineté sus les lays positives" (fols. 231d–232a, p. 274b) and "la souveraineté de la garde de teles lays" (fol. 269d, p. 311b).

[154] *Le Livre de Politiques* 3. 17. (fol. 101c, p. 142a); 3. 24. (fol. 118c, p. 158a); 5. 25. (fol. 201d, p. 243a).

There are differences between the use Oresme made of seigneur and its variants, and the use he made of souvrain and its variants. These differences suggest that the latter word indicates some of the characteristics of sovereignty as it has been described here. One sign that the two words are not synonymous is that we see in the *Livre de Politiques* expressions like "souverain seigneurie," which would make no sense if the two words had the same meaning.[155] Oresme gives us a hint of the difference in the "Table des Notables" at the end of his text. One of the entries under "Translation de princeys" reads: "How the sovereign temporal majesty and the greatest worldly *seigneurie* or glory has been translated from one country to another, and by what means. . . ."[156] Here there is a suggestion of equivalency between sovereignty and an extended degree of seigneurie, as though the difference between the two were merely quantitative. In a gloss from 3. 13., however, Oresme contrasted seigneurie with "souveraine dominacion." Aristotle had said that in a state where the few have ultimate authority, it is safe and advantageous to allow the many a share in deliberation and judgment, in order to keep them from becoming discontented.[157] Oresme explained this arrangement:

In the context of this chapter, he means, it seems to me, first that it is better that a few virtuous men have, not all the *seigneurie* but the sovereign domination. . . . [But] it does not follow from this that the whole people has the authority to govern, as is the case in democracy; only a chosen few have it in this case.[158]

There appears to be a qualitative difference between the general governmental power described as seigneurie and the superior or final authority described as "souveraine dominacion." We may also recall Oresme's definition of princey, in which seigneurie is made a synonym of princey (both indicating a general sort of power), while emperors were called "souverains princes."

A more specific characteristic of supreme authority was attributed by Oresme to those he called souvrain. This was the prerogative of hearing appeals, and of deciding cases between inferiors. In *Politics* 6. 3. 1318a, Aristotle had mentioned the use of sortition as a means of settling disputes. Oresme's gloss on this section begins with an explanation of this unfamiliar practice, then continues:

For in this state there was no sovereign prince to whom such a doubtful matter could be taken. And, supposing that there had been such a prince, there might have been a

---

[155] For example, in 3. 8. (fol. 87d, p. 128a), Oresme said: "Il entent par monarchie le princey la ou un seul a souveraine seigneurie." Similarly: "Et par ce semble que les possessions des prestres estoient toutes determinees et que il en estoient souverains seigneurs" (3. 21. [fol. 108a, p. 148b]): ". . . souverains seigneurs de tout, et de esperituel et de temporel" (4. 16. [fol. 150b, p. 189b]) and 7. 10. (fol. 248b, p. 290b). In a gloss from the *Livre de Ethiques* 8. 13. (fol. 168d, p. 434 in Menut's edition), he said: "Et *monarchie*, c'est la ou .i. tous seul a souveraine seigneurie sur une communité." For "seigneurie en souveraineté," see below, chap. 5, n. 116.

[156] Fol. 325a, p. 369b.

[157] *Politics* 3. 11. 1281b (Barker, pp. 124–125).

[158] Fol. 95b–c, p. 135b.

case in which the laws and regulations appeared to contradict each other, while the legal authorities were not in agreement and the prince was uncertain.[159]

Oresme touched upon a more specifically juridical aspect of sovereignty in his definition of *pretoire* in the "Table des expositions des fors mos de Politiques": "Generally this is an assembly of those who hold jurisdiction. And this is what is called the sovereign court, from which there is no appeal. And sometimes the word is used for the place where the court sits, and where judicial proceedings are held."[160]

The fullest discussion of judicial sovereignty, and the one most relevant to the government Oresme knew, occurs in the long gloss on universal monarchy. Here Oresme was presenting an argument favoring universal monarchy, and thus opposing "the right side in this question," but this does not affect his use of terms:

. . . one man should be sovereign in spiritual things . . . great temporal questions should be under his jurisdiction, or under the jurisdiction of another temporal sovereign . . . disputes which arise between the subjects of princes all terminate in the sovereign courts [of these princes] . . . the only cases to come before the sovereign monarch are those which are between princes and which cannot be settled by negotiators. . . .[161]

Here the judicial sovereignty of the national monarch was emphasized as clearly as it was in the response of King Charles to the appeal of the Gascon barons.

Oresme's choice of terminology suggests that he had a conception of sovereignty which distinguished it from other kinds of authority. Seigneurie was to him a general and possibly intermediate sort of power, which, like feudal power, often had to do with possession. Souveraineté was something with a more absolute quality,[162] which was associated with the judicial supremacy of the royal government under Charles V.

We have tried to sift some of Oresme's ideas out of his glosses; now we digress a bit to consider his sentiments. Aristotle shows little local loyalty.[163] Nor do the early *Politics* commentators give us a sense of place. But we find

---

[159] *Le Livre de Politiques* 6. 3. (fol. 220a, p. 261a).

[160] Fol. 329a, p. 373a.

[161] Ibid., 7. 10. (fol. 249a, p. 291a). Similarly the *Songe du Vergier* 1. 146. (ed. Brunet, p. 174) says that the king "estoit prest de recevoir leurs appellacions [he is speaking of the barons of Guyenne; see nn. 54–55 above], et de user de sa souveraineté et derrain ressort. . . ."

[162] This is more true of souveraineté than of souverain, which as we have seen (n. 137) was used more loosely as an adjective. For example, in the prologues to the *Livre du ciel et du monde* (fol. 1a, p. 38 of Menut and Denomy's 1968 edition) and to the *Livre de Politiques* (fol. 3c, p. 44a) Oresme referred to Charles as the "tres souverain et tres excellent prince." We have seen that sovereignty was sometimes described as though it could be merely relative (see n. 44) but it is likely that in these cases we have examples of inflated praise.

[163] Certainly Aristotle illustrates his ideas with examples from Greek history, but, as T. A. Sinclair has said in the introduction to his translation of the *Politics* (Harmondsworth, Middlesex and Baltimore, 1962), 17: "No one would ever guess from reading the *Politics* that Aristotle himself was a Macedonian or that a Macedonian king was then conquering the world." Alan Gewirth makes a similar comment in his notes to *The Defender of Peace* (2: xxviii), comparing the work of Aristotle with that of Marsilius of Padua.

in the glosses of Oresme traces of national sentiment, slight patriotic bris-
tlings of the sort which have caused him to be considered a propagandist.
These details are worth mentioning, though they have little to do with the
Politics itself, because they surely have something to do with the way
Oresme felt about France as a nation and about the royal government.

It is hardly surprising that Oresme made flattering references to his royal
patron. He praised Charles as an individual, for his wisdom, and, what is
less to be expected, for his courage.[164] He also gave Charles the more general
honor due a king of France, calling him king by the grace of God.[165] He
spoke of him as the defender of the faith and the most Catholic king.[166]
There seems to be no reference to the royal touch, though Oresme did refer
to a miraculous cure of, not by, a French king.[167] Oresme mentioned in
addition to French monarchs some of the institutions of the royal government.[168]

In several of the glosses in the *Livre de Politiques* Oresme showed a loyalty
and attachment to France as a whole.[169] Where Aristotle said that kings
should be of the same stock as their subjects, Oresme, once again enlarging,
that is, transforming the polis, said that the natural and mutual affinity of

---

[164] In the prologue to the *Livre de Ethiques* (fol. 1b, p. 98 in Menut's edition) Oresme said: "Si
me semble que nous devons beneïr et loer le Roy du ciel qui a son pueple pourveü de tel Roy
terrien plain de si grant sagesce. . . . il est soubz Dieu, aprés le pape, principal deffenseur [of
the Catholic faith]. . . ." Farther on (fol. 1d, p. 100) he said: ". . . nostre bon roy Charles puet
estre dit Charles grant en sagesce; et que de tres saint mouvement et de tres noble courage. . . ."

[165] In the prologue to the *Livre de Ethiques* (fol. 1a, p. 97), we read: ". . . tres noble et tres
excellent prince Charles, par la grace de Dieu roy de France . . . ," and at the end of this work
(fol. 224b, p. 547) we read: "Du commandement de tres noble, puissant et excellent prince
Charles par la grace de Dieu Roy de France. . . ." In the prologue to the *Livre de Politiques* (fol.
3c, p. 44a) we read: "A tres souverain et tres excellent prince Charles, quint de ce nom, par la
grace de Dieu roy de France." Nearly identical phrases occur in the *Livre du ciel et du monde*
in the prologue (fol. 1a, p. 38 in the Menut and Denomy 1968 edition) and at the end of
the translation (fol. 203c, p. 730).

[166] ". . . le roy de France, qui est tres catholique et vrai filz et champion de Sainte Eglise et le
plus excellent de touz les princes terriens qui sunt en ce munde. Et il a fait mettre en lumiere
ceste doctrine de politiques, qui pourroit moult valoir a tele reformacion" (*Le Livre de Politiques*
3. 24. [fol. 125a, p. 161b]). Similarly, the author of the *Songe du Vergier* said in the conclusion to
part 2 (2.282, ed. Brunet, p. 146): ". . . car vous estes le vray champion de la foy catholicque."

[167] "Aussi ay je oy dire que es hystoires de Reins est que l'en vouloit debouter .i. roy de France
du royalme pource que il avoit une leideur en le oil, mes toutesvoies il demoura, et cuide que il
fu gueri par miracle" (*Le Livre de Politiques* 3. 23. [fol. 116c, p. 156a]). Apparently Oresme did
not approve of dismissing kings because of physical imperfection. Where Aristotle says that
rulers should be physically and mentally outstanding (*Politics* 7. 14. 1332b), he noted that "le
vaillant roy Pepin fu petit du corps" (7. 29. [fol. 280b, p. 323b]).

[168] He mentioned the *parlement* several times (2. 20. [fol. 64d, p. 107b]; 4. 23. [fol. 161a, p.
200b]; 5. 31. [fol. 210a, p. 251b]; 6. 2. [fol. 218a, p. 258b]; 6. 12. [fol. 231c, p. 274a]). The peers of
France were mentioned in 3. 13. (fol. 94d, p. 135a), the *chambre des comptes* in 5. 31. (fol. 210a,
p. 251b); 6. 2. (fol. 218a, p. 258b) and 6. 12. (fol. 231b, p. 274a). The assizes and exchequer were
mentioned in 7. 18. (fol. 264c, p. 306a), the exchequer alone in 4. 23. (fol. 161b, p. 200b), and, in
the same gloss, the bailiffs and provosts (fol. 161a).

[169] As Strayer says in "Normandy and Languedoc" (from *Medieval Statecraft*), p. 57: "Some
of the earliest expressions of French patriotism, or of protonational sentiments, come from men
who were born in the two conquered provinces [that is, Normandy and Languedoc]."

the French makes them like members of one lineage.[170] Not only were France and Paris especially blessed.[171] In addition, France had inherited the former majesty of Persia, Greece, and Rome, and with it the most extensive of powers and the greatest worldly prosperity.[172] He mentioned some of the legendary traditions of France, for example the fleur-de-lis and the supposed descent of the French from Hector. (The latter appears in the *Livre de Ethiques.*)[173]

The problems of Oresme's own lifetime were mentioned in his glosses. Like other writers of his time,[174] he showed an interest in laws of succession which would bar the English claim to the crown of France.[175] When he says in his universal monarchy gloss that it is unnatural for people speaking one language to rule over people who speak another, this may surely be seen as another reference to the war. Oresme also mentions Jacques d'Artevelt twice as an example of a demagogue.[176] And finally, and most strikingly, Oresme chose his fellow Norman, Duke William, as an example of a conqueror who justified his action through the imposition of superior government: "[Another way benefactors can deserve to rule] is by conquering a country in order better to govern it, and in a just war, as the first dukes or kings of France conquered this country, or as Duke William, duke of this Normandy, conquered England."[177]

It is possible to piece together a conception of national sovereignty from the glosses of Oresme, although we find not puissance souveraine but preeminence of the royal or national government, not nationalism but na-

---

[170] *Le Livre de Politiques* 1. 15. (fol. 28c–d, p. 71b) (from *Politics* 1. 12. 1259b).

[171] Ibid., 7. 7. (fol. 244d, p. 286b).

[172] Ibid., 7. 13. (fol. 256a–b, p. 298a).

[173] For the fleurs-de-lis, see 7. 3. (fol. 238d, p. 280b), where Aristotle (7. 2. 1324b; Barker, p. 285) mentions soldiers' armlets and Moerbeke (Susemihl, p. 248, lines 10–11) has ". . . aiunt ornatum ex liliis . . . quotcunque militiis militaverint." Oresme's text is: "Il leur lisoit prendre paremens de fleurs de lilz. Et par aventure, a l'exemple de ce, les armes de France sunt de teles fleurs." For Hector, see the *Livre de Ethiques* 7. 1. (fol. 132b, p. 364): "De cestui Hector descendirent les François; ce dit un expositeur, et ainsi le dient les hystoires." See Wisman, "L'éveil du sentiment national," 293, for an example of the Trojan legend, from Christine de Pisan.

[174] See n. 29 above.

[175] Since the English claim was based on descent from a woman we can understand the point of remarks such as this from 2. 21. (fol. 65d, p. 109a): "[Succession] doit estre maintenue selon les conditions approuvees, escriptes ou acoustumees, si comme seroit . . . que femme ne peust succeder, ne homme par femme, ne homme de estrange nacion. . . ." Similarly, in another discussion of rules of succession (3. 23. [fol. 116b, p. 156a]), he said "Une autre regle seroit que nul ne succede en royalme par femme ou moiennant femme . . . car autrement pourroit succeder un qui seroit d'autre nation et de estrange pere." Again female succession is linked with alien rule. See Lewis, "War-Propaganda and Historiography," p. 9.

[176] "Et tel demagoge fu en Flandres, un appellé Jaques d'Artevele" (4. 7. [fol. 135b, p. 174a]). Artevelt is also given as the example of a demagogue in the "Table des fors mos" (fol. 326c–d, p. 371a), and described as one who "par adulation ou flaterie demeine le menu peuple a sa volenté et qui les esmeut a rebellion contre les princes ou le prince."

[177] *Le Livre de Politiques* 3. 20. (fol. 107c, p. 147b). It may be noted that Oresme, who mentioned "ceste Normendie" several times in his glosses (see also: 4. 23. [fol. 161b, p. 200b]; 5. 21. [fol. 195a, p. 236a]; 7. 18. [fol. 264b, p. 306a]: "ceste Normendie" again; and 7. 39. [fol. 293a, p. 338b]), was probably writing these glosses in Paris.

tional sentiment. We can see in the *Livre de Politiques* an understanding of the qualities which make the communitas perfecta the political unit best able to fulfill the ends of the state and thus to deserve sovereignty. Oresme like other medieval Aristotelians struck a balance in his use of the hierarchy of communities, using it to dispute the pretensions of the empire and at the same time enlarging it to include the nation or kingdom. He did not, like Dante, support the claims of universal monarchy by making extreme interpretations of Aristotle's political and metaphysical conceptions. Instead, he opposed the empire and defended individual kingdoms in a practical and realistic spirit not unlike that of Aristotle. We can see Oresme's notion of sovereignty not only in the way he used the text of Aristotle but in his choice of words as well. In his use of terms like souveraineté there are reflections of the practice of the French government under Charles V. Finally, we see Oresme as a philosopher and a proud and self-conscious Frenchman, whose occasional displays of national sentiment provide a particular complement to his general notions of the "multitude de citoiens par soy souffisante" and "communité parfeite."

IV. THE PUBLIC STATE AND THE COMMON GOOD

National governments had to put an end to competition from other jurisdictions, local and imperial alike. At the same time, they needed to foster allegiance to an impersonal, eternal state or crown in order to replace private and particular loyalties. They had to think of their kingdoms as political communities, not as interlaces of warriors or as estates held in fee by the monarch, to look to the nation as an institution rather than a backdrop for a procession of kings. Political writing must also expand, to speak of states rather than of rulers.[1] We can see all this happening in the fourteenth century, when changes in theory and practice were rapid and concurrent. By this time, western Europe had seen the creation of "the substance if not the accidents of the State,"[2] of an entity which existed in anticipation of a name.[3]

The continuity of the monarchy was emphasized in France by the royal religion and by the notion of the *corona regni*, which has been described by Strayer as the "mass of rights and powers associated with the royal government, held by each king as successor to the monarchy rather than as an

---

[1] For bibliography, see chapter 3, nn. 1 and 70. Among those listed in n. 1, the works of David, Riesenberg, Kantorowicz, Post, Guenée ("État et nation en France"), Wahl (see also his article "Immortality and Inalienability: Baldus de Ubaldis," *Mediaeval Studies* 32 [1970]: 308–328), and Strayer's essays (collected in *Medieval Statecraft and the Perspectives of History*) will be most important here. Reference will also be made in this introductory section to the works on the France of Charles V, especially those of Lavisse, Dodu, Chaplais, and P. S. Lewis.

On organic and corporatist ideas, see Otto von Gierke, *Das deutsche Genossenschaftsrecht*, 4 vols. (Berlin, 1868–1913) and *Political Theories of the Middle Age*, a translation of a section of the first volume of the former work, done with notes by Frederic William Maitland (Cambridge, 1900). For another point of view, see Maurice De Wulf, "L'Individu et le groupe dans la scolastique du XIIIᵉ siècle," *Revue néoscolastique de philosophie* 22 (1920): 341–357 (see also De Wulf's *Philosophy and Civilization in the Middle Ages* [Princeton, 1922], where the article is essentially reproduced in chapter 10), and Ewart Lewis, "Organic Tendencies in Medieval Political Thought," *American Political Science Review* 32 (1938): 849–876. Lewis denies the assertion of Gierke that "medieval theory conceived the group as having an end of its own distinct from the ends of its individual members" ("Organic Tendencies," 851). The article of Anton-Hermann Chroust, "The Corporate Idea and the Body Politic in the Middle Ages," *Review of Politics* 9 (1947): 423–452, seems to strike a position between Gierke and his opponents. See also Georges de Lagarde, "Individualisme et corporatisme au Moyen Age," in *L'Organisation corporative du moyen âge à la fin de l'Ancien Régime (Études présentées à la Commission Internationale pour l'Histoire des Assemblées d'États)*, 3 vols. (Louvain, 1937), 2: 3–59, and J. P. Canning, "The Corporation in the Political Thought of the Italian Jurists of the thirteenth and fourteenth centuries," *History of Political Thought* 1. 1. (Spring 1980): 9–32. For the doctrine of the *corpus mysticum* and its influence on political ideas, see Henri de Lubac, *Corpus mysticum: l'eucharistie et l'église au moyen âge* (Paris, 1944), and Gerhart B. Ladner, "Aspects of Mediaeval Thought on Church and State," *Review of Politics* 9 (1947): 403–422.

[2] Post, "Reflections," from *Studies in Medieval Legal Thought*, 568.

[3] "État et nation en France," 18.

individual."[4] Although the conception of the crown increased the prestige of the ruler, it limited (in theory) the exercise of his power by making him a steward.[5] He should not, for example, diminish the kingdom by making apanages. Jean II had done this:[6] Charles V preferred to make provisions in land.[7]

Here we see the principle, familiar from Roman and ecclesiastical law, that sovereignty may not be alienated or prescribed against.[8] Louis VII had promised to safeguard the integrity of the corona regni.[9] By the middle of the fourteenth century, the non-alienation clause was an established part of the coronation oath.[10] As J. A. Wahl has said, this doctrine "demonstrated

---

[4] "Defense of the Realm and Royal Power in France," from *Medieval Statecraft*, 293.

[5] Lewis, *Later Medieval France*, 95, cites Jean Jouvenal des Ursins, who said in the fifteenth century that ". . . a proprement parler le roy ny a que une maniere de admin[i]stration et usage pour enjoyr sa vie durant tant seulement" (from *Traictie compendieux de la querelle de France contre les Anglois*, B. N. MS. Fr. 17512, fol. 12ᵛ). See also Herbert H. Rowen, *The King's State. Proprietary Dynasticism in Early Modern France* (New Brunswick, N. J., 1980), chap. 1, and Raymond Cazelles, *Société politique, noblesse et couronne sous Jean le Bon et Charles V* (Geneva, 1982), 578.

[6] Calmette, *Charles V*, 161–162.

[7] Lavisse, "Le pouvoir royal au temps de Charles V," 251.

[8] See Riesenberg's book, the article by Wahl, "Immortality and Inalienability," cited in full in n. 1, and the article by Kantorowicz, "Inalienability: A Note on Canonical Practice and the English Coronation Oath in the Thirteenth Century," *Speculum* 29 (1954): 488–502. Wahl, 327, gives a reference to Post, *Studies in Medieval Legal Thought*, 416 ff., where it is said that, while the oath against alienation may have come from the oaths taken by bishops, its form came from provisions against alienation found in the *Codex*.

[9] Strayer, "Defense of the Realm and Royal Power in France," in *Medieval Statecraft*, 293, with reference to Alexandre Teulet, *Layette du trésor des chartes (Inventaires et documents)*, 5 vols. (Paris, 1863–1909), 1: 77, #143, from 1156, and to Achille Luchaire, *Études sur les actes de Louis VII* (Paris, 1885), 439, #611 (1171–1172).

[10] It seems that a non-alienation clause did not appear in the oath of Philip VI (David, *La souveraineté*, p. 228). Pierre de Cugnières was said to have argued at the Assembly of Vincennes in 1329, against the archbishop of Sens, that the coronation oath contained such a clause (Pierre Toussaint Durand de Maillane, *Les Libertez de l'église gallicane prouvées et commentées*. . . , 5 vols. [Lyon, 1771], 3: 456–457). See Jean-Pierre Royer, *L'Église et le royaume de France au XIVᵉ siècle d'après le "Songe du Vergier" et la jurisprudence du Parlement* (Paris, 1969), pp. 145, 146, 149, and G. H. M. Meyjes, *Jean Gerson et L'Assemblée de Vincennes (1329). Ses conceptions de la jurisdiction temporelle de l'Église* (Leiden, 1978), 60 and n. 22, for discussion of this claim.

Some say the clause was introduced in 1369 (Delachenal, *Histoire de Charles V*, 3: 81; Jean de Pange, *Le roi très chrétien* [Paris, 1949], 413: ". . . Charles V, lors de son avènement, introduit dans le serment royal la clause suivante: 'Je conserverai inviolablement la supériorité, les droits et les dignités de la couronne de France, et je ne les transporterai pas ni les aliénerai'"). Marcel David, "Le serment du sacre du IXᵉ au XVᵉ siècle," *Revue du moyen âge latin* 6 (1950), 258, gives the Latin form of this oath: ". . . superioritatem, jura, et nobilitates corone Franciae inviolabiliter custodiam, et illa nec transportabo, nec alienabo" (François André Isambert, *Recueil général des anciennes lois françaises, depuis l'an 420 jusqu'à la révolution de 1789*, 29 vols. [Paris, 1821–1833], 5: 240).

Charles V borrowed from the ceremony of episcopal ordination the ritual of the benediction of the ring, which was thought by Percy Ernst Schramm (*Der König von Frankreich. Das Wesen der Monarchie vom 9. zum 16. Jahrhundert*, 2 vols. in one [Weimar, 1939], 1: 237 ff.) to imply the marriage of the king to his realm and thus the principle of non-alienability. But Kantorowicz (*The King's Two Bodies*, 222, n. 84) feels that the decisive words for this interpretation do not occur in the ceremony. At any rate, in 1401, under Charles VI, the *roi mineur* cited the example of his predecessors in guarding the rights of the crown: ". . . nos prédécesseurs . . . ont juré

the assured position of the realm as an object of public law rather than as one of the king's personal possessions."[11] Similarly, in accordance with the provisions of Roman law, it was held that promises made against public authority were invalid.[12]

At the same time, Christian, juristic, and Aristotelian ideas were combined in the depiction of the king as a public person and representative of the state, as the head of a body whose interdependent members[13] were joined mystically[14] or organically.[15]

The attention of the writers who expressed these notions of interdependence and common welfare was devoted to the actions of government. Less was said about the responsibilities of the governed, although the two subjects can hardly be separated. A state which is both communitas perfecta and defender of the common good may well make demands upon its citizens, first in time of emergency, and then for regular maintenance. These obligations, while they must serve a purpose and must be more than mere tribute to the government, can no more begin and end with the reign of a particular ruler than can the obligations of the crown itself. This was recognized by some writers[16] and of course by members of the royal administration. But as we shall see, Oresme (and not he alone) was curiously blind to this requirement of national life.[17] As a commentator he clearly recognized

---

et aussi nous jurasmes nous moult solonnelment . . . garder lesdiz droiz de nostredicte couronne, et aussi ledit demaine entier, et non le aliéner ne départir en aucune manière, et readmender, readjoindre, et reaünir ce qui en seroit aliéné . . ." (Isambert, Recueil général, 7: 10–11, cited in David, La souveraineté, p. 231).

[11] "Immortality and Inalienability," p. 318.

[12] In the case of Guyenne (see above, chap. 3, n. 55), it was claimed on behalf of the king that "laissier aucune chose de ses ressors et souverainetez" would be "contre son sairement et son honneur et ou detriment de son ame" (Delachenal, Chronique des règnes, 2: 177, cited in David, La souveraineté, 230). The author of the Songe du Vergier said: "De rechief cest chose impossible que le roy estant roy puisse renoncer à la souveraineté, s'il ne renonce a tout son royaulme" (1.146., ed. Jean Louis Brunet, in vol. 2 of Pierre Dupuy, Traitez des droits et libertez de l'église gallicane, rev. ed., 4 vols. [Paris, 1731–1751], 178). See also 2. 251.; Brunet, 107. See also Wahl, "Immortality and Inalienability," 325, for references to the Digest.

[13] See Kantorowicz, The King's Two Bodies, 209–210. This idea was associated with the Aristotelian hierarchy of communities. See Kantorowicz, "Pro Patria Mori in Medieval Thought," American Historical Review 56 (1950–1951), 486, where he speaks of the five corpora mystica distinguished by the lawyers: the village, the city, the province, the realm, and the universe, with reference to Gierke's Das deutsche Genossenschaftsrecht, 3: 545, n. 64, and to Fritz Kern's Humana civilitas (Leipzig, 1913).

[14] See especially John of Salisbury, Policraticus 5. 2. (ed. Clemens C. I. Webb, Ioannis Saresberiensis Episcopi Carnotensis Policratici sive De Nugis Curialum, Libri VIII, 2 vols. [Oxford, 1909], 1: 282–284). See H. Liebeschütz, "John of Salisbury and Pseudo-Plutarch," Journal of the Warburg and Courtauld Institutes 6 (1943): 33–39, and A. Momigliano and H. Liebeschütz, "Notes on Petrarch, John of Salisbury and the Institutio Traiani," ibid., 12 (1949): 189–190.

[15] See Henri de Lubac, Corpus mysticum, as cited above in n. 1; Kantorowicz, The King's Two Bodies, 207–232, and Strayer, "The Historical Experience of Nation-Building," from Medieval Statecraft, 344.

[16] See Wahl, "Immortality and Inalienability," 323, for the view of Baldus that "fiscus semper est solvendo," that the dues owed to the unchanging fisc are themselves unchanging.

[17] Oresme could claim the support of Aristotle against taxation (see above, chap. 1, n. 35; below, nn. 50, 89, 103–108), but he might have noted, as he did elsewhere, that the circumstances of a large kingdom are different from those of a city-state.

the preeminence of the royal government over local communities. As a member of the court he must have been aware that the responsibilities and expenses of the royal government were immense. Yet he saw taxation as royal rapacity and called for the king to live on his own. This inconsistency, however, which appears clearly only in hindsight, was shared with most of his contemporaries.

Although the application of this broadened conception of the state was incomplete or occasionally disingenuous, its effects were pervasive and profound. As we see in political practice a continual recourse to notions of the crown, the public utility, and the inalienable prerogatives of the state, so we see among political writers a virtually unanimous use of the common good as the standard of government.

The Public State and Aristotelian Theory

Aristotle began his description of political life by speaking of communities rather than of rulers. This contrasts strongly with the narrow scheme of the *specula principum* which characterized political writing between Augustine and the reintroduction of Aristotle.[18] In the *Politics* the subject of political philosophy was not the ruler but the state itself, a community directed toward a common goal.[19]

According to the latter conception of the state, government must be judged by its service to the community as a whole.[20] This need not imply the sacrifice of the individual. Aristotle did not go so far as Remigio da Girolami, who said that one who is not a citizen is not a man, and that man as a social animal must give up even his soul for the sake of the group.[21] It is true that

---

[18] See Lester K. Born, "The Perfect Prince: a Study in Thirteenth- and Fourteenth-Century Ideals," *Speculum* 3 (1928): 470–504; Wilhelm Berges, *Die Fürstenspiegel des höhen und späten Mittelalters* (Leipzig, 1938); and Dora M. Bell, *L'Idéal éthique de la royauté en France au moyen âge d'après quelques moralistes de ce temps* (Geneva, 1962). See also Georges de Lagarde, in "La philosophie sociale d'Henri de Gand et Godefroid de Fontaines," *Archives d'histoire Doctrinale et Littéraire du Moyen Age* 18–20 (1943–1945): 109.

[19] For material on theories of the public state and their relation to the common good, see the works mentioned above in n. 1, and the following: Richard Egenter, "Gemeinnutz vor Eigennutz. Die soziale Leitidee im 'Tractatus de bono communi' des Fr. Remigius von Florenz (*1319)," *Scholastik* 9 (1934): 79–92; I. Th. Eschmann, "A Thomistic Glossary on the Principle of the Pre-eminence of a Common Good," *Mediaeval Studies* 5 (1943): 123–165; idem, "Bonum commune melius est quam bonum unius. Eine Studie über den Wertvorrang des Personalen bei Thomas von Aquin," ibid., 6 (1944): 62–120; Lorenzo Minio-Palluelo, "Remigio Girolami's De bono communi: Florence at the Time of Dante's Banishment and the Philosopher's Answer to the Crisis," *Italian Studies* 11 (1956): 56–71; and Richard Crofts, "The Common Good in the Political Theory of Thomas Aquinas," *The Thomist* 37 (1973): 155–173.

[20] In *Politics* 3. 6. 1278b (Barker, p. 111), Aristotle said that although men are drawn to live socially by natural impulse, "they are also drawn together by a *common interest*, in proportion as each attains a share in the good life [through the union of all in a form of political association: Barker's brackets]." In the same chapter (3. 6. 1279a; Barker, p. 112), Aristotle says that "constitutions which consider the common interest are *right* constitutions, judged by the standard of absolute justice. Those constitutions which consider only the personal interest of the rulers are all *wrong* constitutions, or *perversions* of the right forms."

[21] Remigio borrowed the Aristotelian dichotomy between actuation and potential to support his contention that the parts of a community exist only in potentiality: "Totum enim ut totum

Aristotle attributed to the political association a qualitative superiority over less perfect groups, and that he said that any man not a beast or a god was by nature a member of a polis.[22] Nevertheless, he saw no fundamental conflict between the interests of the individual and those of the state: both seek the good life.[23] Aristotle spoke not so much of the subordination of the individual citizen as of the subordination of the less worthy interests of the rulers. His rulers were bound to promote the good of the community, or be tyrants and despots.[24]

It is worthwhile to give a few examples of Aristotle's ideas of tyranny, because medieval writers, who were most familiar with rule by one man, took a special interest in its good and bad forms. Also, the word "tyranny" was extended by Aristotle to other perverted forms of government, as for example in *Politics* 5. 10. 1312b, where he says that democracy is "in its extreme form . . . [a] tyranny of the masses."[25] The definition of tyranny was flexible as to the manner of ruling as well as to the number of rulers. In 4. 10. 1295a Aristotle said that the "most commonly understood" form of tyranny is one existing "where a single person governs men, who are all his peers or superiors, without any form of responsibility, and with a view to his advantage rather than that of his subjects."[26] We shall see a similar variety of definitions in the glosses of Oresme.

---

est existens actu, pars vero ut pars non habet esse nisi in potentia secundum Philosophum in 7 physic." (cited by Egenter, "Gemeinnutz vor Eigennutz," p. 83, n. 10, from *Tractatus de bono communi,* fol. 99ʳb of the Florence MS. Bibl. Naz. Cod. Conv. Soppr. C.4. 940). Remigio's statement, "si non est civis, non est homo, quia homo est naturaliter animal civile secundum Philosophum in 8 eth. et in 1 polit." is found ibid., fol. 100ʳa (Egenter, p. 84, n. 10). For the sacrifice of the soul, see Egenter, 89 and n. 24, citing fol. 104ᵛa of the Florence manuscript. For a less extreme view of the relations between public good and morality, see Gaines Post, "Philosophy and Citizenship in the Thirteenth Century—Laicisation, the Two Laws, and Aristotle," in William C. Jordan, Bruce McNab and Teofilo F. Ruiz, eds., *Order and Innovation in the Middle Ages* (Princeton, 1976): 401–408; 567–570.

[22] *Politics* 1. 2. 1253a. Aristotle also lent support to corporatist ideas; see the "stone hand" of *Politics* 1. 2. 1253a.

[23] Ibid., 3. 6. 1278b (Barker, 111): "The good life is the chief end, both for the community as a whole and for each of us individually." Barker says in his introduction (l–li): "It is easy to glide into the view that the state and its 'well-being' (in the full Greek sense of that term) are thus [i.e., by the moral purpose and dominance of the polis] made into a higher end to which the individual and his personal development are sacrificed. Generally stated, such a view is erroneous: it involves a return, in another form, of that antithesis between political society and the individual which Plato and Aristotle refuse to recognize. The state (they believe) exists for the moral development and perfection of its individual members: the fulfilment and perfection of the individual means-and is the only thing which means-the perfection of the state; there is no antithesis."

[24] In *Politics* 3. 6. 1279a (Barker, 112–113), Aristotle says that the wrong or perverted forms of government which consider the personal interest of the rulers are despotic (as Barker's note says, that means "calculated on the model of the rule of a master, or 'despotēs', over slaves"), "whereas the polis is an association of freemen." Among these perverted forms of government, tyranny is the form which corresponds to the good form of monarchy: in 3. 7. 1279b (Barker, p. 115), he says: "Tyranny is a government by a single person directed to the interest of that person. . . ." There is a similar definition in *Ethics* 8. 10. 1160b.

[25] Barker, 239. A similar text is in 4. 4. 1292a (Barker, 168).

[26] Barker, 179. See also *Rhetoric* 1. 8. 1366a.

Good law and the common good are associated more than once in the *Politics*. In 3. 13. 1283b Aristotle asks who should benefit from legislation, if the Many are "actually better, taken as a whole, than the Few."

We may reply [that the benefit of neither ought to be considered exclusively: Barker's brackets]; that what is "right" should be understood as what is "equally right"; and what is "equally right" is what is for the benefit of the whole state and for the common good of its citizens. . . .[27]

Aristotle also lays down the principle that "laws must be constituted in accordance with constitutions," and that "laws which are in accordance with right constitutions must necessarily be just, and laws which are in accordance with wrong or perverted constitutions must be unjust."[28] Thus, if the common good is for Aristotle the most important criterion of good government, we can infer that a just law will be a law which serves the common good.

At the same time, laws might be bent, broken, or simply overlooked, in accordance with the principle of equity, which operates to preserve the intention of the legislator.[29] Aristotle did not directly associate equity and the common good. If equity looks to the intention of the law-giver, however, it must in a good polity look to the benefit of all.

Aristotle's discussion of the common good was taken up as widely among medieval writers as was his version of the hierarchy of communities.[30] In fact, the qualitative superiority of the common good is analogous to the

---

[27] Barker, 134.

[28] *Politics* 3. 11. 1282b (Barker, 127).

[29] *Ethics* 5. 10. 1137b: ". . . equity, though just, is not legal justice, but a rectification of legal justice. The reason for this is that law is always a general statement, yet there are cases which it is not possible to cover in a general statement" (translated by Harris Rackham [New York, 1926], p. 315).

[30] It would be foolish to deny that there were other sources for the notion of the common good, as we are reminded by Eschmann in "A Thomistic Glossary on the . . . Common Good." It is true as he says that such a principle occurs in Roman and patristic sources available to medieval writers long before the recovery of Aristotle. This does not make it impossible to speak of the Aristotelian contribution to medieval notions of the common good and the public state. For one thing, Eschmann's Roman and patristic sources seem by his own account to lack some characteristics of the medieval notion they allegedly fathered. Cicero's notion lacks "a fixed term of relation in the community as such, viz. the political community" (p. 127). And the *bonum commune* of the Stoics "no longer has a definitely political meaning, but rather a general social one" (ibid.). Eschmann also implies that for Augustine this was an ethical principle, not a political principle related to a "concrete social whole" (141).

The citations in this chapter, on the other hand, concern political questions and come close to the text of the *Politics*. They are far from the universalism of Eschmann's Stoics, whose common good fell "under the tutelage of the whole of nature" (p. 128). Thus one can say that the use of the *Politics* brought to the foreground the specifically political aspects of this notion. It would be hard to account for much of the material in this chapter without mentioning Aristotle.

An additional, minor point might be made about the Eschmann article. He uses Aquinas, it seems, to draw conclusions about the sources of medieval writers in general. But the *Politics* was made available to Aquinas only during the last years of his life, so that he was able to comment on less than half of its text. Thus it is dangerous to assume that later writers were influenced by this treatise only to the same (great or small) extent as Aquinas.

qualitative preeminence of the communitas perfecta.[31] Once accepted, this principle could be used to stress the unity and independent moral value of the state.[32]

The commentators and publicists who preceded Oresme accepted these ideas with an enthusiasm transcending every difference of opinion. Papalists and imperialists, monarchists and republicans, all took up service to the common good as the criterion of good government.[33] Marsilius of Padua was among those who accepted this criterion, but he added the consent of the governed as an additional, and more weighty, requirement.[34] Some medieval writers considered government for the common good to be the test of freedom as well as good government, following the general conception of the *Politics*.[35] Here again Marsilius of Padua placed consent before the common good as a principle of government.[36]

---

[31] This may seem to contradict Aristotle's belief that the goods of the individual and the community are the same. But Aquinas, for example, agreed with Aristotle that the ends of the individual and the state were the same, while saying that there was a qualitative difference between them. In *Summa Theologica* 2ª 2ᵃᵉ, qu. 58, art. 9 (from *Opera omnia* [Rome, 1882–], 9 [1897], p. 17), he said: ". . . bonum commune est finis singularum personarum in communitate existentium, sicut bonum totius finis est cuiuslibet partium." In the same question, art. 7 (p. 15), however, he said: ". . . bonum commune civitatis et bonum singulare unius personae non differunt solum secundum multum et paucum, sed secundum formalem differentiam; alia enim est ratio boni communis et boni singularis, sicut et alia est ratio totius et partis." For support he cited Aristotle, from the first chapter of the *Politics* (1252a) on the difference between the self-sufficient community and the lesser human organizations: "*non bene dicunt qui dicunt civitatem et domum et alia huiusmodi differre solum multitudine et paucitate, et non specie*" (Aquinas's version).

[32] Kantorowicz, *The King's Two Bodies*, 211–212. Victor Martin has seen the connection between these political developments and political thought as early as Beaumanoir in the late thirteenth century (*Les origines du Gallicanisme*, 2 vols. in one [Paris, 1939], 1: 147).

[33] Thomas Aquinas, *De Regimine Principum* 1. 1. (ed. Joseph Mathis [Turin, 1924], p. 3): "Si igitur liberorum multitudo a regente ad bonum commune multitudinis ordinetur, erit regimen rectum et justum, quale convenit liberis"; John of Paris, *De regia potestate et papali* 1. (ed. F. Bleienstein [Stuttgart, 1969], p. 75): "Ad bonum multitudinis ordinatum ponitur ad differentiam tyrannidis oligarchiae et democratiae, ubi rector solum intendit bonum suum et praecipue in tyrannide"; Giles of Rome, *De Regimine Principum* 3. 2. 2. (Rome, 1556, p. 268): "si in aliquo dominio aut principatu intenditur bonum commune et omnium civium secundum suum statum, sic est aequale et rectum"; James of Viterbo, *De regimine christiano* 2. 2. (ed. H.-X. Arquillière [Paris, 1926], p. 166): "Qui autem presunt aliquibus, non bonum subiectorum sed proprium commodum intendentes, a vere gubernationis ratione degenerant, que convenit rationabilibus creaturis"; John of Jandun, comm. on *Metaphysics* 1. 18. (Venice, 1553, p. 15): "Recta politia est qui habet principem qui principatur et dominatur propter commune bonum, ut propter politicum, sed transgressa politia est in qua dominatur princeps propter proprium bonum, et hoc patet per 3. politice"; and William of Ockham, *Dialogus* 3. 1. 2. 6. (ed. Goldast, *Monarchia*, 2: 794): "Si ordinetur ad bonum commune, sic est principatus temperatus et rectus. Si non ordinatur ad bonum commune, est principatus vitiatus et transgressio. . . ."

[34] *Defensor Pacis* 1. 9. 5. (ed. Richard Scholz [Hanover, 1932], p. 44): "Haec igitur duo predicta principatum temperatum et viciosum separant, ut apparet ex Aristoteles [citing *Politics* 4. 8.] aperta sentencia, simpliciter autem aut magis subditorum consensus." See also the English version by Alan Gewirth, *The Defender of Peace*, 2 vols. (New York, 1951–1956), 1: 60.

[35] At one point Aristotle did describe freedom as living according to one's wishes (*Politics* 6. 2. 1317b [Barker, 258]): "Liberty has more than one form. One of its forms [is the political, which: Barker's brackets] consists in the interchange of ruling and being ruled. . . . Such is the first form of liberty, which all democrats agree in making the aim of their sort of constitution. The other form [is the civil, which: Barker's brackets] consists in 'living as you like'. Such a life,

The common good was also used as the criterion for law-making and law-breaking.[37] Even Marsilius, who thought that valid laws were those which could be enforced, mentioned it.[38] It was sometimes held that laws contrary to public utility could be rejected even after enactment, so that the common good was preferred to technical legality. Similarly, medieval writers associated equity with the common good. Aquinas did so, though without mentioning Aristotle.[39] Henry of Ghent approved of making exceptions from strict observance of the law in order to preserve the welfare of the state.[40]

---

the democrats argue, is the function of the free man, just as the function of slaves is *not* to live as they like." In general, as we have seen, Aristotle considered the first meaning of liberty to be the more admirable.

Among medieval examples we have Thomas Aquinas, *Summa Theologica*, pars prima, qu. 96, art. 4 (*Opera omnia* [Rome, 1882 –], 5 [1889]: 429): "Tunc vero dominatur aliquis alteri ut libero, quando dirigit ipsum ad proprium bonum eius qui dirigitur, vel ad bonum commune"; idem, *De Regimine Principum* 1. 1. (ed. Mathis, p. 3); James of Viterbo, *De. reg. christ.* 2. 2. (ed. Arquillière, p. 166): "Qui autem presunt aliquibus, non bonum subiectorum sed proprium commodum intendentes, a vere gubernationis ratione degenerant. . . . Qui enim sic gubernantur non reguntur libere. . . ."; William of Ockham, *Dialogus* 3. 1. 2. 6. (ed. Goldast, 2: 794): "[the subjects of a good monarchy] sibi non sunt servi, sed naturali libertate gaudent: quia ad naturalem libertatem spectat, ut nullus possit uti liberis propter utilitatem utentis. . ." (also ibid., 3. 2. 2. 20. [Goldast, 2: 918]); Dante, *De Monarchia* 1. 12. (ed. L. Bertalot [Florence and Rome, 1920], p. 28): ". . . politie recte libertatem intendunt, scilicet ut homines propter se sint."

For a discussion of how Dante alters Aristotle's conception of liberty, and of the way conceptions of liberty are related to government and the common good, see Larry Peterman, "Dante's *Monarchia* and Aristotle's Political Thought," *Studies in Medieval and Renaissance History* 10 (1973): 10–17. Perhaps Peterman confuses the argument somewhat, by speaking only of one form of liberty, the one which consists in "living as you like."

For other ideas of liberty, see Aquinas, *Summa Theologica* 1ᵃ 2ᵃᵉ, qu. 97, art. 3 (*Opera omnia* [Rome, 1882 –], 7 [1892]: 191): "Si enim sit libera multitudo, quae possit sibi legem facere. . . ." and Peter of Auvergne, *In Libros Politicorum Aristotelis Expositio* 8. 1. (ed. Raimundo M. Spiazzi and listed under Thomas Aquinas, who began the commentary [Rome, 1951], 414): ". . . homo liber est, qui est suipsius causa et in ratione causa moventis et in ratione finis. . . ." Of course the differences of opinion seen in these texts reflect to some extent the several definitions of Aristotle himself. In the *Livre de Politiques* 6. 2. (fol. 217b–c, p. 258a), Oresme translates without significant comment the section of the *Politics* cited at the start of this note.

[36] Marsilius of Padua, *The Defender of Peace*, 1: 220. As Gewirth says, Aristotle and Marsilius differ "in that they regard men as free when they are, respectively, the final causes and the efficient causes of the political power which is exercised over them."

[37] For example, see Thomas Aquinas, *Summa Theologica* 1ᵃ 2ᵃᵉ, qu. 90, art. 2 (*Opera omnia* [Rome, 1882 –], 7 [1892]: 150): ". . . cum lex maxime dicatur secundum ordinem ad bonum commune, quodcumque aliud praeceptum de particulari opere non habeat rationem legis nisi secundum ordinem ad bonum commune."

[38] ". . . ex universe multitudinis auditu et precepto tantummodo feratur lex optima, supponendo cum Aristotele 3° Politice, capitulo 7°, legem optimam esse, que lata est ad commune conferens civium" (*Defensor Pacis* 1. 12. 5. [ed. Scholz, p. 65]). The reference to *Politics* is actually to 3. 13. 1283b, cited above at n. 27.

[39] *ST* 1ᵃ 2ᵃᵉ, qu. 96, art. 6 (Rome, 1882 –), 7 (1892): 187: "Quia igitur legislator non potest omnes singulares casus intueri, proponit legem secundum ea quae in pluribus accidunt, ferens intentionem suam ad communem utilitatem. Unde si emergat casus in quo observatio talis legis sit damnosa communi saluti, non est observanda."

[40] *Quodlibeta* 8, qu. 22 (in the Venice, 1613, edition of 2? vols, 2: 44): ". . . statui non debet, nisi propter bonum, et pacem reipublicae. . . . Unde si essent casus aliqui in quibus legem huiusmodi statuti observare nullo modo vergeret in pacem, et bonum reipubl[icae] casus huiusmodi excipi deberent." (See Lagarde, "Henri de Gand et Godefroid de Fontaines" [as cited above, n. 18], p. 108).

Common good notions could be mixed with corporatist and communal ideas of Aristotelian or non-Aristotelian origin. It had often been said, for example, that the king exists for the state, and not the state for the king, or that the state does not belong to the king. We see this in the *Policraticus* of John of Salisbury, in Ptolemy of Lucca, and in Dante.[41]

Oresme and the Public State

From the start of his commentary Oresme brings these themes into his discussion. In one of his earliest glosses on the common good, Oresme makes a distinction between the way the common good is served by private persons and public persons. Aristotle had claimed that under Plato's system of common ownership citizens would not be motivated properly to care for the goods of the community.[42] In fact, Aristotle said, the state will best be served if each tends to his own affairs. In his gloss Oresme tries to reconcile the apparent conflict between this attitude and Aristotle's general regard for the common good:

But it seems that what Aristotle says in the first chapter of the *Ethics* is contrary to this, for he says that the more general a good is, the more divine and worthy of love it is. . . . To this I say, first, that granted one should care more for the common good, in fact most people take more care for their own good. . . . Still, it is true that princes and [other] public persons should care more for the common good than for their own. . . . But private persons should take more care for their own good, and, in so doing, they will be taking care for and sufficiently aiding the common good . . . perhaps a wine-maker, though he loves and wishes for the victory of his prince more than for the fertility of his vineyard, expends more labor and care on the vineyard [than in the service of his prince].[43]

---

[41] See the edition of Webb (cited above, n. 14), 1: 250. See also Ernst Kantorowicz, "Christus-Fiscus," *Synopsis-Festgabe für Alfred Weber* (Heidelberg, 1948): 227–235. As so often occurred, ecclesiological ideas paralleled (or in this case, anticipated) secular ideas: "Canonists had already determined that the Church did not belong to the Pope so now it was easy to argue in a parallel fashion that the fisc did not belong to the Prince" (J. A. Wahl, "Immortality and Inalienability," p. 322). For Ptolemy of Lucca, see *De Regimine Principum* 3. 11. (ed. Mathis, p. 61): ". . . regnum non est propter regem, sed rex propter regnum." For Dante, see *De Mon.* 1. 12. (ed. Bertalot, p. 28). See also Henry of Ghent, *Quodlibeta* 8. 22.

[42] *Politics* 2. 3. 1261b.

[43] *Le Livre de Politiques* 2. 3. (fol. 35c–d, p. 78b). For the citation from the *Ethics*, see 1. 2. 1094b, and for the text, see above, chap. 3, n. 83, and the texts of Aquinas using this, in chap. 3, nn. 77–78. According to Robert Linhardt (*Die Sozialprinzipien des heiligen Thomas von Aquin* [Freiburg im Breisgau, 1932], 151, cited in E. Lewis, *Medieval Political Ideas*, 2 vols. [New York, 1954], 1: 347), he cited it over sixty times. See, for example, *ST* $2^a 2^{ae}$, qu. 99, art. 1, and *De Reg. Princ.* 1. 9. It is not surprising that Remigio da Girolami made use of this principle: ". . . quanto bonum est communius, tanto est magis amandum, scilicet bonum civitatis magis quam bonum unius civis [a chain carried up to the good of the church]" (fol. 97ʳ of the Florence MS. Bibl. Naz. Cod. Conv. Soppr. C. 4. 940, cited in L. Minio-Palluelo, "Remigio Girolami's *De bono communi*," p. 62). Nicolai Rubenstein shows the usefulness of this principle to the Italian communes in "Marsilius of Padua and Italian Political Thought of His Time," in John R. Hale, J. R. L. Highfield, and Beryl Smalley, eds., *Europe in the Late Middle Ages* (Evanston, Ill., 1965), 56. For the divinity of the common good in the work of Roger Bacon and Henry of Ghent, see Lagarde, "Henri de Gand et Godefroid de Fontaines" (as cited above, n. 18), 86–87.

We see here an example of the closeness between the principles of the common good and of the hierarchy of communities, the examples from Aquinas given above having come from discussions of this hierarchy.

Thus Oresme suggests almost literally that the good citizen can best aid the state by cultivating his own garden. (In the *Livre de Ethiques*, however, when discussing the active and contemplative lives, he said that when the state is in danger, there is no occupation too noble to be set aside in order to defend the public good.)[44] Oresme continues his discussion of private and public goods by making a distinction between the good which is common and political by its nature, and the good (or one might say goods) judged to be private and divisible by nature:

Now in the first chapter of the *Ethics* [Aristotle] is talking about the good which is common by its nature, and which concerns everyone, for example justice and the peace of the country, and divine worship. But here he is speaking about the good which can by its nature be parceled out, for example, children, women, and the fruits of the soil. . . .[45]

Of course it is the first sort of good or common good which most frequently concerned Oresme, and will concern us here.

In applying the notion of the common good, Oresme followed Aristotle and his own medieval predecessors.[46] In his longest gloss on the common good, Oresme described the benefit which the ruler must seek. He took from the *Ethics* a classification of goods as "the noble, the expedient, and the pleasant,"[47] or in his words, "bien honneste," "bien profitable," and "bien delectable,"[48] and applied it in his discussion:

. . . just as in a household there are two authorities, one called *despotic* and the other *economic*, similarly in states there are generally two forms of authority. One of

---

[44] ". . . si comme dit Tulles, il n'est nulle speculacion quelconques tant soit haute et noble que l'en ne deüst laissier pour secourir et pour obvier as perilz du bien publique" (*Le Livre de Ethiques* 10. 14. [fol. 212c, p. 524 in the edition of Menut]).

[45] *Le Livre de Politiques* 2. 3. (fol. 35d, p. 78b).

[46] When Oresme spoke of the common good in his translation of the text, he was translating phrases like "ad commune conferens" from Moerbeke. This is the phrase Moerbeke used, for example, in his version of *Politics* 3. 7. 1279a (Barker, p. 114; Susemihl, p. 178, lines 7, 12, and p. 179, line 3). Oresme spoke here (*Le Livre de Politiques* 3. 8. [fol. 87c, d, p. 128a]) of the "profit publique" and "commun profit." "Expedit communi" (*Politics* 3. 7. 1279b; Susemihl, 180, lines 2–3) becomes "est expedient a tout le commun" in Oresme (3. 8. [fol. 88a, p. 128b]). "Propter communiter expediens" (*Politics* 3. 3. 1276a; Susemihl, 158, line 6) becomes "pour le commun expedient" in Oresme (3. 2. [fol. 76b, p. 117b]). "Ad conferens totius civitatis et ad commune civium" (*Politics* 3. 13. 1283b; Susemihl, p. 207, line 4) becomes "au profit de toute la cité et au commun profit de tous les citoiens" in Oresme (3. 17. [fol. 101d, p. 142a]).
The majority of Oresme's references to the common good, however, occur in his glosses. Here the expression most frequently used is "bien commun." The most common variant is "bien publique," which occurs at least thirty times. Other expressions used by Oresme include: "profit commun" (as in 2. 21. [fol. 66c, p. 109b]); "santé de tout le commun" (3. 7. [fol. 86b, p 127a]); "profit des subjects" (3. 7. [fol. 86d, p. 127a]); "bien de leur subjects" (3. 7. [fol. 86c, d, p. 127a]); and "profit publique" ("Table des . . . fors mos" [fol. 326c, p. 370b, and fol. 328b, p. 372b]). "Commun policie" (as in the "Table des . . . fors mos," fol. 326c, p. 370b), however, is an expression used to describe good government by the multitude, as in a timocracy or polity.
For a discussion of the "visual glosses" on good government from the manuscripts of the *Livre de Politiques*, see Claire Richter Sherman, "Some Visual Definitions in the Illustrations of Aristotle's *Nicomachean Ethics* and *Politics* in the French Translations of Nicole Oresme," *The Art Bulletin* 59 (1977): 326–328.

[47] *Ethics* 2. 3. 1104b (Rackham, p. 81): *Le Livre de Ethiques* 2. 4. (fol. 28a–b, p. 153).

[48] *Le Livre de Politiques* 3. 7. (fol. 86c, p. 127a).

them is similar to despotic authority, and in this the rulers seek what is expedient or profitable for them. . . . And as for the noble good of virtue, if such princes are unjust, they do not seek it. . .[49]

This is contrasted with the rule of those who subordinate their material well-being (but not their virtue) to that of their subjects:

. . . there is another sort of authority similar to economic authority, in which the rulers seek and pursue what is expedient for their subjects, principally and before all else, and seek only secondarily what is expedient for themselves. And this is true especially of the king, who should be materially self-sufficient and not depend on others for support, as is clearly evident from *Ethics* 8. 13. But . . . such princes love and seek their own [noble or virtuous] good above that of their subjects. . . .[50]

As Oresme says more simply in his next gloss," . . . to be a prince is to labor without personal gain."[51]

In another general discussion of good and bad forms of government, Oresme compares Aristotle's classification to that of Augustine, and the Greek polity to the Roman *res publica*:

. . . Saint Augustine, in *The City of God* 2. 22., made a similar distinction, which Cicero, speaking in the person of Scipio, set forth in the third book of *The Republic*. . . . But what Aristotle calls *oligarchy*, he calls *faction*, and he gives no name to the other kinds, beyond calling *democracy* a *tyranny*. In addition, Aristotle designates these governments under the name of *polity*, while Cicero designates them as *republics*, and says that in the three bad forms of government the public order is not depraved . . . but is simply and entirely invalid. . . . Nevertheless, they are governments, but they are depraved ones.[52]

---

[49] Ibid., fol. 86c, p. 127a.

[50] Ibid., fol. 86d, p. 127a. Oresme's citation from *Ethics* is from 8. 10. 1160b: "For a monarch is not a king if he does not possess independent resources, and is not better supplied with goods of every kind than his subjects; but a ruler so situated lacks nothing, and therefore will not study his own interests but those of his subjects. (A king who is not independent of his subjects will be merely a sort of titular king.)" The translation is that of Rackham, 491.

[51] Ibid., fol. 87a, p. 127b. Speaking of profit in his "Table des Notables," he said "Que tous bons princes gouvernent au profit commun et ad ce tendent principalment et plus que a leur propre profit . . ." (fol. 322c–d, p. 367a).

[52] Ibid., 3. 8. (fol. 88b, p. 128b). In *De civ. Dei* 2. 21. (Loeb ed. as cited above, chap. 3, n. 116, 1 [with trans. by George E. Cracken], p. 220), Augustine gives a summary of Cicero's division, which Oresme has reproduced with general accuracy: ". . . esse rem publicam, id est rem populi, cum bene ac iuste geritur sive ab uno rege sive a paucis optimatibus sive ab universo populo. Cum vero iniustus est rex, quem tyrannum more Graeco appellavit, aut iniusti optimates, quorum consensum dixit esse factionem, aut iniustus ipse populus, cui nomen usitatum non repperit, nisi ut etiam ipsum tyrannum vocaret, non iam vitiosam, sicut pridie fuerat disputatum, sed, sicut ratio ex illis definitionibus conexa docuisset, omnino nullam esse rem publicam, quoniam non esset res populi. . . ."

For the Cicero, see *De re publica* 3. 23. (ed. Per Krarup [Milan, 1967], p. 121): ". . . sunt enim omnes, qui in populum vitae necisque potestatem habent, tyranni, sed se Iovis optimi nomine malunt reges vocari. Cum autem certi propter divitias aut genus aut aliquas opes rem publicam tenent, est factio, sed vocantur illi optimates. Si vero populus plurimum potest, omniaque eius arbitrio reguntur, dicitur illa libertas, est vero licentia," and 3. 43. (ibid., 135): "Ergo ubi tyrannus est, ibi non vitiosam, ut heri dicebam, sed, ut nunc ratio cogit, dicendum est plane nullam esse rem publicam." We may note the similarity between Cicero's *licentia* and Aristotle's "living as you like" (see above at n. 35).

Here Oresme glosses over a significant difference between Aristotle and
Cicero. It is not the same thing to say, as did Aristotle, that a government is
perverted when it is not "directed to the advantage of the whole body of
citizens,"[53] as it is to say, following Cicero, that a government without
justice, like these perverted forms, is no government at all. When Oresme
says that "they are governments, but they are depraved ones," he is perhaps
close to Augustine, who, after explaining why Cicero would not call Rome a
commonwealth, concluded that it probably was some sort of commonwealth, after all.[54] Oresme is in any case following Aristotle in not denying
to depraved systems the title of government, and of course in emphasizing
service to the common good.

Of the forms of government judged according to the "bien commun" in
the *Livre de Politiques*, tyranny appears most frequently. Several of Oresme's glosses describe the tyrant as one who governs for his own profit.[55]
For example, in a gloss from the text containing Aristotle's advice to tyrants,
where it was said that a tyrant should act the role of a king, he said:
"[Aristotle] means that tyrants adopt the precautions which follow. And
some are guileless, while others dissemble, in order to seem like kings. But
they are not [kings], for they seek and promote principally their own gain
and not the public good."[56]

After describing the expedients of tyrants, Aristotle said that their governments are seldom durable. Oresme supports this statement with scriptural
references to a principle of common good:

. . . this is similar to what Our Lord said through a prophet to those who were
tyrannizing over the people of Israel, that they ruled them cruelly and by force:
". . . you ruled over them with rigour and with a high hand" [Ezech. 34:4; Douay
Version]. And they seek their own benefit and not that of their subjects: ". . . the
shepherds fed themselves and fed not my flocks" [Ezech. 34:8; Douay Version]. And
for this reason he says afterwards that he will make them fall, and that their tyranny
will not endure: "Behold . . . I will . . . cause them to cease from feeding the
flock any more: neither shall the shepherds feed themselves any more" [Ezech.
34:10; Douay Version].[57]

In this gloss we see another characteristic of tyranny: cruelty.[58] Two other
glosses, both of which mention the common good, provide additional char-

---

[53] *Politics* 3. 7. 1279b (Barker, p. 115).

[54] "Secundum probabiliores autem definitiones pro suo modo quodam res publica fuit" (*De
civ. Dei* 2. 21. [ed. cit, 224]).

[55] We have seen that this definition was also applied by Oresme to despotism (above, n. 49)
as it had been by Aristotle in *Politics* 3. 6. (above, n. 24) Oresme followed him, saying in his
gloss that the government of free men is "celui qui est au profit des subjects" (while despotism
resembles a master's domination over slaves: *Le Livre de Politiques* 7. 29. [fol. 281b, p. 324b]).

[56] Ibid., 5. 29. (fol. 207a, p. 248a), from *Politics* 5. 11. 1314a. He made similar comments
about another of Aristotle's counsels for tyrants, that against raising individuals to greatness:
". . . les tirans le funt pour leur propre profit. Et donques quant as roys, ce sunt regles; et quant
as tirans, ce sunt cauteles" (5. 31. [fol. 208d, p. 250a], from *Politics* 5. 11. 1315a).

[57] *Le Livre de Politiques* 5. 32. (fol. 211c–d, p. 253a).

[58] See also ibid., 5. 27. (fol. 205b, p. 246b) for the "horribles crudelités qui ont esté entre les
tirans et leur proceins." In the manuscript illustrations of the *Livre de Politiques* which are

acteristics of this form of government. In a gloss from 5. 24. Oresme explained how kings fall when they behave like tyrants. Here Aristotle described tyranny as the taking of prerogatives beyond the law. Oresme combined this characteristic with disregard of public benefit.[59] In a gloss on Aristotle's description of barbarian kingship (*Politics* 3. 14. 1285a), which resembles tyranny but is desired by its servile subjects, Oresme attributed to true tyranny both violence and the suppression of the will of the people.[60] Here he approached the definition of Marsilius, who described bad government as that which is not in accord with common benefit and common consent.[61] Oresme mentioned consent again in 3. 21., where he applied Aristotle's definition of barbarian kingship to the government of Biblical Israel. Here, however, he retained service to the common good as the criterion of proper rulership.[62] And in a gloss from 2. 22., he implied that governing for the good of the ruler is the chief characteristic of tyranny:

. . . the word "tyrant" is used in two or three senses. . . . First, a tyrant is said to be one who directs a monarchy for his own benefit and against the public benefit. . . . In addition, anyone who governs for his own benefit and against the common good, whether alone or in a group, can be called a tyrant. . . . Furthermore, anyone who commits any cruel act can be called a tyrant. Thus one could say that Diocletian and Maximian were tyrannical toward the Christians, however little they may have intended to prefer their own benefit over the public or common benefit. . . .[63]

As tyranny is a paradigm of the bad constitution and as it supplies negative definitions of the good constitutions, it is unnecessary to say a great deal about Oresme's treatment of the other forms of government. The common good is mentioned in Oresme's discussions and definitions of monarchy, aristocracy and oligarchy.[64] One of Oresme's glosses speaks of democracy as

---

reproduced in Menut's edition (pp. 6–7, from Brussels, Bibl. Royale MS. 2904, fols. 1ᵛ and 2ʳ), the three bad forms of government, *tyrannie, olygarchie* and *democracie*, are represented by scenes of torture and execution, with the rulers in military dress, while the three good forms, *royaume, aristocracie,* and *tymocracie,* are represented by scenes of peaceable counsel, with the rulers in civil dress. See Claire Richter Sherman, "Some Visual Definitions" (as cited above in n. 46), 328.

[59] Fol. 199c–d, p. 241a.

[60] Ibid., 3. 20. (fol. 106c, p. 146b). See also 4. 22. (fol. 160d, p. 200b) where Oresme, discussing types of election as they relate to forms of government, said: "Et en tirannie il n'i a ne sort ne election fors seulement la volenté du tirant, qui use de pleniere posté."

[61] See above, n. 34. Marsilius described tyranny as a "principatus viciatus, in quo dominans est unicus ad conferens proprium, preter voluntatem subditorem" (*Defensor Pacis* 1. 8. 3. [ed. Scholz, p. 38]).

[62] ". . . Et par le texte de l'Escripture il appert que le droit dessus dit [Samuel's predictions about the exactions to be made by the future king of Israel: I Sam. 8:10–22] est ou profit du prince et appert aussi que le peuple d'Israhel vouloit avoir tel roy. . . . Et ce est le royalme que Aristote appelle *barbarique* et non pas vray royalme" (fol. 109b, p. 149b). In the same gloss, Oresme referred to the common good without mentioning it, saying that the "droit dessus dit" was clearly for the profit of the prince and not for his subjects, for the Bible tells "comment le roy appliqueroit ce que il prendroit sus eulz non pas en la neccessité de la deffense du paíz, mes en ses propres usages et en aucuns deshonnestes . . ." (ibid., fol. 109d, p. 149b).

[63] Ibid., fol. 68d, p. 112a. The text of Aristotle's remark is from *Politics* 5. 10. 1312b, which is discussed above at n. 25.

[64] See 4. 22. (fol. 160d, p. 200b), and 5. 20. (fol. 193d, p. 234b), for monarchy as the opposite of tyranny, with regard to the common good. A similar opposition between aristocracy and

lawless as well as serving only the interests of the rulers.[65] In his definition of *democratie* in the "Table des expositions des fors mos," however, he mentions self-interested rule as the characteristic of democracy.[66]

Private citizens serving as advisers must, like the ruler, think of the common benefit. Where Aristotle said that the associates of the king should also be the friends of the government or state, Oresme commented:

> . . . whoever bears a true love for the king, loves the kingdom as well; and whoever does not love the kingdom does not truly love the king. For as Cicero says, the first law of friendship is that one must not treat one's friend dishonestly. And therefore whoever tries to please the king by counseling him to do something contrary to the public good of the kingdom, is not the friend of the king.[67]

If governments are to be judged according to their service to the common good, what should be done if they are found wanting? Here again the common good is the standard by which actions are to be judged. Oresme was willing to allow the correction of princes in the name of the common good, but only if the correction was done by a "reasonable and honorable multitude."

> . . . there should be one sovereign or several, who have the power of governing and exercise it according to law. . . . But such a multitude might have the decisive authority in three matters. . . . [First] in the choice of those who govern. . . .

---

oligarchy is in glosses from 2. 21. (fol. 66c, p. 109b), 5. 1. (fol. 167a, p. 205b) and 5. 12. (fol. 181c, p. 222a). He mentioned the family resemblance between oligarchy and tyranny in 4. 22. (fol. 160c, p. 200a), and an "expedient of oligarchs," rather like the expedients of the tyrants mentioned earlier, that is, the construction of great buildings to impress and deceive the people, is mentioned in 6. 9. (fol. 228c–d, p. 270b). In 2. 21. (fol. 68a, p. 111a), Oresme gave the "propre profit" definition of oligarchy, and then said, rather surprisingly, that "par ce le peuple subject a cause de faire sedicion." We shall soon see that this remark does not in itself give an adequate impression of Oresme's views on sedition.

[65] Ibid., 4. 19. (fol. 155a, p. 194a). The reference here for Aristotle is *Politics* 4. 14. 1298a; see n. 25 above for a similar comparison of democracy and tyranny.

[66] "*Democratie* est une espece de policie en laquele la multitude populaire tient le princey a leur profit. Et ne est pas bonne policie. Et olygarchie, ou les riches qui sunt en petit nombre le tiennent, est pire, et tyrannie tres malvese" (*Le Livre de Politiques*, fol. 326d, p. 371a). Of democracy's opposite he said: "*Commune policie* est la ou une grande multitude tient le princey au profit publique. . . . Et ceste policie Aristote appelle *tymocracie* ou .xiii.ᵉ chapitre du .viii.ᵉ d'*Ethiques*, mes en cest livre il l'appelle *policie*, par le commun nom. Et pour faire difference, je le ay tousjours nommee *commune policie*" (ibid., fol. 326c, p. 370b). Moerbeke's version of "commune policie," from *Politics* 3. 7. 1279a (Susemihl, p. 179, lines 2–4) is ". . . quando autem multitudo ad commune conferens vivit, vocatur communi nomine omnium politiarum politia."

[67] *Le Livre de Politiques* 3. 25. (fol. 120c, p. 162a). For the Cicero, see *De Amicitia* 13. 44. (trans. William Armistead Falconer [London and New York, 1923: Loeb Classical Library], 154): "Haec igitur prima lex amicitiae sanciatur, ut ab amicis honesta petamus . . . ." In 5. 25. (fols. 201d–202a, p. 243a), Oresme said, in a gloss suggested by Aristotle's discussion of moderate kingship and its stability (*Politics* 5. 11. 1313a): "Meismement que ceulz qui sunt entour eulz [i.e., kings] et pres de eulz ne leur conseillent pas [i.e., to keep the royal power at a moderate level] . . . Et aiment plus leur propre profit que la continuation ou duree du royalme pour le temps avenir." In 7. 32. (fol. 285d, p. 329b), he followed Aristotle's treatment of the good use of leisure (*Politics* 7. 15. 1334a) to consider how counselors can lighten the load of the king: "Item, il ne doit pas prendre gens qui quierent principalment le promotion et le profit de eulz ou de leur amis; car il convient que aucune foiz il conseillent contre le bien publique et du prince."

[Second] in the correction of those who govern, when they abuse the honor of their office, and dissipate or destroy the public good. . . . Third, in the establishment, adoption, and alteration of the law. . . . For it is said that what touches all should be approved by all.[68]

If correction fails, sedition may follow.[69] But sedition may be praised as a proper defense of the ends of the community, or condemned as impious resistance against the instrument of divine punishment. This was not a simple conflict, in which classical doctrine sanctioned sedition (under certain circumstances) and Christian doctrine forbade it. For example, Oresme repeated an argument of Peter of Auvergne, that sedition undertaken for public benefit may do more harm than good.[70] Oresme agreed that even a well-intentioned revolt, and one likely to succeed, would be wrong if it led to "any great evil, for example thievery or murder."[71] Oresme doubted that sedition could occur without such evils.[72] He also doubted that more than a few revolts are undertaken for the common good.[73] He followed these arguments with Biblical admonitions against sedition, citing especially the epistles of Paul.[74]

On the other side, Oresme mentioned Aristotle's description of the common good as divine,[75] and thus worth preserving, and his statement that

---

[68] *Le Livre de Politiques* 3. 17. (fol. 101c, p. 142a). For the origins of the maxim, "Quod omnes tangit," see Gaines Post, "A Romano-Canonical Maxim, 'Quod Omnes Tangit,' in Bracton," *Traditio* 4 (1946): 200–209.

[69] For a "visual gloss" on sedition from the *Livre de Politiques*, see Claire Richter Sherman, "Some Visual Definitions" (as cited above in n. 46), 328–330. As Sherman notes (p. 330), such scenes were all too familiar to King Charles, after his experiences as regent.

[70] The gloss is in the *Livre de Politiques* 5. 1. (fols. 164d–166b, pp. 203b–205a). The argument from Peter of Auvergne appears in fols. 164d–165a, p. 203b. In 5. 1. of his commentary (as cited above in n. 35: p. 247), Peter gave a reason why good men may choose not to make sedition: ". . . frequenter contingit propter dissensionem detrimentum boni communis. Sapiens autem ut plurimum plus diligit bonum commune quam proprium; et ideo non facit dissensionem." Oresme said: ". . . souvent avient que le bien commun est esjené ou blechié par tele dissention et un bon homme aime plus le bien commun que le sien propre." For a similar argument, without mention of Aristotle, see Thomas Aquinas, *De Reg. Princ.* 1. 6. (ed. Mathis, 8–10).
Similarly, in a commentary not on Aristotle but on *The City of God*, John Ridewall used Augustine's argument that, while killing a tyrant may be good "simpliciter et absolute" it might be bad if, for example, the murder caused a civil war. (See Beryl Smalley, "John Ridewall's Commentary on *De Civitate Dei*," *Medium Aevum* 25 [1955–1956]: 151–152, which cites Corpus Christi MS. 186, fols. 163–163v.)

[71] ". . . aucun grant mal, si comme seroit larrecin ou homicide" (fol. 165a, p. 204a). For a similar point of view, see Thomas Aquinas, *Summa Theologica* 2ª 2ᵃᵉ, qu. 42, art. 2, ad 3 (*Opera omnia* [Rome, 1882–], 8 [1895]: 321): "Ad tertium dicendum quod regimen tyrannicum non est iustum: quia non ordinatur ad bonum commune, sed ad bonum privatum regentis, ut patet per Philosophum, in III. *Polit.* [cap. 5] et in VIII. *Ethic.* Et ideo perturbatio huius regiminis non habet rationem seditionis: nisi forte quando sic inordinate perturbatur tyranni regimen quod multitudo subiecta maius detrimentum patitur ex perturbatione consequenti quam ex tyranni regimine."

[72] Fol. 165a, p. 204a.

[73] Ibid.

[74] Ibid., fol. 165b, p. 204a–b. Oresme cited 2 Corinth. 12:20 and Romans 13:1.

[75] Ibid., fol. 165c, p. 204b, and see above, chapter 3, nn. 77, 78, and 83, and, in this chapter, n. 43.

"those who are pre-eminent in merit would be the most justified in attempting sedition."[76] Then he spoke of princes as scourges for their peoples.[77] He acknowledged that, just as an unjust prince may cause his people to suffer justly, so can unjust sedition cause a prince to suffer justly, as Caesar and King David suffered.[78] Still, his conclusion is the one we might expect: "it appears from the evidence of reason, and by the authority of Aristotle and of the Holy Scripture that sedition is not to be recommended," in large part because it tends to damage the common good.[79]

Oresme gave additional weight to the public or common aspect of the state by treating the prince as an official. We have seen an example of the way Oresme set apart the public and the private, in the gloss from 2. 3., cited above.[80] Here he said that private persons can serve the public good by managing their own affairs, while princes and other "personnes publiques" must prefer and attend to the common good. We have also seen that the counselor's duty is to serve the state, not to please a friend.

Rex propter regnum was the view of Oresme, who objected more than once to the proprietary conception of kingship. In a discussion of the relative merits of election and hereditary succession, he said ". . . a kingdom is not like a private possession or a source of a family's revenue, but rather it is a dignity and lordship, and an honorable estate which requires industry [in its rulers] to govern it and protect the common good of the people."[81] This is part of an argument against hereditary succession, an argument which does not advance the conclusion of Oresme.[82] But we can tell by looking at the

---

[76] *Politics* 5. 1. 1301a; Barker, p. 204. This statement, which Oresme translates (fol. 165c, p. 204b) as "les bons feroient tres justement sedition" is followed in Aristotle's text by the phrase "(though they are the last to make the attempt)." This is not a very strong argument in favor of sedition: we can see that Oresme realized this by reading his remarks in the conclusion of the gloss (fol. 166a, p. 205a): ". . . Aristote ne dit pas absolument que les bons *funt* seditions, mes il dit *feroient*. Ce est assavoir se ce estoit chose a faire, et dit apres que il ne les funt pas. Et par ce appert que ce ne est pas bien; car autrement il pecheroient se il ne les faisoient, meismement pour la reformation et salvation du bien publique." Thus the gloss from 2. 21. (cited above, n. 64) which speaks of the subjects of an oligarchy who have "cause a faire sedicion" is not speaking of the justification of sedition but of the likelihood of sedition, which was avoided by an oligarchy which encouraged the diffusion of wealth (*Politics* 2. 11. 1273b; Barker, 87).

[77] Oresme cited Job 34: 30, Proverbs 22: 3, Amos 5: 13, and Ecclesiasticus 13: 4 (*Le Livre de Politiques* 5. 1. [fols. 165d–166a, p. 204b]).

[78] Fol. 166a, pp. 204b–205a.

[79] Fol. 166a, p. 205a.

[80] See above at n. 43.

[81] *Le Livre de Politiques* 2. 21. (fol. 65d, p. 109a). Compare this to the remark of Jean Jouvenal des Ursins, above in n. 5.

Wahl ("Immortality and Inalienability," 327), speaking of the usage in writs and similar documents, says the term *dignitas* (which had become common during the thirteenth century) "referred to the uniqueness of the royal prerogatives and the sovereignty as it rested in the king," while *corona*, with which it was often associated, "referred 'chiefly to the sovereignty of the collective whole of the realm'" (Wahl here quotes Kantorowicz, *The King's Two Bodies*, 384). It is probable that Oresme is thinking of something like this meaning when he calls royal government a "dignity." The "honorable estate" (*honourableté*), on the other hand, seems to be a more private conception (as in the definition of this word in the "Table des . . . for mos," fol. 327d, p. 372a).

[82] For Oresme's support of hereditary succession, see the *Livre de Politiques* 2. 21. (fol. 66a, p. 109a).

remainder of the gloss that this is not an insincere statement. Oresme combined support for hereditary succession with an insistence that it be regulated

. . . according to approved practice . . . for example, if the eldest son of the king were to succeed, or the one nearest to him, etc. And a woman cannot succeed, nor a man through a woman, nor a foreigner, nor a blind man, nor a bewitched man . . . And [a man not qualified under these conditions] cannot succeed, however eligible he might be to succeed to the private or personal inheritance of his parents, either in whole or in part.[83]

Here succession is suited to public benefit (which includes, by these rules, the exclusion of English claims to the French throne).[84] Public office must have higher, or at least narrower, standards of qualification, than private succession. After all, royal government is not "a thing which can be sold or divided or willed away . . . Rather, royal government is a noble public office, and a dignity and distinction which requires excellence in character and in judgment and in other qualities, and also requires diligence in order properly to govern the people."[85] Here Oresme objects to "pure succession," according to which the kingdom would go to "any person capable of succeeding to the private inheritance of the preceding king."[86] He once again insisted that a kingdom is not like a private inheritance, so that

. . . of all the common laws which speak of the succession or transfer of [private] inheritances, none have any effect whatsoever on the right to succeed to a kingdom. . . . And if any government is directed or distributed according to the rules of private inheritance, it is not a true kingdom, or [at the least], it is distributed and administered contrary to the [true] nature of a kingdom. And therefore this method of simple succession is not acceptable. . .[87]

Oresme returned to this theme when speaking of succession by an elected dynasty, saying that the excellent qualities for which the dynasty was originally chosen should be the criterion for the succession of individuals, rather than the qualifications which apply in "the common law of private families." In kingdoms the profit of the people is to be considered.[88]

---

[83] Ibid., 2. 21. (fols. 65d–66a, p. 109a). Oresme's apparent belief in witchcraft has been noted above, chapter 1, n. 52.

[84] There was a near-reversal of this application in the translation and commentary on *The City of God* made for Charles V by Raoul de Presles. Here a discussion is made of the *lex Voconia*, a law passed at the time of the Punic Wars, which forbade any sort of female inheritance, and which was criticized by Augustine (in 3. 21.). Raoul de Presles was well aware that this law applied to "des successions des privées personnes et non pas des successions des puissans hommes comme des roy. . . " but he wrote a long exposition on this passage which led up to the exclusion of female royal succession in the *lex Salica* (Shulamith Shahar, "Traduction et commentaire de la 'Cité de Dieu' par un penseur politique sous Charles V," *L'Information Historique*, Jan.–Feb. 1977, 48–49, quoting the Bibl. Nat. MS., Fonds français 17, fol. 174v). Oresme mentions Augustine's criticism in 3. 23. (fol. 116a, p. 155b).

[85] *Le Livre de Politiques* 3. 23. (fol. 113a, p. 153a). Here we have "noble office publique"; see ibid., 6. 2. (fol. 217b, p. 257b) for "office publique honorable."

[86] ". . . toute personne qui pourroit succeder au privé patrimoine de roy precedent" (*Le Livre de Politiques* 3. 23. [fol. 115c, p. 155a]).

[87] Ibid.

[88] Ibid., fol. 115d, p. 155b. He also applied this theme to the succession of women: "Et nientmoins femme peut succeder en privé heritage selon les lays et coustumes communes. . . .

With this background we can guess Oresme's attitude toward those counselors who, like Guillaume de Plaisian, encouraged their masters to make
free with the possessions of subjects: ". . . some are so perverse and so
foolish that they make the prince believe that he is the proprietor of all the
goods in his kingdom, and that he can take for himself or give to another
goods which a subject holds by just title."[89] Nor would Oresme allow a king
to profit from his office. In the long gloss on succession from 3. 23., one
objection made against an elected prince was that he might misappropriate
public wealth "to the detriment of the common good" in order to provide
for the future of his children.[90]

Above all, the prince as public officer and representative of the crown
must preserve the integrity of the state. What Oresme thought of the practice of making apanages, may be inferred from his repeated insistence that a
kingdom cannot be treated like a family possession. In the gloss cited above
from 3. 17., one of the three cases in which a reasonable and honorable
multitude might have decisive authority in a state is in the correction of
princes who "abuse the honor of their office, and dissipate or destroy the
public good." Here again Oresme was speaking of something resembling
the inalienability of sovereignty.

Among the practices by which greedy princes tend to abuse the honor of
their office and injure the common good is the alteration of currency. We
have seen that Oresme devoted a treatise to this subject long before he
began his translations of Aristotle: this had been his earliest service to the
French monarchy. The ideas of this treatise are carried into his glosses on the
Ethics and the *Politics*.[91] In the *Livre de Ethiques* Oresme modified Aristotle's
view that currency is entirely conventional, and may thus be changed or
invalidated. Aristotle said in *Ethics* 5. 5. 1133a that "demand has come to be
conventionally represented by money; this is why money is called *nomisma*
(customary currency), because it does not exist by nature but by custom
(*nomos*), and can be altered and rendered useless at will."[92] Here is the gloss
of Oresme:

---

la succession a royalme ne doit pas estre conduite ne menee par teles lays comme sunt succession de heritage; car femme ne doit pas succeder a royalme, comme dit est" (ibid., fol. 116a).

One of the distinctions made by the French legist and canonist Pierre Jame (Petrus Jacobi)
between kings who have the *ius* or *nomen* of emperor (including the French king as emperor in
his realm) and those who have not, is that the latter succeed to their kingdoms as to a private
inheritance (Gaines Post, "Two Notes on Nationalism in the Middle Ages," *Traditio* 9 [1953]:
317–318, citing Jame's *Aurea practica libellorum* [Cologne, 1575], 278–279, #43,44). Another
of the characteristics of lesser kings is that they have an income separate from the public fisc
and have limited powers of taxation (ibid.). Oresme, on the other hand, considered this proper
even for the French king.

[89] *Le Livre de Politiques* 4. 10. (fol. 139b, p. 178b). For Guillaume de Plaisian, see above,
chapter 3, note 50. Of course Plaisian said that it was public utility and defense which justified
the king's appropriation of the possessions of his subjects.

[90] Fol. 114a, p. 154a.

[91] Oresme mentioned his treatise in the gloss from the *Livre de Ethiques* cited here and in the
one cited below, n. 97. In the *Livre de Politiques* the treatise is mentioned in 1. 10. (fol. 21c, p.
64a).

[92] Trans. Rackham, 285. For Oresme's translation see *Le Livre de Ethiques* 5. 11. (fols. 99d–
100a, p. 295).

And it should be known that in Greek the word *nomisma* means "money"; and it comes from *nomo*, which means "law." And for this reason [Aristotle] says that its value is established by law and not by nature . . . nevertheless, natural necessity places restrictions on the use of money. And also there are certain materials which by their nature are better suited to the making of coins than others, as I have said in a *Treatise on the Alteration of Money*.[93]

In *Politics* 1. 9. 1256b–1258a money is again described as the product of convention. Oresme did not object, perhaps because Aristotle did not suggest in this chapter that a convention is easily altered.[94]

Elsewhere, however, objections were made, and these in the name of the common good, which had been identified in the treatise on money as both the final end of currency and the only proper justification for its alteration.[95] In the *Livre de Ethiques* 5. 11., Oresme glossed the statement of Aristotle that money "tends to be comparatively constant":[96]

That is to say, [it should be constant] more than other things [are]: for money should be altered in value and rate only very infrequently, and only in those few cases in which this will serve the public good. For it is the measure of all commodities which are exchanged, and every measure should be certain and stable. And I have spoken more plainly of this matter elsewhere, in a *Treatise on the Alteration of Money*.[97]

In glossing the section of the *Politics* where Aristotle explained the purpose of the stamp or "impression" in making clear the value of each coin,[98] Oresme spoke of the necessity of dependable coinage:

. . . the ruler impressed on [the coinage] his sign . . . in testimony of the trustworthiness of the metal and of its weight . . . [thus] . . . to make a fraud in this matter is a sort of false testimony. . . . Cassiodorus said that to make such a fraud in currency is to corrupt what is ordained for justice, and is a great evil . . . one should not make alterations in the currency for profit, thus deceiving the people: [mutations made] for any reason should occur only infrequently . . . the [exchange-] rate of money is something like a rule or a law.[99]

Then Oresme cited the remarks of Aristotle from *Ethics* 5. 5., and spoke of the wickedness of tampering with the currency:

. . . money by its nature wishes to remain at one value. And Huguccio says that the word "money" is derived from a verb which means "to remain". . . . And of all the deceptions which the prince practices on the people this is the most unnatural and

---

[93] Ibid., fol. 100a, p. 295.

[94] *Le Livre de Politiques* 1., 10.–11. (fols. 20a–23b, pp. 62b–66a).

[95] See *De Moneta* 3 (chapter 10 in the French version): "Rursum nulla talis mixtio facienda est, nisi dumtaxat pro utilitate communi, racione cuius moneta inventa est et ad quam naturaliter ordinatur, ut patet ex prius dictis" (ed. Charles Johnson, *The De Moneta of Nicholas Oresme and English Mint Documents* [London, 1956], p. 8). In chapter 1 of the Latin version Oresme cited Cassiodorus, who said that money had been especially invented "in usum publicum" (Johnson, p. 5, from *Variarum Liber* 5. 39. [Migne, *Patrologia Latina*, 69: 672]).

[96] *Ethics* 5. 5. 1133b; Rackham, p. 287.

[97] Fol. 100d, p. 297.

[98] 1. 9. 1257a.

[99] *Le Livre de Politiques* 1. 10. (fol. 21b, pp. 63b–64a). For the reference to Cassiodorus, see *Variarum Liber* 1. 10., in *PL*, 69: 515.

unreasonable, and the most underhanded and fraudulent, and, depending upon its magnitude, the most harmful to the common good.[100]

Currency was only one aspect of economic policy which Oresme wished to see regulated for the public benefit. He said that monopolies should be established only by public authority, and for public benefit.[101] We have already seen that Oresme did not favor taxation as a means of supporting the state.[102] He thought that a king should live on his own.

. . . a true king is self-sufficient, having no need of the goods of his subjects, especially in keeping his household and in maintaining his royal estate, as was said in *Ethics* 8. 13. And therefore whoever follows this practice [i.e., the rapacity of certain Israelite kings, as predicted by Samuel] would not be a true king.[103]

Here it seems that Oresme favored the conception of a public state by denying that a prince can treat the kingdom and all within it as his own: at the same time he failed to recognize that a national government cannot serve its people without substantial and regular revenue, and did not see that taxation might be considered, not as the private aggrandizement of the ruler, but as the public obligation of the citizen.[104] He spoke of taxation as a tyrannical expedient. Where Aristotle said in *Politics* 5. 3.1302b that the

---

[100] Fol. 21b–c, p. 64a. Menut (p. 64a) gives a reference for the citation of Huguccio, *Magnae Derivationes*, from Bodleian Laud MS. 626, fol. 114c, lines 32–39. Huguccio said that *moneta* was derived from *moneo*, which means "to warn." Oresme seems to be thinking of *maneo*, which does mean "to remain."

[101] "Et ce peut faire la communité ou personne publique pour elle et pour le bien publique, et non pas personne privee se ne estoit, par aventure, par aucun privilege, si comme aucuns en certains temps et lieuz funt monopole de vin que l'en appelle le ban" (*Le Livre de Politiques* 1. 14. [fol. 27b–c, p. 70b]).

[102] See above, chapter 1, n. 35, and, in this chapter, nn. 17, 50, and 89.

[103] *Le Livre de Politiques* 3. 21. (fol. 109d, p. 150a). See also ibid., 3. 19. (fol. 105b–c, p. 145b); 4. 2. (fol. 128c, p. 167a), and n. 50 above.

For the English text from the *Ethics*, see above, n. 50. In the *Livre de Ethiques* 8. 13. (fol. 168d, p. 434) this was translated as: ". . . car celui n'est pas roy qui n'est de soy et par soy souffisant en tous biens. Et tel seigneur ne a mestier, besoing ou indigence de rien. Et donques il ne met pas son entencion a querir ses proffiz, mais les proffiz de ses subjectz. Et le prince qui n'est tel, c'est a savoir par soy souffisant, il est appellé *clerotes*, non pas roy." Oresme rightly said that *clerotes* (i.e., κληρωτός) meant "elected by lot" and added that such a king, chosen by chance rather than reason, should be provided with support, so that "il ne ait mestier des biens de ses subjectz pour son bon estat mener. Mais quant au fait des guerres, il convendroit autre ordenance" (ibid., pp. 434, 435).

[104] This did not make Oresme unusual among his contemporaries. See the studies of John Bell Henneman, *Royal Taxation in Fourteenth-Century France: The Development of War Financing 1322–1356* (Princeton, 1971) and *Royal Taxation in Fourteenth-Century France: The Captivity and Ransom of John II 1356–1370* (Philadelphia, 1976. Memoirs of the American Philosophical Society 116), as well as several articles by the same author, which illustrate in detail the difficulty with which taxation could be imposed except under immediate danger of war, and the skill with which Charles V worked to overcome this resistance and to foster a sense of public responsibility and a recognition of the need for regular revenue. The church had a more sophisticated organization, but it faced the same attitude. See John A. Yunck, "Economic Conservatism, Papal Finance, and the Medieval Satires on Rome," in Sylvia L. Thrupp, ed., *Change in Medieval Society* (New York, 1964): 72–85, who says, speaking of the satirists who did not realize the papacy "had burst the bonds of feudal economics," that "economic theory lagged notoriously behind economic fact in the Middle Ages" (76).

personal advantage which rulers seek "is sometimes sought at the expense of individuals; sometimes at that of the public,"[105] Oresme provided an illustration: "For they impose taxes and exactions upon the people and take the revenues of the public treasury and the goods of the commonwealth and apply them to their own benefit, rather than to public business . . . in taking such gain the prince injures the citizens."[106]

It seems that Oresme saw taxation as simple tyranny, as a corollary of greed. Aristotle himself said of tyrants who weaken their subjects by impoverishing them that "the imposition of taxes produces a similar result."[107] But here Oresme conceded that revenue taken from the people might be applied to the common good:

Such impositions were formerly ordained for the maintenance of bridges and roads, and to support those who guarded against the transfer of false commodities and took care lest anything be taken into or out of [the country] against the precautions made for the public good. But afterwards the tyrants increased these exactions for their own benefit and for the impoverishment of their citizens.[108]

On the whole, however, we do not see in Oresme's glosses a balance between the duties of the governors and the obligations of the citizens, a recognition of the mutual responsibilities of ruler and ruled. In this respect the *Livre de Politiques* is still a mirror for the prince.

That the laws of such a public state must serve the common good was as clear to Oresme (and to King Charles) as it had been to Aristotle.[109] Where Aristotle had associated law and the common good in *Politics* 3. 13. 1283b, Oresme followed,[110] although he was hobbled by a mistranslation. Aristotle had said that in making laws what is "right" or "equally right" is "what is for the benefit of the whole state and for the common good of its citizens. . . ." When Moerbeke translated the Greek word equivalent to

---

[105] Barker, 208.

[106] *Le Livre de Politiques* 5. 4. (fol. 169a, p. 208a). See also ibid., 6. 4. (fol. 221a, p. 262a).

[107] *Politics* 5. 11. 1313b; Barker, 245.

[108] *Le Livre de Politiques* 5. 26. (fol. 205a, p. 246a).

[109] For example, see the citation from the ordinance on the regency, in chap. 3, n. 40, and see Dodu, "Les idées de Charles V," 26–27. Again, the *Songe du Vergier* echoes the royal ideas: ". . . quant les oeuvres du prince ne tendent pas au proufit commun du peuple, mais à son propre et singulier proufit, il doit estre appellé tyrant; il ne seigneurist pas justement" (1. 131.; Brunet, p. 132). The translations of Oresme were intended by the king to serve the same purpose: "Mais pour ce que les livres morals de Aristote furent faiz en grec, et nous les avons en latin moult fort a entendre, le Roy a voulu, pour le bien commun, faire les translater en françois, afin que il et ses conseilliers et autres les puissent mieulx entendre . . ." (*Le Livre de Ethiques*, prologue, fol. 1d, p. 99 in the edition of Menut).

[110] Oresme had already associated the two in his glosses on the *Ethics*. In *Ethics* 5. 1. 1129b, Aristotle said: "Now all the various pronouncements of the law aim either at the common interest of all, or at the interest of a ruling class determined either by excellence or in some other similar way. . ." (Rackham, 259). Oresme's gloss for this is: "Si comme en aucune policie ou aucuns ont la seigneurie non pas selon vertu, mais pour leur richesces ou puissance. Et les ordeneeurs des loys ou estatus en teles policies regardent tant seulement ou principalment au proffit ou a la volenté de telz seigneurs; et de ce sera dit aprés plus a plain et en cest livre et en *Politiques*" (*Le Livre de Ethiques* 5. 2. [fol. 91b, p. 278]).

"equally," he gave to this word its secondary meaning of "perhaps."[111]
Oresme overcame this evidently puzzling mistranslation:

[Text] And perhaps it is just that laws be established for the good of the whole city
and for the common benefit of all the citizens.
[Gloss] He says "perhaps" because, when speaking of what is practical or expedient,
for example riches, it may be that a multitude would be less virtuous, or in greater
danger, if it were richer, just as was said in 2. 12. But when speaking of the noble or
of the expedient, it is not proper to say "perhaps," for laws should be made for the
common good.[112]

Speaking of laws which limit the possessions and power of citizens,
Oresme equated justice and expediency with the common good.[113] His very
definition of "illegal" included a reference to public benefit: "That is illegal
which disregards the laws established for the common good, and which
does not adhere to their conventions, and [so are those who do these
things]."[114]
Law and the common good meet in the notion of government. In speaking of democracies and oligarchies, where Aristotle criticized democrats and
oligarchs for emphasizing only liberty and wealth, respectively, as qualifications for standing in the state,[115] Oresme commented:

. . . because in these polities those who govern give more consideration to things
other [than virtue and good works], . . . their actions and their laws are just only in
an improper sense. And because the principal end [of their state] is unjust, as it is
directed for their own profit rather than for the common good, their laws and deeds
are unjust in a simple sense.[116]

He made a similar point in glossing *Politics* 7. 9. 1328b, where Aristotle
speaks of the distribution of services in an ideal constitution, which "has for
its members men who are absolutely just, and not men who are merely just

---

[111] Barker, p. 134 (*Politics* 3. 13. 1283b). For the Latin, see Susemihl, 207, lines 3–5: "quod
autem rectum sumendum forte: rectum autem forte ad conferens totius civitatis et ad commune
civium." Thus the Greek ἴσως became "forte." See above at nn. 27 and 38, for references to
this passage. See also Gewirth, *The Defender of Peace* 2: 46, n. 10 for Marsilius.

[112] *Le Livre de Politiques* 3. 17. (fol. 101d, p. 142a). We have seen Oresme refer to the *bien
honneste, bien profitable,* and *bien delectable* before (above at nn. 48, 49). The present text is
difficult to translate, because Oresme speaks of an "expedient" which may or may not be the
same as the *bien profitable.* If the two are not meant to be the same thing, then the last sentence
in the gloss should be translated: "But [on the other hand] when speaking of the noble or of the
expedient . . . ." The citation of the second book refers to 2. 7. 1267a, where Aristotle, in
criticizing the plans of Phaleas, says that the property of a state "should not be so large that
neighbouring and more powerful states will covet it, while its owners are unable to repel an
attack . . ." (Barker, 66).

[113] "Et donques les ordenances qui obvient a ce par raison sunt justes et expedientes. Item,
elles sunt pour le commun profit, car il ne est pas bon pour la communité que les possessions
des citoiens soient equales ne quelles soient en grande inequalité . . ." (*Le Livre de Politiques* 3.
19. [fol. 104a, p. 144b]).

[114] Ibid., "La Table des . . . fors mos," fol. 327d, p. 372a.

[115] *Politics* 3. 9. 1280a (Barker, 118).

[116] *Le Livre de Politiques* 3. 10. (fol. 90b, p. 130b).

in relation to some particular standard."[117] In explaining the justice which exists only in relation to the standards of a particular constitution (a justice thus resembling the actions and laws called just only in an improper sense), Oresme said:

By *men who are just not absolutely but are just only according to the assumptions* [*of their constitutions*] he means those who have unjust laws and uphold them; for [these laws] safeguard a proportional distribution of power [as in an oligarchy, presumably] or equality [as in a democracy], but this is done for their own benefit, and not for a good end, and we see [this sort of relative justice] in oligarchy and democracy.[118]

In another place he spoke of the oligarchs or tyrants who govern either "without laws or according to laws which [by not serving the welfare of the community] do not agree with the good laws of the past."[119]

In a long gloss on moderation in kingship Oresme went so far as to imply that laws which are "not just or expedient for the public good" are not true laws. "For just as a bad custom is not a proper custom, but a corruption, similarly such a law if it is contrary to good government is called in Greek *apostudyamenos*: that is to say an imprudently established law, as it appears in *Ethics* 5. 2."[120] We have seen that Roman law supplied a principle of similar import, that is, that laws made against the public good might be considered invalid, and thus be renounced.

For Oresme the importance of laws was in their purpose rather than in themselves. We have just seen him deny that laws "contrary to good government" are laws in the fullest sense of the word. He seemed also to accept the opinion of Aristotle that "laws ought to be made to suit constitutions (as indeed in practice they always are), and not constitutions made to suit laws."[121] Here Oresme did not mention the common good, but here, again,

---

[117] Barker, 301.

[118] *Le Livre de Politiques* 7. 17. (fol. 263c, p. 305a). Moerbeke's version of "men who are absolutely just, and not men who are merely just in relation to some particular standard" is "iustos viros simpliciter, sed non ad suppositionem" (ed. Susemihl, 276, line 9), which was translated by Oresme as "hommes qui sunt justes simplement et non pas a supposition" (fol. 263b).

[119] Ibid., 4. 19. (fol. 155a, p. 194a).

[120] Ibid., 5. 25. (fol. 202c, p. 243b). The source for the "lay indiscretement mise" is *Ethics* 5.1. 1129b: "But the law also prescribes certain conduct: the conduct of a brave man . . . . that of a temperate man . . . . that of a gentle man . . . . and so with actions exemplifying the rest of the virtues and vices, commanding these and forbidding those—rightly if the law has been rightly enacted, not so well if it has been made at random" (Rackham, p. 259). Aristotle's word for "made at random" is ὁ ἀπεσχεδιασμένος. Oresme's translation of the last section of the *Ethics* citation is: "Et la chose est droituriere qui est mise ou faite justement et droiturierement; et celle qui n'est ainsi mise et faite est pire et est appellee *apostudyamenos*, c'est a dire, loys indiscretement mise et faite senz pourvision" (*Le Livre de Ethiques* 5. 2. [fol. 91c, p. 278]).

[121] *Politics* 4. 1. 1289a (Barker, 156). In his gloss on this text (*Le Livre de Politiques* 4. 1. [fols. 127d–128a, p. 166a]), Oresme said: ". . . la policie ou le salut de la policie est la fin pourquoy est la lay . . . . [the founder of a state] doit metre lays convenables et les conformer et appliquer a la policie. Et se il avoit son premier resgart as lays et selon elles il instituoit sa policie, il pervertiroit ordre naturele; car l'en doit premierement resgarder a la fin."

This might be taken to be no more than an explication of Aristotle's text. In 5. 25., however, in

good laws made to suit good constitutions will serve this end. Similarly, he suggested that a state which is governed by laws established for the sole benefit of the rulers might as well be ruled without law.[122]

We have seen that the principle of the common good could be used to justify abrogation of the letter of the law as well as to judge laws. Acceptance of this principle was consistent with Oresme's general attitude toward the law. We have noted that by the time his glosses were written a certain pragmatism had entered the law-making and the use of law in the national monarchies of Europe.[123] Roman law was accepted only voluntarily and selectively, an attitude echoed in the glosses of Oresme. We have seen that in political practice only good custom was considered inviolable; Oresme said in similar spirit that law should be regarded not as a venerable authority but as a newly made proposal to be judged according to *prudence politique.*

The principle of equity, which Oresme, like other medieval writers, associated with the common good, also emphasized the ends of laws rather than the laws themselves. In his gloss Oresme added a qualification to the statement of Aristotle that, should a conflict arise between the people and the law, "rightly constituted laws should be the final sovereign":[124]

This means [sovereign] in all things which are determined, or which can be judged, by laws . . . the prince cannot make judgment against the letter of the law except by virtue of a principle called *epieikeia*. For [in applying] this principle he does not act against the intention of the legislator or against justice, as appears more clearly in *Ethics* 5. 31. And [the application of this principle] occurs when the prince dispenses [from the law] or makes remission of punishment for the common good, or for the sake of natural equity, and not for another reason.[125]

Natural equity is not a synonym for natural law. In a gloss from Aristotle's discussion of equity in *Ethics* 5. 10., Oresme said that equity is in accord with natural law and is better than positive law.[126] Natural law and equity are indeed alike in their capacity to override positive law. Nevertheless, Aristotle himself did not speak of natural law in *Ethics* 5. 10. In fact, as Barker

---

a gloss on moderation in kingship, Oresme said (fols. 202d – 203a, p. 244a): "Mes le remede [for excessive attachment to the law] est que l'en se abstraie sans soy adherdre a la lay pour l'auctorité de elle, mes comme se elle fust de nouvel proposee a mettre. L'en doit en juste balance peser la raison de la lay et la raison contraire. Et considerer qui la fist et pour quelle fin et a quelle policie. Car les lays doivent estre mises selon les policies . . . . l'en doit jugier non pas comme legiste sousmis a celle lay, mes comme celui qui a en soy prudence politique."

[122] "Mes il me semble que peu a de difference se aucuns gouvernent selon leur volenté ou se il gouvernent selon lays lesqueles eulz meismes ont faictes sans le consentement de la multitude en leur faveur et a leur profit ou propre conferent et contre le bien publique. Et teles lays sunt proprement olygarchiques et injustes" (ibid., 4. 10. [fol. 139a, p. 178a–b]).

[123] See chapter 3, nn. 17, 61–63, and 136.

[124] *Politics* 3. 11. 1282b. Aristotle himself qualified his statement in the remainder of the sentence quoted here, saying that "personal rule . . . should be sovereign only in those matters on which law is unable, owing to the difficulty of framing general rules for all contingencies, to make an exact pronouncement" (Barker, p. 127).

[125] *Le Livre de Politiques* 3. 14. (fol. 97b–c, p. 137b). See also 3. 24. (fol. 123c–d, p. 160b).

[126] "*Epyekes* est selon droit naturel et est meilleur que droit positif" (*Le Livre de Ethiques* 5. 21. [fol. 112c, p. 324]). This is n. 5 in Menut's edition; see also n. 8 (p. 324) and n. 14 (p. 325).

has noted, speaking of his argument in *Rhetoric,* "'natural law' and 'equity' are distinct. . . . Natural law is the *universal* law: equity is one of the two subdivisions of the unwritten part of *particular* law."[127]

The connection between equity and the common good was more consistent with the notions of Aristotle. Oresme combined these notions when he considered Aristotle's plan to banish from the ideal state any man who seems dangerously powerful:

> . . . it seems that it would be unjust to take away his possessions or to banish him with no further cause, and it would [also] be against the law. [But] I respond . . . [that the state should moderate the power of such a man] . . . if there were good reason to suspect that he wished to harm the state. And the ruler could do this with justice, if he had the consent of the people, or else by a rule called *epiei-keia* . . . . he would be acting in accordance with the intention of the legislator, which was to serve the common good.[128]

Here the consent of the people and the good of the people are both used as counterweights to legal justice.

In discussing the proper age of priests and bishops Oresme supported equity and the common good at the expense of positive and perhaps even natural law.[129] It is apparent in this case, as in Oresme's discussion of equity and the sovereignty of the law, that he did not wish to justify an habitual disregard of the letter of the law. Dispensations or remissions were to be made only according to the intention of the legislator, that is, for the public benefit.

On other occasions, Oresme justified such dispensation on the basis of a principle similar to equity, without using that term. He said that for the common good, regulations prohibiting marriages on the grounds of consanguinity might be relaxed.[130] Elsewhere he spoke of permitting changes in the law for the sake of necessity or utility and with the approval of the people:

> . . . old laws which are bad should be changed, and so should other [laws] when the benefit that would result outweighs the disadvantages which arise when old laws are less firmly observed and respected. And it is necessary [in such a case] that

---

[127] "Aristotle's Conception of Justice, Law, and Equity in the *Ethics* and the *Rhetoric*" (Appendix 2 of his translation of the *Politics,* 372, n. 1). Speaking of the *Ethics,* Barker says: "It may seem . . . that the distinction between law and equity is the same as that between legal and natural justice. No doubt it is a similar distinction; but it can hardly be said to be the same. Justice, in Aristotle's view, is generally connected with law. . . . But equity is, in its nature, something distinct from law-something which 'corrects' law; and *so far as justice is connected with law,* equity must also be separate from justice" (ibid., p. 366).

[128] *Le Livre de Politiques* 3. 19. (fols. 104d–105a, p. 145a). The text of Aristotle is *Politics* 3. 13. 1284b.

[129] ". . . determinent les Decrés l'eage des prestres et celui des evesques; et qu'il soient eagiés, ce est droit naturel; mes determiner quel eage, ce est droit positif. Et de ce ne peut nul dispenser fors par le droit appellé *epieyke,* pour le bien publique ou de l'office" (*Le Livre de Politiques* 7. 19. [fol. 267a, p. 308b]). The text of Aristotle is from 7. 9. 1329a. Oresme applied the principle of equity to the church in other places, as we shall see in the next chapter. (The common good was not mentioned in these cases, however.) We shall also see that the conciliarists used this principle and sometimes linked it to the common good (see below, chap. 5, n. 29).

[130] *Le Livre de Politiques* 2. 4. (fol. 37b, p. 80a).

the benefit [to be gained] be very great, and that it represent the desire of all the people, as a matter of necessity and evident utility.[131]

This is a striking example of Oresme's attitude toward the claims of law and of public utility because it is also one of the few glosses in which he clearly disagreed with Aristotle. Aristotle had presented four reasons in favor of changing laws: change has benefited other practical arts; change has removed unreasonable old customs; the makers of ancient laws were no wiser than we; and necessarily general law must be altered in detail as experience is gained. He did not mention necessity or the consent of the people. Against changing laws, he argued that "the benefit of change will be less than the loss which is likely to result if men fall into the habit of disobeying the government."[132] Oresme did not entirely accept this, and as for the last three of Aristotle's reasons in favor of changing the law, he said that no response was made to them because they were correct.[133] Thus for Oresme public utility justified abandoning some of the "great caution" which Aristotle considered necessary in the changing of laws.

In another place Oresme mentioned necessity as part of the phrase "necessity of the defense of the realm," which he equated (somewhat indirectly) with the common good. This example belongs only peripherally to this discussion because the defense of the realm was not used to justify extraordinary measures.[134]

Oresme showed himself an excellent pupil of Aristotle in the matter of the common good. His glosses also had something to say about the corporatist analogy which further emphasizes the unity of the state. He did not make very much of this analogy, but the text of Aristotle gave him little occasion to do so.

In some cases Oresme encountered such an analogy in his text and glossed it without significant comment;[135] in others he introduced such

---

[131] Ibid., 2. 15. (fol. 56b, p. 99a). See below, chap. 5, n. 82, for the application of this to the church. Necessity, utility and equity are linked in 3. 24. (fol. 118d, p. 158a). One lesson of politics, according to the prologue of the *Livre de Ethiques* (fol. 1b, p. 98) is the changing and correction of laws.

[132] *Politics* 2. 8. 1269a (Barker, 73).

[133] *Le Livre de Politiques* 2. 15. (fol. 56b, p. 99a).

[134] ". . . il appert clerement que le droit dessus dit [i.e., the cruelties of Israelite kings as predicted by Samuel] estoit au profit du prince et non pas des subjecs. Car l'Escripture met comment le roy appliqueroit ce que il prendroit sus eulz non pas en la neccessité de la deffense du païz, mes en ses propres usages et en aucuns deshonnestes . . ." (ibid., 3. 21. [fol. 109d, p. 149b]). See above, n. 103, for an example from the *Livre de Ethiques* in which war is given as a cause for disregarding the requirement that kings must live on their own. (Necessity and the defense of the realm are not mentioned as such.)

[135] He had little to say about the analogy of the stone hand from *Politics* 1. 2. 1253a (*Le Livre de Politiques* 1. 2. [fol. 8c–d, p. 49b]). In *Politics* 4. 4. 1290b, Aristotle said that, just as in animals a great variety of combinations of organs will produce a great variety of species, so can many combinations arise from the different parts of the state. Oresme's gloss (4. 5. [fol. 132a–b, p. 170b]) merely explains the text, offering examples of species among animals.
In *Politics* 3. 11. 1281b (Barker, 123), Aristotle said that the collective intellect of the many may produce "a single person, who—as he has many feet, many hands, and many senses— may also have many qualities of character and intelligence." Here again Oresme had little to

analogies himself.[136] In two cases they were used to emphasize the importance of the state as a whole. In *Politics* 2. 2. 1261a, Aristotle said in objection to Plato's communism that a polis must have "a difference of capacities among its members."[137] Where Aristotle said that "a real unity, such as a polis, must be made up of elements which differ in kind,"[138] Oresme elaborated:

As are the parts of a man, that is to say the flesh, the bones, and the various limbs. But [he does not speak] thus of an incomplete thing like the earth, or another [such] element. And thus the men who are part of the city [should] differ in their accidental qualities, not in their essential qualities, as is said above.[139]

In the *Livre de Politiques* 8. 1. Oresme used a corporal analogy to describe the interdependence of the citizens in a state. Aristotle had said that the citizen belongs to the state, not wholly to himself, and that provisions for each individual must be adjusted to provisions for the state as a whole.[140] Oresme used a similar statement from Cicero:

---

say in his gloss (3. 13. [fol. 93d, p. 134a]). This section of the text is important, however, because it is said to have inspired the decision of Charles V to hold elections for the office of chancellor (see Menut's note on p. 134a, and Siméon Luce, "De l'élection au scrutin de deux chanceliers de France sous le règne de Charles V," *Revue historique* 16 [1881]: 91–102, and idem, "Le principe électif, les traductions d'Aristote et les parvenus au XIVᵉ siècle," *La France pendant la guerre de cent ans: épisodes historiques et vie privée au XIVᵉ et XVᵉ siècle*, 2 vols. [Paris, 1890–1893], 1: 179–202).

Oresme had more to say in 5. 4. (fol. 170b–d, pp. 209b–210a), commenting on Aristotle's warnings (5. 3. 1302b–1303a) against the disproportionate increase of one part of the body (or state). As we shall see below (chap. 5, n. 95), Oresme applied this warning to the church, saying that the clergymen should not care most for their "propre profit."

[136] In 5. 6. (fol. 173a–b, p. 212b), Oresme used the analogy of the human body to illustrate the contention of Aristotle that "discords among the notables involve all the state in their consequences" (*Politics* 5. 4. 1303b; Barker, 212). In 5. 24. (fol. 199b–c, p. 240b), Oresme compared a city to a "corps bien complexionné" in speaking of the susceptibility of the city to external dangers. In 5. 32. (fol. 210c, p. 252a) Oresme used a corporal analogy in a gloss on the short duration of tyranny (from *Politics* 5. 12. 1315b), saying that tyranny is "comme un corps qui est en maladie incurable." Similarly, in his treatise on currency Oresme compared a tyrant to a misshapen monster (see the citation above, chap. 3, n. 68, from the French version; for the Latin version, see Charles Johnson, *The De moneta of Nicholas Oresme* . . . [London, 1956], 43–44).

He said in his long gloss on universal monarchy (7. 10. [fol. 249b, p. 291a]) that neither a republic nor a human body should be allowed to become a giant, with a reference to "Plautarcus," that is, to the corporal analogy cited by John of Salisbury in the *Policraticus* (see above at n. 14) and attributed to Plutarch's *Institutio Traiani*. Oresme had also mentioned this analogy and the *Policratique* (one of the books translated for Charles V) in the gloss from 5. 4. which is mentioned in the previous note. In the same long gloss (fol. 251a, p. 292b) he said that "la multitude de tous les hommes ne est pas un corps ne chose qui puisse estre ordenee sous un homme," and denied that a world with many princes would be like a monster with many heads. He further denied (fol. 251a–b) that all of mankind forms a *microcosmus* which should be governed by one man, claiming rather that each man or kingdom is a "petit munde." In 7. 27. (fol. 279b, p. 322a) he introduced a statement from *De caelo et mundo* (2. 4. 287b 15?) that a perfect whole cannot be made of corruptible parts, and applied this to the human body, in discussing whether all those in a good state can be virtuous (from *Politics* 7. 13. 1332a).

[137] Barker, p. 41.

[138] Ibid.

[139] *Le Livre de Politiques* 2. 2. (fol. 34c, p. 77a).

[140] *Politics* 8. 1. 1377a (Barker, p. 333).

For a city or a community is like a body whose members or parts serve one another while principally serving the whole, just as Saint Paul said, and as was said in chapter 5. 4. above. And for this reason [Cicero] said that we are not born for ourselves alone, but for our friends and for our country.[141]

By another route Oresme has come close to the principle of the common good.

The hierarchy of communities gives prominence to the state by locating the level of government which best serves the ends of political life. The doctrine of the common good locates the highest end or purpose within the state. What these two conceptions have in common is essential to serious political inquiry: that is, they identify a qualitative superiority, and distinguish qualitative superiority from mere quantitative superiority. The communitas perfecta, as Aristotle made clear, differs in kind from the lower communities. In the same way the state through its association with the common good and its comparison to corporations and *corpora mystica* becomes something more than the sum of its parts.

Oresme does not oblige us with a theory of the public state, but his glosses on the common good make it clear that he accepted these distinctions. He made a thorough acceptance of Aristotle's emphasis on the preeminence of the whole over the part, the office over the holder of the office. He applied these notions where Aristotle applied them, and went beyond him—in application, by directly associating equity with the common good, and in opinion, by justifying change in the law for the sake of the common good. Perhaps he did this as an active commentator. It is also possible that he made so much of the common good because the unity of a large monarchy is less obvious and more precarious than that of a polis. Moreover, it is clear that he wished to oppose proprietary notions of government, whether personified

---

[141] Fol. 295b–c, p. 339b. The reference to Saint Paul is probably to I Corinth. 12:12: "Sicut enim corpus unum est, et membra habet multa, omnia autem membra corporis cum sint multa, unum tamen corpus sunt: ita et Christus." Oresme had already cited this verse in the gloss from 5. 4. (see n. 135 above).

Menut's reference for the Cicero is *De amicitia* 18; however, a more likely source seems to be *De officiis* 1. 7. 22. (p. 22 in the Loeb edition with trans. by Walter Miller [London, 1947]): "Sed quoniam, ut praeclare scriptum est a Platone, non nobis solum nati sumus ortusque nostri partem patria vindicat, partem amici, atque, ut placet Stoicis, quae in terris gignantur, ad usum hominum omnia creari, homines autem hominum causa esse generatos. . . ." In a note to *Politics* 8. 1. 1377a (p. 333) Barker gives *Laws* 923 A as the source of a statement similar to that of Aristotle's above; this is perhaps the source of Cicero's reference to Plato. The text of Plato is: ". . . both you yourself and this your property are not your own, but belong to the whole of your race, both past and future, and . . . still more truly does all your race and its property belong to the State" (in the Loeb edition with trans. by R. G. Bury, 2 vols. [London and New York, 1926], 2: 421); see also *Epistles* 9. 358 A (pp. 592–593 in the Loeb edition with trans. by R. G. Bury [Cambridge, Mass. and London, 1929]).

Oresme cited this remark of Cicero in 1. 2. (fol. 8d, p. 49b), in his discussion of the "stone hand" analogy, and in 7. 7. (fol. 243a, p. 285b) in a discussion of the active and contemplative lives. It is also found in the *Livre de Ethiques* 8. 1. (fol. 157c, p. 412). The author(s) of the *Somnium Viridarii* and its French version the *Songe du Vergier* cited the remark at the start of the treatise, with reference to Plato rather than to Cicero (Georges de Lagarde, "Le 'Songe du Verger' et les origines du gallicanisme," *Revue des sciences religieuses* 14 [1934]: 19).

by the seigneur of a half-independent enclave, or by a perverse counselor like Guillaume de Plaisian (or by tax-collectors in general). Oresme's scale was broader than that of the classical Greek state, where the citizen body might take an active part in government. The citizens, or rather subjects, in the *Livre de Politiques* seem to be involved only passively in the common good. Promoting the benefit of the whole is a matter for the government, so much so that taxation is condemned. This could not please King Charles, but, apart from this, Oresme's notion of the commonwealth must have been very much like his own.

V. THE *POLITICS*, THE *LIVRE DE POLITIQUES*, AND THE CHURCH

To doubt that Aristotle intended the *Politics* for ecclesiology is beside the point here. Aristotle gave little encouragement to medieval writers bent on discussing the church, but little was sufficient. More than earlier commentators, Oresme applied the text of the *Politics* to the church as well as to the state, and in fact he did so, as he might have said, "pour cause." For if the church in its origins and as an ideal was unlike any community known to Aristotle, it was in fourteenth-century practice similar to and more developed than its counterparts, the secular states. In this century changes occurred both in church and in state: centralization, articulation of governmental processes, movement of jurisdiction to higher levels of government, and consequent disruption of local or feudal ties. The glosses of the *Livre de Politiques* reflect these events in the church as well as in the state, with approval in the latter case, and disapproval in the former case.

In the background of many of these glosses, linking together apparently separate subjects, is a great theme of fourteenth-century church history: the expansion of papal prerogative. The papal government became ubiquitous in a mechanical, habitual way, extending a uniform influence by making itself indispensable, rather than asserting a direct and occasional power, by making itself feared.[1] If we look at the questions which must interest the historian of the late medieval church, and which did interest Oresme, for example, the making of appointments, the jurisdiction of the clergy, the role of the cardinals and the council, and the difficult integration of the mendicant orders into the church, we see everywhere the effects of concentrated power.

During the very years when Oresme was working on his translations of Aristotle, the papacy, under the last of the Avignon popes,[2] had attained what was perhaps its widest extent of jurisdiction.[3] The assertion by Gregory XI of his right to appoint "to all patriarchal, archiepiscopal and episcopal churches, as well as to all houses of monks and friars, regardless of their

---

[1] Yves Renouard, *The Avignon Papacy 1305–1403* (Hamden, Conn., 1970), trans. by Denis Bethell from *La papauté à Avignon* (Paris, 1954), 96, calls the Avignon papacy the "high point" of centralization in the church. See also Francis Oakley, *The Western Church in the Later Middle Ages* (Ithaca, N.Y. and London, 1979), 46.

[2] On the Avignon papacy, see G. Mollat, *La collation des bénéfices ecclésiastiques sous les papes d'Avignon (1305–1378)* (Paris, 1921); idem, *Les papes d'Avignon* (Paris, 1924); B. Guillemain, *La cour pontifical d'Avignon* (Paris, 1963), and Renouard as cited in the note above.

[3] Mollat, *Les papes d'Avignon,* 390; Guillemain, *La cour pontifical,* 104.

revenue, wherever and however they fell vacant"[4] was not the result of his idiosyncrasy, but was instead the culmination of the accumulation of general and special reservations, which had increased at Avignon with uniform intensity, and with a devastating effect on the principle of election.[5] In addition to the exercise of ordinary collation Clement V had claimed all appointments in the hands of bishops.[6] Benedict XII extended papal control over local elections.[7] After his death the expected largesse of Clement VI brought over a hundred thousand office-seekers to Avignon.[8] At the same time, papal revenues were augmented by payments from the increasing multitudes of papal appointees,[9] and papal jurisdiction grew as popes intervened in the affairs of religious orders and of the universities, further weakening local authority.[10]

The popes who had gathered to themselves so much of the administrative power in the church were not disposed to share their prerogatives in deliberation and legislation. During the residence in Avignon there was only one ecumenical council, that of Vienne in 1311–1312. This council was more a reinforcement of, than an exception to, the rule of strict papal monarchy. The chronicler Walter of Hemingburgh said that the gathering did not deserve the name of council, as the pope did everything there *ex capite proprio*.[11] The Great Schism had not yet forced the issue of conciliar government.

Papal relations with the mendicant orders acted as a pivot in the controversies which continued into the fourteenth century. There were serious and inevitable disputes over the Franciscan way of life. (These, as it must be admitted, were the questions which most concerned Oresme.) But there was also much conflict over the right of the pope to release the friars from local authority and from the regulations which bound other religious. The Dominican Hervaeus Natalis said in defense of the mendicant privileges that the pope, as ordinary of all within the church and source of the authority of all ecclesiastical officers, could diminish this authority at will.[12] The bitterness caused by such an interpretation of papal power had been most evident

[4] Mollat, *Les papes d'Avignon*, 390. The translation above in the text is that of Janet Love (*The Popes at Avignon* [New York, 1963]), 336–337. Mollat is citing C. Lux, *Constitutionum Apostolicarum de generali beneficiorum reservatione . . . collectio et interpretatio* (Breslau, 1904), 4–10.

[5] Guillemain, *La cour pontifical*, 104; Mollat, *Les papes d'Avignon*, 390.

[6] Richard Southern, *Western Society and the Church in the Middle Ages* (Harmondsworth, Middlesex, 1970), 161.

[7] Ibid., 158, citing *Extravagantes Communes*, 3. 2. 13 (E. A. Friedberg, *Corpus Iuris Canonici*, 2 vols. [Leipzig, 1879], 2: 1266–1267).

[8] Mollat, *Les papes d'Avignon*, 82–83, citing the chronicler Peter of Hérenthals; Southern, *Western Society and the Church*, 161.

[9] Mollat, *Les papes d'Avignon*, 393–394.

[10] Ibid., 387.

[11] Ibid., 388, citing the edition of Walter of Hemingburgh by H. C. Hamilton, 2 vols. (London, 1848–1849), 2: 293; Guillemain, *La cour pontifical*, 96–97. Guillemain provides a reference to E. Mueller, *Das Konzil von Vienne, 1311–1312. Seine Quellen und seine Geschichte* (Münster, 1934).

[12] See B. Hauréau in *Histoire littéraire de la France* 34 (Paris, 1914): 308–351, as cited in John Moorman, *A History of the Franciscan Order* (Oxford, 1968), 340.

in the quarrel between seculars and mendicants at the University of Paris in the middle of the thirteenth century.[13] Dislike and jealousy of the friars had reached such a point there that, after being expelled from the university organization in 1253, the secular masters claimed they would rather lose all their privileges and dissolve their organization than associate with the friars.[14] Although by the mid-fourteenth century this controversy had abated, the issue of privilege was still lively. Mendicant interference in diocesan affairs was one of the chief complaints in Richard Fitzralph's sermons against the orders during the 1350s.[15]

Thus Oresme, when speaking of the church, could apply his text to some of the most general and essential questions of constitution and jurisdiction.

Aristotle and the Church

The writers who had used the *Politics* in discussions of the church[16] generally adopted an attitude consistent with the remarks made at the start of this chapter. That is to say, they regarded the church as the political organization it undoubtedly was, and applied to it Aristotle's notions of proper government. This politicization of the concept of the church, which saw its first consistent expression in the *De regimine christiano* of James of Viterbo,[17] occurred throughout the range of political opinion, just as writers of every persuasion took up the hierarchy of communities and the doctrine of the common good. Moreover, the church was identified with the specifically Aristotelian conception of the self-sufficient community or society, the communitas perfecta.[18]

---

[13] See Decima L. Douie, *The Conflict between the seculars and the mendicants at the University of Paris in the thirteenth Century* (London, 1954).

[14] Pearl Kibre, *Scholarly Privileges in the Middle Ages* (Cambridge, Mass., 1962), 107, citing H. Denifle and E. Chatelain, *Chartularium universitatis parisiensis*, 4 vols. (Paris, 1891–1899), 1: 292–297, #256.

[15] Moorman, *A History of the Franciscan Order*, 342.

[16] The *Politics* was of course not the only work of Aristotle which was applied to questions involving the church. Some of his metaphysical principles, for example the hierarchy of ends and the *ordinatio ad unum*, were used to describe the ends of spiritual and temporal powers, as we shall see in the next chapter. The *Ethics*, with its discussions of the common good and justice, was of course useful in much the same way as the *Politics*.

For material on the use of the *Politics* in ecclesiology, see the general works mentioned above in chapter 3, nn. 1, 70. In E. Lewis, *Medieval Political Ideas*, see especially 2: 357–429, and in Wilks, The *Problem of Sovereignty*, 331–407. See also Gerhart B. Ladner, "Aspects of Mediaeval Thought on Church and State," *Review of Politics* 9 (1947), 403–422; Georges de Lagarde, *La Naissance de l'esprit laïque au déclin du moyen âge*, 6 vols. (Paris, 1934–1946); Thomas M. Parker, "The Medieval Origins of the Idea of the Church as a 'Societas Perfecta,'" *Miscellanea Historiae Ecclesiasticae* (Louvain, 1961): 23–31; and Gordon Leff, "The Apostolic Ideal in Later Medieval Ecclesiology," *Journal of Theological Studies* 18 (1967): 58–82.

[17] Lewis, *Medieval Political Ideas*, 1: 182, says that this treatise was "the first book to treat the church consistently as a *regnum*." For example, we find this in the first chapter: ". . . nam ecclesia communitas quaedam est" (ed. H. -X. Arquillière, as *Le plus ancien traité de l'église, Jacques de Viterbe, De regimine christiano* [Paris, 1926], p. 89). See also *De reg. christ.* 1. 4. (ed. Arquillière, p. 128): "nulla communitas dicitur vere res publica nisi ecclesiastica, quia in ea sola est vera iustitia et vera utilitas et vera communio."

[18] Lewis, *Medieval Political Ideas*, 2: 367. See also McIlwain, *The Growth of Political Thought*, 225. For Aristotelian and other sources of the conception of the church as a self-sufficient community, see Parker, "The . . . Church as a 'Societas Perfecta.'"

This identification took several forms. Thomas Aquinas combined the idea of the self-sufficient community with that of the City of God.[19] James of Viterbo described the church as a *societas perfecta* to show its superiority to the state.[20] For him the secular state was only "an earlier, partial, and undeveloped approximation" of the perfection to be found in the church.[21] Augustinus Triumphus thought that a city acquired perfection as the seat of a bishop, the perfect priest.[22] The canonist Johannes Monachus said that the church fulfilled Aristotle's definition of perfection.[23]

The government of this Christian society was judged according to Aristotle, and by the standards of the common good. Opponents of absolute papal power, like John of Paris and Pierre d'Ailly, applied Aristotle's arguments for mixed government to the church.[24] Papal supporters like Giles of Rome and Johannes Turrecremata used his arguments in favor of monarchy.[25] Augustinus Triumphus compared papal government to one of the

---

[19] "Haec civitas est ecclesia. Ps. LXXXVI: 'Gloriosa dicta sunt de te, civitas Dei, etc.' Tria sunt in ista civitate quae sunt de ejus ratione. . . . Secundum est quod habeat sufficientiam per se. . . . Et haec sufficientia est in Ecclesia: quia quidquid necessarium est ad vitam spiritualem, invenitur in ea. . . . Tertium est unitas civium: quia ab hoc, scilicet ab unitate civium, civitas nominatur; quia civitas quasi civium unitas. Et haec est in Ecclesia" (*Expositio in Ps. XLV [Opera omnia*, 25 vols. (Parma, 1852–1873), 14 (1863): 526]). See also Ladner, "Aspects of Mediaeval Thought," 420.

[20] See *De reg. christ.* 2. 7.: ". . . institutio potestatis temporalis materialiter et inchoative habet esse a naturali hominum inclinatione, ac per hoc, a Deo in quantum opus nature est opus Dei; perfective autem et formaliter habet esse a potestate spirituali. . ." (ed. Arquillière, 232). Similarly, Giles of Rome, in *De ecclesiastica potestate* 2. 7., denied that anyone not "regenerated" by the church could attain perfect justice, or have proper *dominium*.

[21] McIlwain, *The Growth of Political Thought*, 260.

[22] "Alia est communitas civitatis . . . et ista est communitas perfecta secundum Philosophum, quia si civitas bene ordinata est, in ea debet inveniri quidquid necessarium est ad vitam humanam. . . . In [ista] vero praesunt episcopi quia civitas quaelibet est communitas perfecta sicut quilibet episcopus est sacerdos perfectus, cum possit simile generare" (*Summa de ecclesiastica potestate* 1. 1. [Rome, 1479], 8).

[23] "Nam secundum Philosophum, totum et perfectum idem, vel proximum secundum naturam. Nam illud est perfectum quod totum habet, et nihil ei deficit, et illud etiam totum est, quod omnia habet" (*Extravagantes tum Viginti D. Ioannis Papae XXII tum Communes suae Inte[g]ritati una cum Glossis Restitutae* 1. 8. i. s. v. *sponso*, from *Liber Sextus Decretalium D. Bonifacii Papae VIII, Clementis Papae V Constitutiones Extravagantes tum Viginti D. Ioannis Papae* . . . [Venice, 1615], 413).

[24] ". . . licet regimen regium, in quo unus singulariter principatur multitudini secundum virtutem, sit melius quolibet alio regimine simplici, ut ostendit Philosophus III Politicorum, tamen si fiat mixtum cum aristocratia et democratia melius est puro, in quantum in regimine mixto omnes aliquam partem habent in principatu. . . . tale erat regimen a Deo optime institutum, in populo illo [among the ancient Hebrews]" (John of Paris, *De regia potestate et papali* 19. [ed. Fritz Bleienstein (Stuttgart, 1969), p. 175]). In the *Tractatus de ecclesie . . . autoritate* (ed. Louis Ellies Dupin, *Joannis Gersonii opera omnia*, 5 vols. [Antwerp, 1706], 2: 946), Pierre d'Ailly said: ". . . non expedit Ecclesie . . . quod ipsa regatur regimine Regio puro, sed mixto cum Aristocratia et Democratia . . . ." Here he follows John of Paris: see Francis Oakley, *The Political Thought of Pierre d'Ailly. The Voluntarist Tradition* (New Haven and London, 1964), 53, 117–119.

[25] ". . . quod ait philosophus in Politicis de omni principe, potissime verificari habet de summo pontifice. Vult enim ipse, quod quilibet princeps debet esse homo multorum oculorum, multarum manuum et multorum pedum; debet quidem sibi coacervare multos industrios et sapientes, per quos possit videre que spectant ad regimen principatus sibi commissi. . ." (Giles of Rome, *De eccles. pot.* 3. 9.; ed. Richard Scholz [Weimar, 1929], p. 194). This reference seems to be to *Politics* 3. 11. 1281b, where Aristotle is actually speaking of the people who in the

monarchies of the *Politics*, but attributed to papal monarchy power beyond that granted by Aristotle, combining in him the civil and military powers separated by Aristotle.[26] Furthermore, the doctrine of equity, of which Aristotle was a principal source,[27] could be applied to the church as well as to the state to justify extraordinary action in times of emergency. William of Ockham used his "threefold doctrine of equity, necessity, and the common weal" to support the imposition of extraordinary taxes upon the clergy in times of war and the assembling of a general council without the consent of the pope.[28] Equity has been described as a "magic word" for conciliarists.[29]

These writers were not attempting to justify the existence of ecclesiastical government. Though supporters of the state might find in Aristotle a vindication of secular autonomy, his work offers little support for an ecclesiastical polity. But once the necessity of the church was accepted, as it was by virtually all medieval writers, it could be treated like a state. Then Aristotle could be used, not as a warrant for the existence of the church, but to justify

---

aggregate may have the qualities of "a single person, who — as he has many feet, many hands, and many senses — may also have many qualities of character and intelligence" (Barker, 123).

For Turrecremata, see *Summa contra Ecclesie et Primatus Apostoli Petri Adversarios* 2. 71. (Rome, 1489). Here he says in his fifth conclusion, that the plenitude of power was not given to the church as a corporation or to its members, and offers as proof the statement that philosophers, including Aristotle (in *Ethics* 8. 10. and *Politics* 4. 2.), consider monarchy noble and thus to be preferred by God. (This summary comes from the English translation in Lewis, *Medieval Political Ideas*, 2: 427.) Lewis gives *Politics* 3. 11. as the source of Aristotle's preference for monarchy, but 4. 2. (1289a–b) seems more likely to me.

[26] *Politics* 6. 8. 1322a–b, and *Summa de eccles. pot.* 6. 6. ad 2. Marsilius of Padua, on the other hand, ascribed both functions to the secular ruler (*Defensor Pacis* 1. 14. 9.; p. 83 in the edition of Scholz [Hanover, 1932]).

[27] See above, chap. 4, n. 29.

[28] Charles C. Bayley, "Pivotal Concepts in the Political Philosophy of William of Ockham," *Journal of the History of Ideas* 10 (1949), 215. For his justification of extraordinary taxes, see ibid., 205, from the treatise *An princeps pro suo succursu, scilicet guerrae, possit recipere bona ecclesiasticarum etiam invito papa* (from Ockham's *Opera politica*, 3 vols. [Manchester, 1940–1963], 1 [ed. Jeffrey G. Sikes]: 253). For the assembling of the general council, see *Dialogus* 1. 6. 84. (ed. Goldast, 2: 603). Ockham even said that the ecclesiastical monarchy established by Christ could be altered for the sake of *communitas utilitas* (*Dialogus* 3. 1. 2. 20. [Goldast, 2: 807]).

[29] Bernhard Bess, *Johannes Gerson und die kirchenpolitischen Parteien Frankreichs vor dem Konzil zu Pisa* (Marburg, 1890), 6, cited in E. F. Jacob, *Essays in the Conciliar Epoch* (Manchester, 1943), 9, n. 2. Henry of Langenstein mentioned *epieikeia* itself (*Consilium pacis*, in Dupin, *Joannis Gersonii opera omnia*, 2: 831). Pierre d'Ailly interpreted equity to mean that the laws of the church should not be invoked to the prejudice of the church: "Jura positiva, quae communiter dicunt quod absque auctoritate papae non est fas generale concilium congregari, debent civiliter intelligi. . . . Patet ex praedictis, et ex doctrina Aristotelis in Ethicis, ubi loquitur de epicheia" (*Propositiones utiles* 9, from Edmond Martène and Ursin Durand, *Veterem scriptorum . . . amplissima collectio*, 9 vols. [Paris, 1724–1733], 7 [1724?]: 911). This text is discussed in Oakley, *The Political Thought of Pierre d'Ailly*, 160–161.

Jean Gerson, according to E. F. Jacob (*Essays in the Conciliar Epoch*, p. 9) "is never tired of dwelling on the virtues of *epikeia*." In *Tractatus de unitate ecclesiae* (in Palémon Glorieux, *Oeuvres complètes de Jean Gerson*, 10 vols. [Paris and New York, 1960–1973], 6 [1965]: 144) he said: "Unitas Ecclesiae ad unum certum Christi vicarium dum procurator per epikeiam seu bonam aequitatem, non exigit in sic epiekeientibus seu legum positivarum interpretibus quod habeant evidentiam mathematicam seu demonstrativam; sed satis est si certitudinem moralem seu civilem et politicam attulerint."

within the church institutions considered necessary to all government.[30] The institution of property, for example, was the base of the controversy over the mendicant orders. Thomas Aquinas used the *Politics* to demonstrate that private property is natural,[31] and the advisers of John XXII used it to defend individual ownership.[32]

The politicization of the church has gone a good distance when Aristotle enters a dispute on behalf of the papacy. It is clear that theorists were eager to apply the text of the *Politics* to questions involving the church, but it should be noted that these applications were seldom made in commentaries on the *Politics*. In these commentaries religious institutions were given little more prominence than they had been given by Aristotle. In this regard the *Livre de Politiques* represents a departure from the earlier commentary tradition.

The Church in the *Livre de Politiques*

There are over one hundred and fifty references to the institutional church in the glosses of the *Livre de Politiques*. (This figure does not include references to the Bible and to Christian authorities.) Many of these references to the church were made only incidentally,[33] but frequently they were

---

[30] As Barker says in the introduction to his translation of the *Politics* (p. l): "The State is therefore natural when, or in so far as, it is an institution for that moral perfection of man to which his whole nature moves. All the features of its life—slavery, private property, the family—are equally justified, and also natural, when, or in so far as, they serve that sovereign end." For Aristotle's criticism of the community of property, see *Politics* 2. 5. 1262b–1264b.

[31] Aquinas said that imperfect things, for example natural objects, exist for the sake of more perfect things, like man: "Et ex hac ratione Philosophus probat, in I. *Polit.*, quod possessio rerum exteriorum est homini naturalis" (*Summa Theologica* 2ª 2ᵉ, qu. 66, art. 1 [*Opera omnia* (Rome, 1882–), 9 (1897): 84]). He also said (ibid., art. 2) that the need to serve the ends of human life caused the institution of private property to be added to natural law.

[32] For example, Guido Terreni cited the second book of the *Politics* in his *De perfectione vitae* 3. 2. (fol. 84ʳ of the British Museum manuscript Add. 16632). I owe this reference to Thomas P. Turley.

On the other hand, the first part of Plato's *Timaeus* (as translated by Chalcidius) provided a dangerous source of support for common ownership—dangerous because Plato advocated communal marriage and child-rearing (Stephan Kuttner, "Gratian and Plato," in C. N. L. Brooke, et al., eds., *Church and Government in the Middle Ages* [Cambridge, 1976]: 93–118). Kuttner remarks that Terreni, "who read the Decretum very much with the eyes of a fourteenth-century school-man, would comment upon [Plato's communism] only to point out that Aristotle in the *Politics* had criticised the communism of Plato's state" (p. 109).

[33] Among these are baptism (7. 37. [fol. 291d, p. 336b]); bishops (3. 21. [fol. 108b, p. 148b]); canons and canon chapters (6. 2. [fol. 217c, p. 258a], 6. 13. [fol. 232d, p. 275a]); canon law (1. 12. [fol. 25a, p. 68a], 2. 21. [fols. 67d–68a, p. 111a], 4. 23. [fol. 161c, p. 201b], 5. 15. [fol. 187a, p. 227b], 5. 22. [fol. 197d, p. 239a], 7. 10. [fol. 252a, p. 293b], 7. 19. [fol. 265b, p. 307a], 7. 19. [fol. 266b, p. 308a], 7. 19. [fol. 267a, p. 308b], 7. 21. [fol. 270b and c, p. 312a], 7. 36. [fol. 291a, p. 335b]); cardinals (5. 5. [fol. 171b, p. 210b]); choir (7. 25. [fol. 275d, p. 318a], 8. 11. [fol. 306d, p. 353b]); churches (5. 30. [fol. 208c, p. 249b]); clergymen or "gens d'Eglise" (6. 11. [fol. 230c, p. 272b]) or "estat sacerdotal" (7. 36. [fol. 290d, p. 335b]); cloister (7. 25. [fol. 275a, p. 317a], and 7. 25. [fol. 276b, p. 318b]); confession (8. 3. [fol. 298d, p. 343a]); convents (4. 14. [fol. 144c, p. 184a], 5. 5. [fol. 171b, p. 210b], 7. 7. [fol. 243b, p. 285b]); councils (3. 23. [fol. 116c, p. 156a], 6. 9. [fol. 228b, p. 270a], 6. 12. [fol. 232b, p. 274b]); curates (6. 13. [fol. 232d, p. 275a], 7. 7. [fol. 243b, p. 285b]); excommunication (3. 23. [fol. 116d, p. 156a], 7. 21. [fol. 271c, p. 313a]); fraternities in honor of saints (6. 6. [fol. 224a, p. 265b]); "habit de religion" (3. 23. [fol. 116d, p. 156a]); holy

part of substantial discussions. This is remarkable in an exposition of the
Politics; in fact the number of references to the church in these glosses far
surpasses the number of such references in the earlier commentaries. One
must of course remember that these matters could properly be discussed
only by one trained in theology, whereas some of the earlier commentators,
for example Peter of Auvergne[34] and Jean Buridan,[35] were masters of arts.
On the other hand, Albertus Magnus, Thomas Aquinas and Walter Burley
had degrees in theology, and said little about the church.

In the *Livre de Politiques,* by contrast, we find many discussions of the
government of the church, but we find them accompanied by a seemingly
equal number of disclaimers, in which Oresme displayed a certain humility
or bashfulness about his attempts to discuss this subject. He questioned the
use of the *Politics* itself for such a purpose, for he realized that the priests of
Aristotle's time were not like those of the Christian church:

. . . neither the priesthood of our Christian faith nor its jurisdiction, whether
purely spiritual or not, is comprehended in this science. For this worthy office was
especially instituted by one who was both God and man, and is maintained by him.
And [the priesthood] of which Aristotle speaks was established by a human rather
than a divine founder. Furthermore, our priestly office is ordered toward a blessed
happiness not of this world, while that of which Aristotle speaks is meant principally
to promote the wisdom or happiness which can be attained in this world by natural
means.[36]

He elaborated upon his comparison between the two priesthoods and
declared that he intended to treat the subject "comme pur philisophe."[37]

---

hermits, who are mentioned in connection with Aristotle's statements about men who live out
of society as "beasts or gods," from *Politics* 1. 2. 1253a (1. 2. [fol. 7d, p. 48b], 1. 2. [fol. 9a, p.
50a], 7. 7. [fol. 243b, p. 285b]); holy orders (2. 9. [fol. 46c, p. 89a], 6. 9. [fol. 228b, p. 270a], 7. 19.
[fol. 265c, p. 307a], 7. 36. [fol. 289c, p. 334a]); martyrs (5. 11. [fol. 180d, p. 221a]); the Mass (8. 3.
[fol. 298b, p. 343a], 8. 7. [fol. 302a, p. 348a]); the mendicant orders (7. 19. [fol. 267a, p. 308b]);
monks (6. 13. [fol. 232d, p. 275a], 7. 38. [fol. 292c, p. 337b]); oratory (7. 34. [fol. 287d, p. 332a]);
prelates (5. 5. [fol. 171b, p. 210b], 7. 7. [fol. 243b, p. 285b]); refectories (7. 20. [fol. 268a, p.
309b]); relics (2. 22. [fol. 69d, p. 113a], 7. 16. [fol. 261d, p. 303b]); rural and "cardinalz" priests
(6. 9. [fol. 228b, p. 270b]); sacraments (7. 7. [fol. 243b, p. 285b], 7. 16. [fol. 262d, p. 304a]);
sacred places, for example *chapelles* and *oratoires* (7. 25. [fol. 275a, p. 317a]); saints' legends (1.
6. [fol. 15b, p. 57a], 3. 21. [fol. 108b, p. 148b], 7. 21. [fol. 271c, p. 313a]); and treasurers or
secretaries of churches (6. 13. [fol. 232c, p. 275a]).

In many of these cases, ecclesiastical terms were introduced to serve as analogies to things
mentioned in the text of the *Politics;* for example, the cardinals and the constitutional changes
they might introduce were mentioned in connection with constitutional changes in Eubeoa
(*Politics* 5. 3. 1303a).

[34] Conor Martin, "Some Medieval Commentaries on Aristotle's *Politics,*" *History* 36 (1951):
36.

[35] Buridan did mention ecclesiastical government (in very broad terms) in his *quaestio* 8. 5.:
" . . . utrum universitati mortalium expediat quod universo sit unus solus secularis princeps," but here he wished to deny that arguments against universal temporal government
could be turned against universal spiritual government. For the text, see above, chapter 3, n.
133.

[36] *Le Livre de Politiques* 7. 21. (fol. 269c, p. 311a–b).

[37] Ibid., 311b. Similarly, in 6. 12. (fol. 232a, p. 274b) he said: "Mes discuter de puissance qui
vient de Dieu sans moien et qui est donnee'par miracle divin, ce est une chose qui transcende et
passe ceste science, si comme je touchay ou .xiiii.ᵉ chapitre du tiers." (See 3. 14. [fol. 97c, p.

Even in this restricted role he doubted the worthiness of his opinions, and subjected himself (though not, perhaps, without a certain irony) to the correction of those with better knowledge of the subject.[38] Political science is after all a practical science, which is meant to deal with subjects other (and lower) than theology. Even a trained theologian might restrict himself when commenting on the *Politics*. Oresme may have been thinking of this when he cautiously suggested, submitting himself "to those who know and understand the way the church is governed now and was governed in the past," that his discussion of the identity of the state might usefully be applied to the government of the church.[39]

It is hard to know what to make of these disclaimers. It would not have been impossible for Oresme to write a commentary on the *Politics* without mentioning the church: the work of Oresme's predecessors, and his own comments, suggest that this might be the most appropriate response to such an uncongenially secular text. But neither precedent nor diffidence prevented Oresme from making judgments about the proper government of the church. In fact, several of his disclaimers occur in long and pointed discussions of this subject. Perhaps his true attitude can be seen in the

---

137b] for a similar remark.) In 3. 21. (fol. 108b, p. 148b) he said that discussions of the administration of goods within the church "appartient a autre science." We have seen (chapter 3, n. 108) that Oresme excepted the papacy from his discussion of the merits of universal government, for "celle monarchie esperituele vient de Dieu par grace especial" while temporal government comes "de Dieu par autre influence et par autre maniere" (7. 10. [fol. 251c, p. 293a]). For a disclaimer in the *Songe du Vergier*, see 2. 117., mentioned in Jean-Pierre Royer, *L'Église et le royaume de France au XIVe siècle d'après le "Songe du Vergier" et la jurisprudence du Parlement* (Paris, 1969), 68.

[38] These disclaimers are not limited to the risky topic of ecclesiology. See, for example, *Le Livre de Politiques* 2. 21. (fol. 66a, p. 109a), a discussion of election and succession; 3. 23. (fol. 114d, p. 154b), another such discussion; 6. 12. (fol. 232b, p. 274b), on the role of the multitude in government; 7. 10. (fol. 253b, p. 294b), on universal monarchy. See also the *Livre de Ethiques* 9. 3. (fol. 181c, p. 461), on friendship, and 9. 5. (fol. 183d, p. 465), on the soul.

We see this tone in Oresme's scientific writing as well. He said of demons in his *Questio contra divinatores* with *Quodlibeta anexa*: "Moreover, if the Faith did not pose their existence, I would say that from no natural effect can they be proved to exist, for all things [supposedly arising from them] can be saved naturally" (cited in Marshall Clagett's article on Oresme in the *Dictionary of Scientific Biography*, 16 vols. [New York, 1970–1980], 10 [1974]: 225, with reference to MS. Paris, B. N. lat. 15126, fol. 127v). Clagett also refers (ibid.), in speaking of another passage, to "the technique of expression used by Oresme and his Parisian contemporaries, which permitted them to suggest the most unorthodox and radical philosophical ideas while disclaiming any commitment to them."

We may also recognize in some of Oresme's glosses on the church the ill-concealed pride which Edward Grant finds in his scientific speculation: "As with so many sceptics in the history of western thought his profession of ignorance was not an act of humility, but rather of arrogance, a transparent attempt to conceal the self-confidence of a brilliant and learned mind" (from "Scientific Thought in Fourteenth-Century Paris: Jean Buridan and Nicole Oresme," in Madeleine Pelner Cosman and Bruce Chandler, eds., *Machaut's World: Science and Art in the Fourteenth Century* [New York, 1978], 111).

[39] *Le Livre de Politiques* 3. 3. (fol. 79a, p. 120a). In 3. 24. (fol. 122c, p. 159b) he said: "Et ce que je diray, je soumet a toute bonne correction et tousjours en supposant et tenant fermement estre vraie de la posté divine du Saint Pere de Romme ce qu'en croit Sainte Eglise." See also 4. 8. (fol. 137b, p. 176b), 4. 16. (fol. 150c, p. 189b), and 5. 14. (fol. 184d, p. 225b), for further examples. Cf. the prologue to the *Songe du Vergier* (ed. Brunet, p. 8).

comments in which he respectfully acknowledged the difference between the quality of temporal power and the quality of spiritual power, while suggesting that natural philosophy (and his interpretation of natural philosophy) might yet have something useful to say about the church. In a long gloss on church government in 3. 24., he interrupted his argument in order to justify it, as though rapidly and reflexively disposing of an expected objection:

Now . . . to determine whether, according to this science, any things should be reformed in this ecclesiastical polity (supposing always, as was said before, that [the church] is not subject to [political] science, but [that] it is not a bad thing to see what a philosopher might say about it, for perhaps, just as the well-being of the soul is aided by natural philosophy, toward the understanding of what one ought to believe, so can moral philosophy aid in knowing what one should do) . . . saving all worthy correction, it seems to me that the Philosopher would say that this polity should be reformed principally in three areas. . . .[40]

A more complete and leisurely expression of his attitude occurs in 7. 25. He noted that "Aristotle does not speak more in this book about the clergy as a special and notable subject,"[41] and then gave reasons for applying Aristotle's earlier remarks to the church.[42] Oresme then considered the connections between the secular and ecclesiastical polities which make profitable such an interchange of ideas: ". . . [the church] is a mirror and exemplar for all secular governments. . . . And the converse is also true, for if the secular government is badly ordered, it is a sign of defect among the clergy."[43] Then he spoke of the uses of natural philosophy in a way which reminds one of Augustine's "Egyptian gold" argument.

According to Saint Augustine and Saint Jerome and many other doctors [of the church], natural philosophy greatly aids and assists in the understanding and defense of the articles of the faith, and at the same time the moral philosophy of ethics advances the commandments and counsels of God. And similarly, political philosophy can minister to the ecclesiastical polity. For this science is not so foreign to [the church] . . . that there are not [to be found] in this book several lessons and considerations which may be of value to the church especially [in practical matters]. . . .[44]

---

[40] Fols. 123d–124a, p. 160b. In 5. 25. (fol. 201c–d, p. 243a) he said that although the power which comes directly from God by the special grace of the Holy Spirit is not subject to Aristotle's remarks on royal government, and transcends political science, "fors par aventure en tant comme se aucunes choses profitables a tele policie povoient estre adivisees par ceste philosophie en lumiere naturele, par raison et par prudence humaine."

[41] Fol. 277a, p. 319b. The importance of this discussion is shown by a reference to it in the "Table des Notables" at the end of the translation (fol. 321c, p. 366a), with this designation: "Les causes pourquoy en exposant cest livre a esté souvent faite mention de la policie et de la gent d' Eglise."

[42] "Premierement, car ceste policie par soi consideree est tres notable. . . . Item, cest policie de l'Eglise en tant comme separeement consideree est tres principale et universele par tout" (fol. 277a–b, p. 319b).

[43] Fol. 277b, p. 319b. See also 4. 16. (fol. 149d, p. 189a).

[44] Ibid., fol. 277b–c, pp. 319b–320a. For the "Egyptian gold" argument, see *De doctrina christiana* 2. 40. 60. (in Migne, *Patrologia Latina*, 34, col. 63). Oresme also spoke of the church as the mirror of other governments in 4. 16. (fol. 149d, p. 189a), and in 4. 21. (fol. 157a, p. 196a).

In applying the ideas of Aristotle to the church, Oresme followed the usage of his predecessors. He seemed to divide questions concerning the church into two categories. Questions involving the justification of its authority (especially in relation to that of secular states) were difficult to treat within the framework of the *Politics*. In fact, Oresme did not have a great deal to say about the problems of *regnum* and *sacerdotium*, as we shall see. But once the role of the church was accepted, it could be treated as a member of the class of political societies. This allowed him to use a single standard of judgment. As Oresme said, "the law of Jesus Christ is not discordant with [good] government."[45]

Oresme made over twenty references to the "polity of the church."[46] His fullest discussion of the church as a political society occurs in his gloss on the identity of the city, in 3. 3.:

. . . the multitude of those who are or have been [members] of the universal communion in the faith of Jesus Christ may be called a city. And according to this [usage] Saint Paul said to the newly converted Ephesians: "Now therefore you are no more strangers and foreigners: but you are fellow citizens with the saints, etc." [Ephesians 2:19; Douay Version].[47]

Then he introduced the narrow definition of the church as the clergy.[48]

Oresme also referred to clergymen as princes or magistrates, as in this gloss from 4. 21.

. . . priesthood is a magistracy, and consequently priests are magistrates. Again, this sacerdotal magistracy is not the same thing as a political magistracy, that is to say a secular magistracy. . . . And formerly those who governed [the ecclesiastical polity] were called *principes sacerdotum*.[49]

---

[45] *Le Livre de Politiques* 2. 6. (fol. 40c, p. 83b).

[46] References to the "policie de l'Eglise," or nearly identical expressions, are found in the *Livre de Politiques* 3. 1. (fol. 73b, p. 114b): "nostre policie de Saincte Eglise, qui est la Cité de Dieu"; in 3. 24. (fol. 122c, p. 159b): "la policie de l'Eglise"; 3. 24. (fol. 123a, p. 160a): "la policie de le Eglise"; 3. 24. (fol. 123d, p. 160b): "policie de l'Eglise"; 3. 24. (fol. 124a, p. 160b): "ceste policie"; 4. 8. (fol. 137b, p. 176b): "la policie des gens de l'Eglise"; 4. 10. (fol. 139a, p. 178a): "la policie de l'Eglise"; 4. 16. (fol. 149d, p. 189a): ". . . la communité de ceulz que nous appellons *gens d'Eglise* peut estre dicte cité. Et ont une policie qui est universele. . ."; 4. 16. (fol. 150a, p. 189b): "policie ecclesiastique"; 5. 5. (fol. 171b, p. 210b): "nostre policie"; 5. 5. (fol. 171b, p. 210b): "la policie ou le gouvernement de l'Eglise"; 5. 14. (fol. 184d, p. 225b): "la policie de Sainte Eglise"; 5. 14. (fol. 185d, p. 226b): "la policie de l'Eglise"; 5. 25. (fol. 201c, p. 243a): "la policie sacerdotal ou de l'Eglise"; 6. 12. (fol. 232a, p. 274b): "la policie de Sainte Eglise"; 7. 10. (fol. 247b, p. 289b): "la policie presente de l'Eglise"; 7. 19. (fol. 266c–d, p. 308a): "la policie de Saincte Eglise"; 7. 25. (fol. 277a, p. 319b): "la policie de Saincte Eglise"; 7. 25. (fol. 277b, p. 319b): "cest policie de l'Eglise"; 7. 25. (fol. 277c, pp. 319b–320a): "la policie de l'Eglise"; 7. 25. (fol. 277c, p. 320a): "la policie ecclesiastique"; and in the "Table des Notables" (fol. 314b, p. 359b): "la policie de l'Eglise" and as a heading of a section in the "Table" (fol. 321b, p. 366a): "Policie de Eglise."

[47] Fol. 78d, p. 120a.

[48] "Item, quelcunques partie principal du peuple qui a en soy aucun especial gouvernement peut estre dite cité, et en ceste maniere ceulz que nous appellons gens de Eglise sunt comme une cité; car il ont une policie quant a la gubernacion, distribution et ordenance d'aucunes possessions et d'aucune honorabletés publiques" (fol. 79a, p. 120a).

[49] Fol. 157a, p. 196a. For similar references see 3. 24. (fol. 122d, p. 159b); 4. 10. (fol. 139b, p. 178b); 4. 22. (fol. 160c, p. 200a); and 6. 12. (fol. 232a, p. 274b). Oresme's definition of *prince* in the "Table des . . . fors mos" (fol. 329a, p. 373a) is "celui qui tient princey ou qui participe en

Later he qualified this by saying that one could speak of clergymen as kings (or princes, presumably) only by metaphor.[50] This was nevertheless a metaphor upon which Oresme was willing to base extended discussions.

In these discussions Oresme (speaking, as always, with humility and hesitation) applied to the church Aristotle's analysis of constitutions.[51] Limited monarchy seemed to him to be the best form of government for the church. This limitation chiefly consisted in avoiding two of the characteristics of tyranny: domination over the multitude and disregard of the laws. Oresme applied to the papacy the notion of Aristotle that the king should have more power than any individual within the kingdom, but less than the people as a whole.[52]

. . . it is proper that the above-mentioned multitude [that is, the "reasonable" multitude] should have sovereignty over positive laws. In addition . . . the power of the king should be moderated to such a degree that it will be greater than the power of any individual [citizen] or of several of them. But it should be smaller than that of the multitude or of its weightiest part . . . this is one of the differences between a king and a tyrant. . . .[53]

The force of Oresme's next remark is hardly mitigated by the disclaimers which will follow them in the gloss:

---

tenir princey." This can be understood in connection with Oresme's discussion of *princey* (see above, chapter 3, nn. 138–141). In the cases mentioned here, it seems that a prince is something more than a magistrate.

[50] "Car combien que les plus grans de la gent sacerdotal soient appellés roys, si comme il fu dit ou .xiii.ᵉ chapitre du sexte, ce est seulement par methaphore et par similitude pour l'excellence de ceste dignité" (7. 21. [fol. 269d, p. 311b]). The ".xiii.ᵉ chapitre du sexte" corresponds to *Politics* 6. 8. 1322b, where Aristotle spoke of the managers of public sacrifices, who were sometimes called kings.

[51] In 4. 22. (fol. 160c, p. 200a), he suggested what Aristotle *would* say ("diroit") about a hypothetical development in the church. Whether this is an example of his hesitation about applying "ceste science" to the church, or simply an acknowledgment that Aristotle was unable to comment on the problems of the church, is difficult to say. For the text of this gloss, see below, n. 57.

[52] *Politics* 3. 15. 1286b. Oresme did not mention the church when he glossed this passage (3. 23. [fol. 117c–d, p. 157a]).

[53] *Le Livre de Politiques* 6. 12. (fols. 231d–232a, p. 274b). This "plus vaillant partie" recalls the *valentior pars* of Marsilius of Padua (*Defensor Pacis* 1. 13. 2.). Oresme uses the French expression also in the *Livre de Politiques* 3. 14. (fol. 96c, p. 137a and fol. 97b, p. 137b), also mentioning the *Defensor Pacis* and speaking of the role of the "weightiest part" in making laws. It also appears in 3. 23. (fol. 117d, p. 157a) where Oresme added to the statement of Aristotle that the power of the king should be less than that of the whole multitude (from *Politics* 3. 15. 1286b, as above in n. 52 and as mentioned in the section cited above), "Ou de la plus vaillant partie." Similar usages occur in the *Livre de Politiques* 5. 24. (fol. 200a, p. 241a) and 7. 7. (fol. 242c, p. 285a), where Oresme speaks of a city fortunate because the weightiest or most powerful part of its citizens is fortunate. Similar expressions occur in 4. 12. (fol. 141d, p. 181a); 4. 17. (fol. 150c, p. 190a), as part of his translation of *Politics* 4. 12. 1296b, Marsilius's source for the expression; and in 7. 27. (fol. 279c, p. 322b).

As Gewirth says (*Marsilius of Padua. The Defender of Peace*, 2 vols. [New York, 1951–1956], 1: 184), the use of this phrase is "an almost certain sign of Marsilian influence." See Gewirth, 1: 182–199, for a discussion of the origin and use of this expression, and his Appendix 1 (2: 433–434), where he shows how Marsilius misinterpreted Aristotle in his treatment of the *valentior pars* (from *Politics* 4. 12. 1296b).

. . . if the government of Holy Church were not directed by a supernatural power and by the special grace of the Holy Spirit, it would not bring honor to this polity according to [Aristotle] if one said that the pope is above the law and above the General Council, for thus [the government] would be more like a tyranny than a monarchy.[54]

Here, although Oresme spoke conditionally, he made his opinion clear. After seeing this gloss we can appreciate another of his hypothetical discussions of monarchy in the church:

And if someone were to say that, according to Aristotle . . . the ecclesiastical or sacerdotal polity resembles a royal government, and that for this reason its sovereign mortal ruler should have [only] a moderated power over [his] subjects . . . and should be under the law, or run the risk of causing [sedition], especially if his power were greatly extended, far beyond the rule of moderation [proposed by Aristotle], I would respond. . . .[55]

His response is of course another disclaimer based on the insufficiency of political science to deal with the church;[56] this familiar two-step (or three-step) does little to distract the reader from Oresme's argument.

Oresme mentioned service to the common good as a criterion of good government in the church as well as in the state:

[Debased forms of government] exist when a group which is small . . . , or a single man, governs at will and with unlimited power, without laws or by laws . . . made in favor of the rulers and against the public good of the state and the good legislation of the past. And . . . the sovereign [rulers] of the church should, even more than others, take great care lest their government be changed into such a [debased] form. For according to this philosophy, which in this case accords with Holy Scripture, they would thus place in peril the estate of Holy Church.[57]

He also warned against oligarchy and tyranny in the church without mentioning the common good as such. In 3. 24. he called down upon the church the judgment of Ezekiel:

For if it were true, as some say, that the government of the court of Rome be changed into the likeness of an oligarchy or tyranny (which God forbid!), then it could be said of [those at Rome] what Our Lord said through his prophet Ezekiel, in the thirty-fourth chapter: "Woe to the shepherds of Israel that fed themselves, etc." [Ezekiel 34:2; Douay Version].[58]

---

[54] *Le Livre de Politiques* 6. 12. (fol. 232a, p. 274b).

[55] Ibid., 5. 25. (fol. 201c–d, p. 243a).

[56] For a summary and citation of this disclaimer, see above, n. 40.

[57] 4. 19. (fol. 155a–b, p. 194a). Similarly, in 4. 22. (fol. 160c, p. 200a), Oresme said, in a discussion of the oligarchical method of appointment by a section taken from a section (*Politics* 4. 15. 1300a): " . . . se les princes de l'Eglise faisoient ainsi, Aristote diroit que ce seroit comme chose olygarchique ou tirannique."
John of Paris was another who thought that the government of the church, and specifically the papacy, should serve the common good: "Ad hoc rationes adduci possunt ex parte quidem causae finalis, quia non eligitur aliquis in papam nisi propter bonum commune ecclesiae et gregis dominici. Ad hoc enim praeest ut prosit" (*De reg. pot. et pap.* 24 [ed. Bleienstein, p. 200]).

[58] Fols. 124d–125a, p. 161a. Oresme must have liked this passage from Ezekiel; he also cited it in 4. 10. (fol. 139b, p. 178b), in 5. 32. (fol. 211c–d, p. 253a), and in his sermon before Urban V (see below, n. 101). See also the *Songe du Vergier* 2. 282. (ed. Brunet, 146).

Oresme also applied to the church Aristotle's recommendations for balancing the classes in a state. Aristotle favored the state dominated by the stable middle class.[59] Oresme felt that the church itself should be a "policie moienne,"[60] avoiding a dangerous disparity between the wealth of prelates and the poverty of simple priests.

> . . . it might seem to many that [the church] is very far from the middle polity which Aristotle considers excellent, for some who are priests or are [especially in holy orders/ in a certain holy order] are as poor and lowly as are laborers or rabble. . . . And others are [very rich]. . . . And thus it follows by what [Aristotle] says that such a government will not be secure.[61]

This problem of disproportion will come up again when we see what Oresme said about the distribution of goods within the church.[62]

We know that Oresme thought the pope must, like a secular ruler, respect both the law and the people, and exercise a moderated power. The pope was also, according to the glosses of the *Livre de Politiques*, to follow the advice of Aristotle on the proper distribution of goods. In 3. 15. Oresme described the criteria for distribution, which applied, as he said, to "the ruler, be he pope, or king, or another." Offices were to be given with regard only to the fulfillment of their ends; favoritism of any sort was to be judged a sin.[63]

---

[59] *Politics* 4. 11. 1295b–1296b.

[60] Barker translates this as "polity"; for example, on p. 183, line 4.

[61] *Le Livre de Politiques* 4. 16. (fol. 150a–b, p. 189b). This middle-class polity is not the mixed government advocated with the support of Aristotle by opponents of papal absolutism (see above, n. 24), though both ideas emphasize the need for balance.

[62] Oresme mentiqned popes and the papacy many times, sometimes only incidentally, for example in 3. 3. (fol. 78b–c, p. 119b), where he quoted the maxim "Ubi papa, ibi Roma," as a correlative to "Ubi senatus, ibi Roma," in a gloss on the identity of the city. This in turn countered the notion, of some interest at the time of the Babylonian Captivity, that "le pape ne doit onques demourer ailleurs que ou lieu de Rome." Allusion was made to the same maxim, to the effect that the "souverain prestre des Crestiens" need not "tousjours tenir son siege en celle place," in the long gloss on universal government (7. 10. [fol. 250b, p. 292a]).

Several popes were mentioned by name in the glosses: Innocent III was mentioned four times, of which two are the occasions noted in the preceding paragraph. The third reference came in a discussion of the disposition of benefices, from the gloss cited at the beginning of this section (3. 15. [fol. 99c, p. 139b]). The fourth reference was to Innocent's doctrine of the two "grans luminaires . . . l'auctorité sacerdotal et la posté royal" (7. 10. [fol. 248b, p. 290a]). Urban V was mentioned twice, both times for the sermon delivered before him by Oresme on Christmas Eve, 1363 (4. 16. [fol. 150c, p. 189b], and 5. 14. [fol. 185d, p. 226b]). Alexander III was mentioned in connection with the Lateran Council of 1179 (3. 24. [fol. 123b, p. 160a]). Popes Celestine I and Leo I were mentioned for their decrees on the election of bishops (3. 24. [fol. 122d, p. 159b]). One of the letters of Innocent I was cited in 7. 19. (fol. 265b, p. 307a), and Nicholas I contributed the statement that "les lays des emperieres sunt aucune foiz contraires a verité" (7. 10. [fol. 252a, p. 293b]; see Migne, *Patrologia Latina*, 187: 51–52).

[63] ". . . se le prince, soit pape ou roy ou autre, donne office ou benefice a aucun en aiant resgart et consideration a ce qu'il est de son lignage ou de son païs ou en faveur d'autre chose qui ne fait au propos dessus dit, il peche. . . . se le prince ou prelat prefere a tel office le moins souffisant, combien qu'il soit souffisant, devant le plus souffisant il fait injustice; car il pervertist et fausse le equalité de la proportion qui doit estre entre les merites et les louiers" (fol. 99a–b, p. 139b).

In the *Livre de Ethiques* 8. 13. (fol. 169b, p. 435 in the edition of Menut), Oresme said: "Si come il advenoit en la policie de l'Eglise, que ceulz qui ont la souveraineté distribuassent les dignités et les biens as indignes, et que ilz en preïssent pour euls trop largement et feïssent que la

Oresme also considered the possibility of bad appointments made by corrupt or misguided prelates, and went so far as to suggest that a chapter or convent could do better making appointments by lot, than a pope thus led astray.[64]

Clearly, Oresme did not favor allowing the pope a wide prerogative in the distribution of benefices. He applied to the papacy the rule of Aristotle that those who render judgment or distribute offices should know the characters of the persons involved.[65] In a long gloss on the government of the church, Oresme complained that "many who are adulators or ignorant have persuaded the Holy Fathers to use the plenitude of power and to make extraordinary reservations and new exactions, and to give expectations which seem *prima facie* to be contrary to the ancient laws of the church."[66] He continued:

. . . if the papal government . . . which has thus drawn to itself this distributive jurisdiction, uses it improperly . . . [it] would not last long if God did not maintain it by a special grace . . . it is not possible by nature that one man should be able properly to order a large multitude; rather, this is a divine work, as can be seen according to Aristotle, in 7. 10. . . . For a mortal man with only a natural understanding cannot be acquainted with the character and merits of all the clergy. . . .[67]

Oresme limited the power of the pope both as a monarch who must respect the law and the multitude, and as a distributor of offices, who like a secular ruler can exercise his authority only to the extent of his knowledge and wisdom. Later we shall return to the problem of distributive justice: having seen what Oresme expected of those who appoint in the church, we shall see what he expected of those who are appointed.

The breadth of Aristotle's treatment of political life encouraged its users to discuss not only the papal monarchy but its alternatives as well. For example, Oresme, speaking of the identity of the state and its rulers, presented several opinions about who speaks for the church. Aristotle had said that some hold the state responsible for actions taken by the group, while others say that the government is responsible.[68] In his gloss Oresme recalled that some had blamed the city of Athens for the death of Socrates, and others the

---

souveraineté demourast a un lignage ou païs particulier; pour certain, selon Aristote, ce seroit oligarchie et la pire policie qui soit après tyrannie." Menut's note is "Or[esme]'s Gallican sympathies are perfectly evident here." See also *Le Livre de Ethiques* 5. 19. (fol. 109b, p. 315) and 9. 3. (fol. 181c, p. 461).

[64] *Le Livre de Politiques* 5. 5. (fol. 171b, p. 210b).

[65] *Politics* 7. 4. 1326b.

[66] *Le Livre de Politiques* 3. 24. (fol. 123b, p. 160a). Compare to chap. 4, n. 89.

[67] Ibid., fol. 123c, p. 160a–b. See above, chapter 3, n. 126, for Aristotle's remark on the divine work of ordering, from *Politics* 7. 4. 1326a. Victor Martin, in *Les origines du Gallicanisme* (2 vols. in one [Paris, 1939], 1: 328), mentions an ordinance of Charles VI (from 18 February 1407) which says that the pope often makes unworthy appointments because he cannot (in Martin's words) "connaître tout le monde."

[68] ". . . the nature of the 'polis', or state, is at present a disputed question; and while some affirm, 'It was the *state* that did such and such an act', others reply, 'It was not the state, but the *government*—the governing oligarchy or tyrant' " (*Politics* 3. 1. 1274b; Barker, p. 92).

government, and mentioned Aristotle's determination not to give Athens a second chance to sin against philosophy. Then he turned to a new subject:

And just as there may be controversy over [the identity of] a city, so can there be over [the identity of] Holy Church, which is the City of God. Some have said that what the pope ordains is done by the church. And others say this is not the case; but that what is ordained by the college of cardinals in Rome [is done by the church]; and still others say this is not the case; but that what is done or approved by the General Council [is done by the church].[69]

Here Oresme did not make a choice. Perhaps he was not primarily interested in the identity of the church. He seemed to accept a monarchical government for the church,[70] as for the state, while insisting in both cases that the monarchy be limited. The question how rulers rule, for example, whether they serve the common good, or whether they are bound by the law, was apparently more important to him than the question how many rulers there are. (When Aristotle had separated the good constitutions from the bad, he too had given more weight to the manner of governing than to the number of the governors.) One might observe that Oresme did not build up his political principles from the ground. First principles he left to others; his was a secondary role, that of a commentator, an adviser, or perhaps a propagandist, who took his text and applied it to the conditions he knew, without transforming either. He accepted configurations of political power as he saw them, and did not inquire deeply into their origins. Though Oresme criticized the papal monarchy, he did not propose a new constitution for the church. But we must recall that he thought it would bring no honor to the church to say that the pope was above the General Council.[71]

A more complete discussion of church government appears in the section of the *Livre de Politiques* which deals with kingship and law. Here Oresme spoke of the need for reform in the church, and of the opinion of Aristotle that reformation or correction belongs to the multitude.[72] Oresme, who had

---

[69] 3. 1. (fol. 73b, p. 114b). Oresme also mentioned councils of the church in 3. 13. (fol. 93d, p. 134b); 3. 23. (fol. 116c, p. 156a); 3. 24. (fol. 122c–d, p. 159b); 3. 24. (fol. 123b, p. 160a); 3. 24. (fol. 124b, p. 160b); 3. 24. (fol. 124b, p. 161a); 3. 24. (fol. 124d, p. 161a); 6. 9. (fol. 228b, p. 270a); 6. 12. (fol. 232a and b, p. 274b); 7. 19. (fol. 265b, p. 307a); and 7. 25. (fol. 277b, p. 319b).

[70] The opinion of Oresme on government by cardinals may be inferred from a gloss in 5. 5. (fol. 171b–c, p. 210b). Speaking of Heracleodorus of Oreus, who became a magistrate and changed an oligarchy into a democracy or "polity" (as the translation of Barker [p. 210] has it: *Politics* 5. 3. 1303a), he said: "Et tele mutation peut estre faite en miex ou en pis, et est aussi come se aucuns estoient faiz cardinalz et il vousissent muer la policie ou le gouvernement de l'Eglise pource qu'il ne leur plaist pas."

Oresme did not speak of the conception of the church, held by Ockham and others, which made the congregation of the faithful the final source of authority in the church (for Ockham, see *Dialogus* 1. 5. 8. [ed. Melchior Goldast, in *Monarchia s. Romani Imperii*, 3 vols. (Hanover, 1611–1642), 2: 478–479]). Perhaps this is because in Ockham the authority of the *congregatio fidelium* was not expressed institutionally but rather existed potentially or residually.

[71] See above, n. 54, from *Le Livre de Politiques* 6. 12.

[72] 3. 24. (fol. 124a–b, p. 160b). This is a reference to *Politics* 3. 11. 1281a–1282b, where Aristotle presented arguments in favor of the sovereignty of the multitude, and said: "There is this to be said for the Many. Each of them by himself may not be of a good quality; but when they all come together it is possible that they may surpass—collectively and as a body, although not individually—the quality of the few best" (Barker, 123).

already used the General Council as an example of Aristotle's multitude whose qualities surpass those of a few superior citizens,[73] said here again that the multitude was assembled in a form similar to that of a church council.[74] Councils should be held, he thought, whenever convocation was necessary and expedient for the reform of the church.[75] He cited a document from the eleventh Synod of Toledo, which complained of the infrequency of councils, and of the ignorance and wrongdoing which had resulted.[76]

Oresme did not present a program of conciliar government. He did speak of councils as a regular part of the life of the church, as something more than instruments for deposing occasional unsuitable popes, but he did not explain how the members of a General Council were to be chosen, or precisely when meetings were to be held. (He mentioned the latter problem in a gloss on sovereignty within the state, but only in general terms.) He had more to say about who should convoke councils. We shall see that he assigned a role to kings; but the primary responsibility rested with the pope. We know that, according to Oresme, God did not wish the "princey de la court de Romme" to resemble an oligarchy or tyranny.[77] Oresme said that, if such debased forms of government were to appear in the church, there would be no councils.[78] It is likely that he accepted the converse of this proposition: if councils were not called, the papal monarchy would resemble a tyranny.

Without describing a conciliar program, Oresme left no doubt of his attitude, just a few years before the Schism of 1378 made the issue more pressing. His insistence on the need for councils and reform by councils puts him in a line with Gallican theorists.[79]

---

[73] "Car aussi comme il est dit devant de ceulz qui contribue en une despense, chescun de pluseurs treuve aucune chose bonne pour la cité. Et tout ensemble est tres bon, et l'en dit qu'en ceste maniere les Apostelz composerent le Credo et pour ce est il appellé *Symbolum.* Car aussi comme en un escot, chescun de eulz en mist une partie. Et semblablement, en Sainte Eglise au commencement et apres quant elle procedoit en prosperité et en croissance, toutes choses notables estoient ordenees par les conciles generals" (3. 13. [fol. 93d, pp. 134a–b]). *Escot* is probably used here to mean "banquet," or possibly and more appealingly, "picnic."

[74] 3. 24. (fol. 124b, p. 160b).

[75] Ibid., fol. 125a, p. 161b.

[76] Fol. 124b–d, p. 161a; see Migne, *Patrologia Latina*, 84: 451–452.

[77] ". . . anciennement fu establi que les conciles de Sainte Eglise se fussent de an en an a certain terme. Item, peut estre que par la lay sunt determinés et designés certains cas lesquelz quant il aviennent, il convient faire ceste assemblee. Si comme en Sainte Eglise pluseurs conciles furent faiz jadis pour discuter et determiner de divisions et divers opinions de la foy" (6. 12. [fol. 232a–b, p. 274b]).

[78] "Car se . . . le princey de la court de Romme se trasist a la similitude de princey olygarchique ou tirannique. . . . jamés par eulz ne seroit faicte tele assemblee. . . " (3. 24. [fols. 124d–125a, p. 161a–b]).

[79] It is difficult to tell whether the translations of Oresme influenced the theorists of the Council of Constance. Pierre d'Ailly and Jean Gerson naturally emphasized, as Oresme had done, the need for councils which could be summoned even without the consent of the pope, but in complexity and comprehensiveness their theories go far beyond the fragments in the *Livre de Politiques.* It is worth noting that Gerson, at least, was familiar with this translation. In a letter addressed to Gerson as "precepteur du dauphin" there is a list of books to be read by Louis, son of Charles VI. The eleventh item on this list is "Yconomica et Ethica et Politica Aristotelis translata in galicum" (Antoine Thomas, *Jean Gerson et l'éduction des dauphins de France* [Paris, 1930], p. 50).

The subject of councils leads us to the subject of reform. Oresme explained what he meant by reform in the long gloss favoring councils, in 3. 24. He introduced three principal headings for reform, which he divided, in the manner of Aristotle, into reforms in matter and reforms in form:

. . . the Philosopher would say that [the church] should be reformed principally in three aspects. . . . One concerns the quantity and unequal [distribution] of honors and goods, which are not in proper proportion. Another is the conduct of individuals. And these two aspects are like the matter of the government. And the third is like the form, and concerns the establishment of good laws or canons in all matters in which the law has jurisdiction, and the removal of any unreasonable novelties which have been established or put into effect [?] in the past.[80]

It was the third or legislative aspect of reform which led Oresme to his discussion of correction by the multitude and of the convocation of councils. We need not return to this, but before going on to consider the first two aspects of reform it will be useful to look at Oresme's commentary on the section of the *Politics* mentioned in this gloss, to see his attitude toward the changing of laws.

Oresme was less persuaded than Aristotle of the need to retain the habit of following old laws.[81] We may recall his statement that when necessity, utility and the desire of the people were combined in support of changing laws, any laws could be changed provided the net result was beneficial. One may add to this Oresme's remark about removing "unreasonable novelties" among the laws of the church, and the opinion which follows, that to obey such laws without violation or alteration would be improper.[82] Thus we see that even in the church respect for the law should be tempered by concern for expediency and circumstance.

If we take the second aspect of reform to refer to the behavior of clerics already holding benefices, we need say little, because Oresme said little.[83] If,

---

We have seen that the conciliarists were fond of the doctrine of equity, and cited Aristotle when invoking it. Oresme did apply this doctrine to the church, but not to conciliarism. In 3. 24. (fol. 123c–d, p. 160b), he applied *epyeyke* to the distributive function of princes and popes, saying that not even by virtue of this principle could they go against the intentions of the founders of benefices (these intentions being reasonable).

[80] Fol. 124a, p. 160b. For a discussion of reactions to change in the centuries before Oresme, see Beryl Smalley, "Ecclesiastical attitudes to novelty c. 1100–1250," in *Church, Society and Politics*, ed. Derek Baker (Oxford, 1975): 113–131.

[81] See above, chapter 4, nn. 128–133.

[82] "Et que teles lays soient tenues sans enfraindre et aussi sans muer, se ce ne estoit en la maniere ou es cas declarés ou secont livre ou .xv.ᵉ chapitre, et par ceulz a qui il appartient, selon ce que fu dit ou .xiii.ᵉ chapitre" (fol. 124a, p. 160b). The reference to the second book of the *Politics* is to 2. 8. 1267b–1269a, where Aristotle discussed the ideas of Hippodamus of Miletus, and gave reasons for avoiding excessive changes in traditional laws. The reference to "the thirteenth chapter" is probably also to the second book (*Politics* 2. 8. in standard numbering), rather than 3. 13. (the start of *Politics* 3. 11.), which gives arguments for rule by the multitude, and is thus a less likely reference.

[83] This is, however, a matter in which Oresme showed his opinions in practice. While serving as dean at Notre Dame de Rouen, he was associated with measures designed to alter the unedifying behavior of the local clergy. (See Menut, *Le Livre de Politiques*, p. 18a, citing Pierre Adolphe Cheruel, *Histoire de Rouen pendant l'époque communale, 1150–1382*, 2 vols. [Rouen, 1843–1844], 2 [1844], 411–430).

on the other hand, we decide that he was referring to the choice of those who were to occupy benefices, we can discuss this aspect of reform along with the first, under the general heading of distribution of goods.

Oresme's treatment of distributive justice in the church may be divided in turn into three sections. First, he was concerned with the worthiness of potential holders of offices and benefices; that is, with the question to whom goods should be given. Second, he was concerned, as is apparent in his discussion of the church and the "policie moienne," with the imbalance or disproportion of goods as they were distributed in the church. Third, he doubted, as we know, that one man could be competent to distribute benefices throughout Christendom; that is, he was concerned with the question by whom goods should be given.

Oresme did not say anything remarkable about the qualities of proper candidates for positions in the church. He considered the two errors of distributive justice to be the promotion of the unworthy and the choice of inferior candidates over those better qualified.[84] He agreed with Aristotle that the most important qualities in candidates are those which promote the ends of offices and governments.[85] One good quality is not sufficient; all the qualities affecting the office must be considered.[86] Improper weighing of qualities is an oligarchic practice, to be avoided by the governors of the church. Oresme gave three reasons why certain oligarchs might be said to resemble one of Aristotle's species of democracy:

One is that [the rulers] distribute honors and goods to unworthy [persons]. Another is that they appropriate such things to a large extent for themselves and their friends. And the third is that they always reserve offices for the same group of people . . . all the rulers of proper governments, and especially those in the ecclesiastical polity, should above all take precautions lest such conditions arise in their government. . . .[87]

Failure to preserve equality in the church and consequent grasping after offices had already led to great evils in the church.[88]

---

[84] 7. 21. (fol. 272a, p. 313b). See above, n. 63, for a citation from the chapter to which he refers here, and below, n. 100, for a similar remark from Oresme's sermon of Christmas Eve 1363.

[85] See n. 63 above. Aristotle said in *Politics* 3. 12. 1283a (Barker, 131): "Claims to political rights must be based on the ground of contribution to the elements which constitute the being of the state."

[86] 3. 17. (fol. 101b, p. 141b). What Aristotle said in the text which provoked this gloss was: ". . . none of the principles [wealth, birth, goodness, and the strength of numbers: Barker's brackets], in virtue of which men claim to rule and to have all others subject to their rule, is a proper principle" (*Politics* 3. 13. 1283b; Barker, 134). This is not quite the same thing.

[87] 4. 10. (fols. 138d–139a, p. 178a).

[88] ". . . ont esté faictes fraudes, deceptions, faveurs, corruptions et divisions es elections. Et ont obtenu gens non vertueus lesquelz ont distribué malvesement les autres mendres benefices et a gens non dignes, contre la doctrine devant mise au .xv.ᵉ chapitre. Et ainsi le estat sacerdotal est empirié en meurs par dissolutions et pompes et par teles choses; et est cause de le empirement des autres estas" (3. 24. [fol. 123a, p. 160a]). For the reference to "chapter 15," see above, n. 63.

In discussing the proper balance of honors in the state, Oresme like Aristotle argued for proportionality rather than strict equality, and emphasized the need to avoid extremes of wealth and poverty. The first of these principles may be inferred from the statement that office-holders should be chosen according to their ability to contribute to the ends of the state. This cannot be reconciled with the equal participation of all the members in the state, unless it is possible that each citizen can make the same contribution to the state. Neither Aristotle nor Oresme believed this, and neither favored government based on a lack of distinction between citizens who were considered equal because they were equally free.[89] Oresme embellished his development of this theme with a musical example, comparing proper (that is, proportional) distribution within a state (the church was not specifically mentioned) to the melody achieved in a harmonious composition.[90]

The church was mentioned when Oresme discussed the need for a wide distribution of goods and offices. We have seen Aristotle's concern for proper distribution in his praise for the middle-class "polity," the ideal which the church, with its extremes of wealth and poverty, had failed to reach. Oresme, like Aristotle, feared that such disproportion could lead to unrest. His warning to the church neatly joined an Aristotelian metaphor to a Christian one:

. . . Aristotle [says], in criticizing this sort of inequality, that no one who wished to do a proper job of boat-making would make the stern or prow, or any other part, larger than proportion requires. And therefore this church, which is called the boat of Saint Peter, is poorly made and likely to be lost, if the governing part or any other part is large beyond measure and proper proportion, and is likely to perish, espe-

---

[89] This idea is explained in *Politics* 5. 1. 1301a (Barker, 204): "Democracy arose in the strength of an opinion that those who were equal in any one respect were equal absolutely, and in all respects. (Men are prone to think that the fact of their all being equally free-born means that they are all absolutely equal.)" This was translated in the *Livre de Politiques* 5. 1. (fol. 164b, p. 203a) with a gloss that adds little to the text. For a discussion of the principal end of a system of distributive justice, see *Politics* 3. 9. 1280a–1281a.

In one of his glosses on this chapter (3. 10. [fols. 89d–90a, p. 130b]), Oresme discussed proportional equality, or equality based upon contributions to the state, mentioning robber bands and debased governments to show that, even if this sort of equality is good in principle, it is not good if the proportion is based on the ends of an evil association. For Aristotle's description of the arithmetical liberty of democracies, according to which freedom makes all equal, see *Politics* 6. 2. 1317a–b. The comments of Oresme (in 6. 2. [fol. 217b–c, pp. 257b–258a]) are purely explanatory and offer no judgment.

[90] ". . . en chant ou en sons quant appropos, .ii. choses sunt a considerer: une est consonancie, et l'autre est melodie. . . . Et quant les sons sunt equalz ou quant il sunt trop inequalz et hors proporcion deue ce ne est pas consonance. . . . Semblablement en cité, quant as possessions et autres choses, se tous estoient equalz ou se il estoient trop inequalz, ce ne seroit pas bonne ordenance ne bonne consonance. . ."(2. 11. [fol. 49c, p. 92a], from *Politics* 2. 7. 1266b). Oresme referred to the "bel exemple" in 3. 19. (fol. 104a, p. 144b) and in 5. 4. (fol. 170c, p. 209b), and added musical references to his glosses in 2. 7. (fol. 42b–c, p. 85a, where Aristotle also mentions music [*Politics* 2. 5. 1263b]); in 4. 16. (fol. 149c, p. 189a); and in 7. 27. (fol. 278d, p. 321b).

Oresme did not invent this analogy, as he acknowledged in 4. 16. It came from *De civitate Dei* 2. 21., and had in turn been borrowed by Augustine from Cicero (*De re publica* 2. 42.).

cially in times of strife, even though [it was promised that] it would endure forever. . . .[91]

Oresme enumerated the advantages of laws prohibiting excessive wealth: they avoid sedition, promote the common good and the virtue of individual citizens, and conform both to the law of nature and to the purposes of great legislators like Solon, Phaleas, and Lycurgus.[92] For these reasons he did not approve of the pluralistic practices which had arisen in the church contrary to the old laws.[93] Oresme further warned against rapid and excessive promotions,[94] and against the disproportionate increase of one part of the state. Using a corporal analogy, Aristotle had explained how, for example, an increase in the number of poor within a state could lead to constitutional change. Oresme took up this analogy, warning that neither secular nor ecclesiastical government should be allowed to become distorted like a monster, or unsound from head to foot, like the people of Israel as described by Isaiah.[95]

The head of the church must not destroy the soundness of its members. We know that Oresme applied to the pope the principle that rulers must know the qualities of potential office-holders, a requirement favoring local independence, and that he feared papal susceptibility to misdirection and prejudice. To avoid the disadvantages of appointments made by a single man, he recommended the venerable practice of election, giving examples from the earlier history of the church.[96] He continued, with plausible diffidence:

---

[91] 4. 16. (fol. 150b–c, p. 189b). See Hugo Rahner, "Navicula petri. Zur Symbolgeschichte des römischen Primats," *Zeitschrift für katholische Theologie* 79 (1947): 1-35. The text of Aristotle is from *Politics* 3. 13. 1284b: "A shipwright would not tolerate a stern, or any other part of a ship, which was out of proportion" (Barker, p. 136).
  Oresme spoke similarly in 3. 24. (fol. 123a, p. 160a): "Et par aventure, que inequalité bien proporcionee selon ceste regle ne a pas assés esté gardee en la policie de le Église, mes a esté et est en ce inequalité immoderee et trop grande, et si comme dit l'Apostle: Un en a peu et l'autre en a trop [I Corinthians 11:21]. . . ."
[92] 3. 19. (fol. 104a–b, p. 144b).
[93] 3. 19. (fol. 104b, p. 144b). Similarly, in a discussion of the goods and property of the church, Oresme said: ". . . [clergymen] doivent avoir honeste estat, si comme il fu dit ou .xix.ᵉ chapitre, et sans excés. . . . Mes lay doit estre mise que il ne puissent acquerir ou tenir oultre certain terme ou mesure. Et est miex que leur possessions soient moderees et franches que elles fussent excessives et que par celles, autres parties de cité fussent meues a les molester par aucunes exactions" (7. 21. [fol. 269a–b, p. 311a]). In 2. 21. (fols. 67d–68a, p. 111a) Oresme applied to the church Aristotle's arguments for a wide distribution of offices (*Politics* 2. 11. 1273b).
[94] 5. 15. (fol. 187a, p. 227b). For Aristotle, see *Politics* 5. 8. 1308b.
[95] 5. 4. (fol. 170c–d, pp. 209b–210a). Oresme was here glossing *Politics* 5. 3. 1302b–1303a, and citing Isaiah 1:5,6.
[96] ". . . il semble que les dignités et les possessions sacerdotalz furent aucune fois distribuees, ce est assavoir les grandes, par lays de election et aucunes a la conscience des esleus, et institués es grandes dignités oveques correction. . . . un concile general fu a Rome environ l'an de grace .viii.ᶜ .xxvi. [14 and 15 November 826], et le tint Pape Eugenius secundus. Et en ceste concile est expressement deffendu que nul ne soit consacré en evesque qui ne est esleu du clergey et requi du peuple. . . . Unde Celestinus Papa dicit: Nullus invitis ordinetur episcopus plebis enim et clericorum et ordinis consensus et desiderium constat esse requirendum. Et Leo

. . . if the ruler, be he a ruler in the church or elsewhere, should . . . give such an honor and the possessions appertaining to it to someone other than the one to whom it is due according to these laws and canons, it seems that he would be doing the same thing as a king who gave an inheritance to a man other than the rightful heir and lawful successor. [But] perhaps these canons, which were made by a divine legislator, and apply to all of Christendom, are unlike the laws of inheritance.[97]

Many of these ideas on reform and distributive justice appear in Oresme's Christmas Eve sermon of 1363.[98] This sermon, delivered before Urban V in Avignon, was not given in a spirit of holiday celebration. It was a violent denunciation of the church, and a warning of the punishment which would come in the absence of reform. Much of it concerned the improper distribution of goods and benefices. Oresme attacked the "scandalous" inequality in the church, where some died of starvation, and others of indigestion, where some were richer than kings and others poorer than the common masses.[99] He deplored the "promotion of the unworthy and the

---

sanctissimus Papa ait: Nulla enim racio sunt ut inter episcopos habeantur qui nec a clericis sunt electi nec a plebibus expetiti" (3. 24. [fol. 122c–d, p. 159b]). For the section quoted above from the *capitula* of the *Concilium Romanum* of November 826, see *Monumenta Germaniae Historica*. Laws. Section 3: Councils 2: 1 (Hanover and Leipzig, 1906): 569. Menut also gives references for Celestine (Migne, *Patrologia Latina*, 84: 689) and Leo (ibid., p. 765). These citations recall the principle that what touches all should be approved by all, which Oresme applied to the political powers of the multitude (see above, chap. 4, n. 68, from 3. 17. [fol. 101c, p. 142a]). See also Yves Congar, "Quod omnes tangit, ab omnibus tractari et approbari debet," *Revue historique de droit français et étranger*, 4th ser. 36 (1958): 210-259.

[97] 3. 24. (fols. 122d–123a, p. 159b). We have already seen Oresme deny that the secular state can be treated like a private inheritance (see above, chap. 4, nn. 81–88); here he suggests an analogy between the laws of private inheritance and the government of the church, then withdraws it with his customary (and perhaps not entirely candid) diffidence.

This long gloss from 3. 24. is one of the most important discussions of the church in the *Livre de Politiques*. It has been cited extensively in the discussion of conciliarism above. Because of its importance it is worth taking some space to mention the curious history of the gloss. In his article "Nicole Oresme et son commentaire à la 'Politique' d' Aristote" (*Album Helen Maud Cam*, 2 vols. [Louvain and Paris, 1960–1961], 1: 125) Mario Grignaschi notes that in the Avranches manuscript of the *Livre de Politiques* this gloss is cut off after the first few sentences. He suggests that it was deliberately suppressed: "Peut-être ce revirement surprenant s'explique-t-il par le désir de ne pas gêner la politique de Charles V, qui avait accordé son appui au pape d'Avignon, par un appel au Concile Général." But Menut, who used this manuscript for his edition, notes (p. 159a) that in the manuscript, at the end of book 3, the remaining part of the gloss (the offending part, according to Grignaschi) is found at the end of chapter 26, rather than chapter 24. (In fact, it originally had been placed at the end of chapter 27.) Thus the gloss is present in the manuscript, a fact Grignaschi may have missed by consulting it only intermittently.

[98] Oresme mentioned this sermon in the *Livre de Politiques*. At the end of a discussion of distribution in the church, he said: ". . . a ce accordent les sainctes propheties . . . si comme je moustray autrefoiz en la presence du Pape Urban quint" (4. 16. [fol. 150c, p. 189b]). In 5. 14. (fol. 185d, p. 226b), speaking of Aristotle's suggestion that revolutions might be avoided by fostering alarms to make citizens hold tightly to the constitution (*Politics* 5. 8. 1308a), he said: ". . . je moustray en un sermon devant le pape Urban quint et les cardinaulz par la Saincte Escripture et par ceste philosophie les perilz, les causes, la proceineté, les remedes qui povoient resgarder ou touchier la perturbation ou mutation de la policie de l'Eglise." References to the sermon here will come from Francis Meunier, *Essai sur la vie et les ouvrages de Nicole Oresme* (Paris, 1857), which contains a thorough summary of its contents (40–48).

[99] "Alius quidem esurit, alius vero ebrius est . . . li quidem . . . majores quam principes saeculi, caeteri dejectiores vulgo" (Meunier, p. 42, n. 3). We have seen the verse which begins this citation (I Corinth. 11:21) used in the *Livre de Politiques* 3. 24. and 3. 19. (nn. 91, 93, above).

disparagement of the worthy."[100] He spoke of the danger of tyranny in the church, recalling the verses from Ezekiel which he often cited in the *Livre de Politiques*. [101] He did not seem to have great hopes of the hierarchy, for he said that only the promise of the preservation of the church and the grace of God, and not the actions of the prelates, had saved the church from ruin.[102] He denounced the clergy's refusal to be corrected.[103]

Oresme also saw misdistribution and misdirection in the life of the mendicant orders. He criticized them in his sermon, and in his commentaries as well.

Once given the opportunity to apply to the church Aristotle's arguments for the naturalness of private property, and his criticism of the communism of Plato, Oresme was not likely to abstain, for he had strong (and by no means favorable) opinions about the mendicant orders.

The controversy over voluntary poverty and mendicant privilege was not over by the middle of the fourteenth century, as is shown by the reaction to the writings and sermons of Richard Fitzralph.[104] For Oresme, a lively dislike of the mendicant orders may have been a result of his years at the University of Paris, where these orders fought their greatest battle with the secular clergy.[105] Or it may be that his skeptical and realistic temper made him distrust the Franciscan imitation of Christ as a false or impossible analogy. Whatever his reasons, Oresme made an enthusiastic attack upon the Franciscans especially, using a combination of practical argument from Aristotle and moral precept from the New Testament.[106]

The second part of this citation is echoed in a remark from 4. 16., cited above in n. 61. Oresme thought that the clergy had the right to live better than the *populares*, but not to practice *superflua pompa*, which incited indignation rather than respect among the poor (Meunier, 42, n. 4). We shall see more of this attitude in the section on property and poverty in the church.

[100] "Promotio indignorum et vilipensio meliorum . . ." (Meunier, 43, n. 3). See n. 84 above.

[101] "Pastores qui non pascunt gregem Domini sed semetipsos . . . Quibus Dominus dicit: *Vos odio habetis bonum et diligitis malum qui violenter tollitis pelles eorum desuper eos et carnem eorum de super ossibus eorum; et ita comederunt carnes populi mei*" (Meunier, 43, n. 2). See above, n. 58, for references to the use of this verse in the *Livre de Politiques*.

[102] Meunier, 43–44.

[103] "Recusationis correctionis . . . Filii mendaces, filii nolentes audire legem, qui dicunt: *Nolite accipere verbo quae vera sunt, loquimini nobis placentia.* . . . Odio habuerunt in porta corripientem et loquentem perfecte abominati sunt" (Meunier, 43, n. 5).

[104] See Louis Leonor Hammerich, *The Beginning of the Strife between Richard Fitzralph and the Mendicants* (Copenhagen, 1938), Aubrey Osborn Gwynn, *The English Austin Friars in the time of Wyclif* (London, 1940), 80–89, and Gordon Leff, *Richard Fitzralph, commentator of the sentences; a study in theological orthodoxy* (Manchester, 1964). Reginald Lane Poole edited a portion of Fitzralph's *De Pauperie Salvatoris* as an appendix to his edition of the *De Dominio Divino* of John Wyclif (London, 1890). See also Yves Congar, "Aspects ecclésiologiques de la querelle entre mendiants et séculiers dans la seconde moitié du XIIIᵉ siècle et le début du XIVᵉ," *Archives d'Histoire Doctrinal et Littéraire du Moyen Age* 36 (1961): 50–51, 100–101, 151.

[105] See Decima Langworthy Douie, *The Conflict between the seculars and the mendicants at the University of Paris in the thirteenth century* (London, 1954).

[106] It is possible that Oresme wrote a separate treatise against the mendicant orders. (He certainly does not fail to make his opinions clear in the *Livre de Politiques*, as we shall see.) Menut, in "A Provisional Bibliography of Oresme's Writings," *Mediaeval Studies* 28 (1969): 295, lists under "Works of Uncertain Attribution" a treatise entitled *Contra mendicationem*, of which he says: "This is a Latin version of Oresme's attack upon the mendicant friars found in French in the long gloss in *Le Livre de Politiques* II, 6; whether written by Oresme is doubtful."

One of his chief practical arguments concerned the necessity and positive good of property in all governments, including the church.[107] He did not, like Marsilius, abandon Aristotle at the church door in order to turn to the New Testament. Rather, Oresme held that the administrators of the church, like any other administrators (according to Aristotle) need leisure, and for this reason require a secure income and property. Mendicancy did not seem to him a good way of gaining a secure income: "And according to this philosophy the legislators of Holy Church formerly ordained that worthy [persons] be promoted to high office, and to the care of souls, and that they be provided with sufficient wealth to lead honest lives without being reduced to begging or to servile labor."[108]

Oresme gave examples, going back to Egypt, to show that provision had always been made for the support of priests.[109] This practice must therefore be natural to human society:

. . . because this thing is or has been so generally observed, in all times and places, it follows that it must be a natural [observance]: and in the *Nature of the gods* and . . . the *Tusculan Disputations* [Cicero] uses this reasoning, saying that we know the existence of God as a sort of law of nature. . . . And consequently, one might say that it is a natural part of human society that religious officials should be [supported] with no need of mendicancy or servile labor.[110]

---

[107] Of course Oresme made his remarks with his customary humility. One of his disclaimers (7. 19. [fol. 266d, p. 308b]) comes at the end of a sharp attack on the mendicants. Elsewhere, Oresme was bolder: ". . . en ceste matiere aucuns ont escript raisons et allegacions de escriptures, et fait descriptions et distinctions de domaine de proprieté et de usage et d'autre choses et pluseurs altercacions d'une partie et d'autre. Mes quant a present, souffise ce que dit est, car selon la doctrine de Aristote, il semble que nul ne peut tenir le contraire, se ce ne est ou par affection desordenee ou par ignorance de philosophie moral ou par inexperience des choses mondaines" (2. 6. [fol. 42a, p. 84b]). This is the gloss mentioned above in n. 106, as the source of the treatise *Contra mendicationem*.

[108] 2. 21. (fol. 67c, p. 110b). The reference for "ceste philosophie" is *Politics* 2. 11. 1273b (Barker, 86), where Aristotle said that legislators should provide support for the "better sort of citizens" for "the period for which they hold office."

[109] ". . . selon Aristote ou Proheme de *Methaphisique,* premierement en Egypte la gent sacerdotal eut liberté de vaquer as sciences quant il eurent les choses neccessaires a vivre. Item, l'ystoire de Thebes, des Grecs, des Romains et briefment en toutes les hystoires des paiens appert ce que dit est. Et pour ce dit Aristote ou .vi.ᵉ chapitre du secont que telz gens estoient appellés princes et roys. Et dire que princes et roys en leur estat fussent mendians, ce est grande absurdité. . . . Item, en especial en l'*Ystoire des Bretons,* qui estoient en la region a present appellee Angleterre, appert comment environ l'an de grace .cl. quant le roy Lucius fu converti a nostre foy. . . . le roy donna as eglises toutes les possessions et territoires des temples et encor plus. . . . Item, en la lay de Moïse est contenu comment ceulz de cest office avoient les dismes, les primices, les oblations, etc. Et en la lay de Grece il ont dismes, oblations, possessions, etc. Et meismes Macomet en son *Alcoran* dit souvent que l'en doit paier les dismes" (7. 19. [fol. 266a–b, pp. 307b–308a]).

For the reference to the *Metaphysics,* see 1. 1. 981b, on Egypt's mathematician priests. I have been unable to find a reference to priests as princes in *Politics* 2. 5. 1263b (Oresme's 2. 6.), which is part of a discussion of Plato's communism. For the reference to Geoffrey of Monmouth's *Historia regum Britanniae,* see the variant edition by Jacob Hammer (Cambridge, Mass., 1951), 84–85 and 85–86, which correspond to Menut's references to 4. 397–412 (or more precisely, 407–412) and 5. 4–5 (or 1–5).

[110] 7. 19. (fol. 266b, p. 308a). The references to Cicero are: *De natura deorum* 1. 17. (pp. 44, 46, of the Loeb edition with translation by Harris Rackham [London and New York, 1933]):

Once again, Oresme, though believing that the Christian clergy was directly established by God, treated it as an institution which shares with human organizations in general, and even pagan and infidel priesthoods in particular, certain requirements for political life.

Support for a priesthood had been a feature of Aristotle's ideal city.[111] According to Oresme, he would have considered voluntary poverty harmful to civil life and to contemplation.

> But it is still more foreign to the ethical conceptions of Aristotle to recommend voluntary poverty, to say that the most perfect estate is to have or to own nothing, either individually or in common . . . such a thing would seem discordant with good government. But the law of Jesus Christ is not discordant with [good government], according to a letter of Saint Augustine. . . . [Moreover] . . . if an abundance of riches is an impediment to contemplation, so also is poverty . . . for this reason, in ancient times contemplatives were accustomed to do manual labor.[112]

According to political science, mendicants are not to be considered part of the city. In 5. 31., where Aristotle said that "a state is composed of two sections — the poor and the rich,"[113] Oresme remarked, "He does not mean mendicants when he speaks of the poor; for according to this science they are no part of the city. Rather, he is referring to small householders, for example laborers and craftsmen."[114]

Oresme considered voluntary poverty not only inconvenient when practiced but unlikely to be practiced at all. He was not impressed by the delicate

---

". . . intellegi necesse esse deos, quoniam insitas eorum vel potius innatas cognitiones habemus; de quo autem omnium natura consentit, id verum esse necesse est; esse igitur deos confitendum est"; *Tusculan Disputations* 1. 13. (p. 36 in the Loeb edition with translation by J. E. King [London and New York, 1927]): ". . . omni autem in re consensio omnium gentium lex naturae putanda est . . . ."

[111] *Politics* 7. 9. 1329a; also 7. 10. 1330a. Oresme referred to this in a gloss from 7. 21. (fol. 269b, p. 311a): "Or avons donques par le .xix.ᵉ chapitre que ceulz d'office sacerdotal doivent avoir possessions, et avons par cestui comment elles doivent estre moderee." See Marcel Pacaut's introduction to G. H. M. Posthumus Meyjes, *Jean Gerson et L'Assemblée de Vincennes (1329). Ses conceptions de la juridiction temporelle de l'Église* (Leiden, 1978), p. xiv, where it is said that for Gerson ecclesiastical property is "une nécessité conforme au bon ordre de la société."

[112] 2. 6. (fol. 40c–d, p. 83a–b). Menut's reference for Augustine is Migne, *PL*, 33: 686, from Epistola 157. 4: "Hic utique dicunt, ideo patres antiquos non vendidisse omnia quae habebant, et dedisse pauperibus, quia hoc eis non praeceperat Dominus."

The life of voluntary poverty was "more foreign to the ethical conceptions of Aristotle," according to Oresme, than the community of possessions proposed by Plato, which was criticized in *Politics* 2. 5. 1263b ("The life which they are to live appears to be utterly impossible"; Barker, 51). This is the chapter Oresme is glossing here.

Oresme spoke similarly in *Le Livre de Politiques* 1. 2. (fols. 8d–9a, p. 50a), speaking of holy hermits who are as gods, not beasts, in Aristotle's distinction. In 4. 12. (fol. 141a, p. 180b) he spoke of the moral harm done by poverty, and in 7. 19. (fol. 266c, p. 308a), he spoke again of the political harm done by mendicancy. The distinction between poverty "prise pour indigence et deffaute" and the poverty "prise pour avoir ce de petit qui souffist," which respectively damage and promote felicity, was made in 7. 27. (fol. 278d, p. 321b), as it is made in the gloss from 2. 6. cited above (in a part which has not been included in the citation). See also the *Livre de Ethiques* 10. 12. (fol. 210d, p. 520), and 10. 16. (fol. 214d, p. 528).

[113] *Politics* 5. 11. 1315a (Barker, p. 249).

[114] Fol. 209d, p. 251a.

distinctions between use and ownership which had been employed to describe the circumstances of the mendicants:

> . . . it is likely that as time passed . . . there would be a reversion to the [present disposition of] possessions, except that there might be common ownership of fields. . . . And in fact things would be just as they are at present, no matter how much it is said: "This thing is not my own [possession]; rather, I am using it." And similarly, there are some who say that they own nothing either singly or in common, and nevertheless [as regards property] they live just like others. And some buy and sell, etc.[115]

The attitude of Oresme toward these theories of property reminds us of his remarks on the empire, where he rebuked those who placed their trust in poetic fictions. "And it would seem according to . . . Aristotle that such opinions [as the community of possessions] are dangerous to states, and are moreover like thought experiments which cannot properly be brought into practice."[116]

As Oresme saw willful misrepresentation in the defense of apostolic poverty, so he saw cynical self-interest in the attack upon clerical possessions. Speaking of demagogues who seek popular favor by "forc[ing] [the notables] to break up their estates"[117] or, as Moerbeke and Oresme have it, by division of property and religious revenue,[118] Oresme said that these "flatterers and adulators of the people" are like "those who preach to the people against clergymen who have possessions."[119]

---

[115] 2. 7. (fol. 43a, p. 85b). Compare this to the citation from 2. 6. which appears above in n. 107. Oresme expressed a similar opinion in his sermon of Christmas Eve 1363: "Fatue disputaverunt de paupertate Christi. . . . In omni gente et lege vulgata de jure, quod est proprie naturale, sacerdotes habuerunt et debent habere unde possent vivere honestius quam populares. . . . Sed ex hoc non conceduntur equitaturae seu familiae superflua pompa quae raro potest absque superbia duci et salva justitia sustineri" (cited from Meunier, *Essai sur la vie et les ouvrages*, 42, n. 4).

[116] 2. 6. (fol. 42a, p. 84b). See above, chapter 3, n. 135, for the discussion of the empire. Gerard of Abbeville had dismissed the distinction of *usus* and *dominium* as a legal fiction (John Moorman, *A History of the Franciscan Order* [Oxford, 1968], 130). Admittedly, this is not quite the same thing as an *ymaginacion*.
Oresme did make use of a distinction between ownership and use, in an example we shall meet again in the discussion of church and state. In 3. 20. (fol. 107c–d, p. 148a) he discussed the ancient kings who were "seigneurs de la presidence qui est selon les guerres et de toutes les substances ou possessions quelcunques que ne appartiennent a prestres." His gloss is: "Et dez autres possessions il ne avoient pas de toutes la seigneurie en propreté ou en usage, que l'en appelle 'dominium utile'; mes il avoient la seigneurie en souveraineté et la jurisdiction, ce que l'en appelle 'dominium directum' " (fol. 107d, p. 148a). It is unfortunate (but irrelevant here) that this gloss is based on a mistranslation of Aristotle.
This distinction was also used in Oresme's discussion of usury (1. 12. [fols. 24d–25b, pp. 67b–68a]).

[117] *Politics* 5. 5. 1305a (Barker, 215).

[118] Oresme said that these demagogues "funt acroire au peuple que les substances et possessions doivent estre parties equalment, ou les rentes qui sunt pour les sacrifices" (5. 8. [fol. 176a, p. 215b]), taking his text from Moerbeke's "vel substantias aeque partiales facientes vel reditus sacrificiis" (Susemihl, 520, lines 4–5).

[119] 5. 8. (fol. 176a, p. 216a). Similarly, in 2. 6. (fol. 40d, p. 84b), he said: "Et par aventure, aucuns qui loent et commendent ceste povreté ne la tiennent pas . . . si comme dit Seneque ou livre de *Declamacions:* Facilius est paupertatem laudare quam ferre. . . . puisque leur oevres

Oresme was not merely a critic of apostolic poverty; like John of Paris he wished to pursue a moderate solution to the problem of property in the church, to be neither a Waldensian nor a Herod.[120] Oresme thought that both parties in the dispute over poverty made exaggerated claims, and were so far from a reasonable accommodation that they endangered the stability of the church:

> . . . in recent times some poor men in this [ecclesiastical] polity have murmured and argued against the others, saying that clergymen should not have [even moderate] possessions. . . . And the others, on the contrary, despised them and said that they were envious, wicked, and [nothing more than] beggars and thieves. And some of them held that [clergymen] should be sovereign lords of all things, both spiritual and temporal. And each party like the other introduced on its behalf [passages from] scripture, and specious arguments unsupported by any evidence. . . . [both of] these opinions are very far from a proper balance. And therefore . . . this government is in danger of disturbance or mutation.[121]

When he presented ethical arguments against voluntary poverty, Oresme did not entirely ignore Aristotle, but he relied more upon the Bible. It is significant that he borrowed from the Bible chiefly moral injunctions; he did not take it upon himself to interpret the records of the lives of Christ and the apostles, which had been the center of much of the controversy over poverty.[122]

Oresme did not criticize those who fell into poverty or mendicancy through no fault of their own, or chose to live with few possessions. Acci-

---

et leur vie est contraire a ce que il dient, leur sermons ne sunt pas a croire. Et pourroit aucun avoir suspicion que il ne dient teles choses fors pour esmouvoir les cuers des genz afin que il soient améz et honoréz et que l'en leur donne." Menut's reference for (the Elder) Seneca is *Controversiae* 2. 1. 18.: *"Facilius possum paupertatem laudare quam ferre"* (in the Loeb edition of 2 vols., with translation by M. Winterbottom [Cambridge, Mass. and London, 1974]; 1: 224).

This remark of Seneca also turns up in the *Livre de Ethiques* 4. 3. (fol. 67d, p. 234), and ibid., 10. 16. (fol. 215b, p. 529). In the same book (4. 24. [fol. 86a, p. 269]) Oresme extended the charge of hypocrisy to the Spartans and the Dominicans. Marsilius of Padua spoke similarly of hypocrites in the *Defensor Pacis* 2. 11. 3., citing *Ethics* 10. 1. 1172a.

[120] John of Paris, *De reg. pot. et pap.*, prohemium (ed. Bleienstein, 69–70): "Nam error Valdensium fuit successoribus apostolorum, scilicet papae et praelatis ecclesiasticis, repugnare dominium in temporalibus nec eis licere habere divitias temporales. . . . Alius vero error fuit Herodis, qui audiens Christum regem natum credidit ipsum regem esse terrenum. Ex quo derivari videtur opinio quorundam modernorum, qui in tantum supradictum errorem Valdensium declinant ad oppositum totaliter deflexi, ut asserant dominum papam in quantum est loco Christi in terris habere dominium in temporalibus bonis principum et baronum et cognitionem seu iurisdictionem."

[121] *Le Livre de Politiques* 4. 16. (fol. 150b, p. 189b). This excerpt comes from the same gloss as the excerpt on disproportion quoted above, n. 91. The connection between disproportion and voluntary poverty is quite clear.

[122] Oresme did mention the requirement that the apostles give up their possessions. This and similar commands had been used by the emperor Julian to justify the confiscation of the goods of the church (see Charles Norris Cochrane, *Christianity and Classical Culture*, rev. ed. [London, 1944], 284). Oresme criticized this imperial hypocrisy: "Et ne entendoit pas la parole de Dieu si comme Julian l'Apostat le alleguoit pour oster as Crestiens leur facultés en colorant son avarice par ce que Jhesu Crist dit: Qui non renunciat omnibus que possidet non potest meus discipulus esse [Luke 14:33]" (*Le Livre de Politiques* 7. 19. [fol. 266a, p. 307b]).

dental poverty was for him a misfortune to be alleviated (certainly not a condition to be praised), while a voluntary simplicity was to be admired as appropriate to a life of contemplation, so long as it was supported by honest labor.[123] On the other hand, Oresme found two great faults in the voluntary poverty of the mendicant orders. This poverty, he thought, was at once servile and degrading to those who practiced it, and unfair to those whose property was used to support it. Thus he followed a single standard, judging poverty in the church as he judged poverty outside it.

We have already seen Oresme's distaste for the practice of mendicancy, for example in the gloss from 2. 21., where he said that the clergy should have enough wealth "to lead honest lives, without being reduced to begging or to servile labor." In his long gloss on the qualities required in priests, Oresme listed mendicancy as an impediment to the priesthood, along with deformity, epilepsy, idiocy, vice, vile or lowly estate, and bigamy.[124] He had harsh words for "those who are called *validi mendicantes,* " whose practice is "vicious and reproved by the law."[125] In the same chapter, he said that it would be a great impropriety if priests chosen (like those of Aristotle's ideal city) from former warriors and deliberators, were to end their days as mendicants.[126]

Oresme's discussion of the second error of the mendicants, that is, their use of the goods of others, made more reference to the Bible, but this concerned the moral teachings of Christ and his followers rather than the lives and practices of the apostles. Oresme recalled that giving is more blessed than receiving (Acts 20:35). Receiving through mendicancy, moreover, seemed to him a source of *sollicitudo:*

And if it is less good to receive than to give, it is even worse to demand [support] and to beg. . . . Saint Clement . . . made [Christians] work, according to the doctrine of Saint Paul. And perhaps in doing this they had less worry and less hindrance to contemplation than they would have had in procuring their necessities through the use of things belonging to others. . . .[127]

Oresme explained the poverty of the early Christians as one of giving rather than receiving:

Also, in 2 Corinthians 8, where Saint Paul commends the poverty of those in Macedonia, saying: ". . . their very deep poverty hath abounded unto the riches of their simplicity" [verse 2: Douay Version], the gloss says: "The highest, that is the great or most noble goodness of mind. They were poor in possessions but rich in

---

[123] 7. 19. (fol. 265c–d, p. 307a–b).

[124] 7. 19. (fols. 264d–266d, pp. 306b–308b).

[125] Ibid., fol. 265d, p. 307b. Oresme continued, citing Virgil on "turpis Egestas" (*Aeneid* 6. 276), Luke 16:3, Psalms 108: 10 and 36: 25, and Jerome's "epistre *Ad Vigilancium*" (see Migne, *PL* 23: 366).

[126] 7. 19. (fol. 267a, p. 308b). See also below, chapter 6, n. 67.

[127] 2. 6. (fol. 41b–c, p. 84a). Here Oresme shows a strong sense of individual property rights. Perhaps he saw both Franciscan mendicancy and royal taxation as violations of these rights, and as evils affecting their subjects as well as their objects. See also the *Songe du Vergier* 2. 267. (ed. Brunet 2: 125).

giving, because governed by a pure conscience, etc." . . . And therefore they did not live without owning anything and did not beg, but they gave, in accordance with what Our Lord said: "Give to the poor" [Matthew 19:21]. And he did not say "Take from the rich."[128]

The alternative to begging was of course work. In the same gloss Oresme further examined the practices of the early church.

. . . it was the doctrine of Saint Paul that [contemplatives] should work, for he said in 2 Thessalonians 3: "For yourselves know how you ought to imitate us. For we were not disorderly among you. Neither did we eat any man's bread for nothing: but in labour and toil we worked night and day, etc." [verses 7, 8: Douay Version]. . . . To which the Apostle adds: "For also, when we were with you, this we declared to you: that, if any man will not work, neither let him eat" [verse 10: Douay Version].[129]

The interpretation of the *Glossa ordinaria* was then introduced to show that this imperative of labor did not contradict the lesson of the lilies of the field, that one must not concern oneself with how one will live.[130] Christians were to be encouraged to provide for themselves "such things as were needful" after the example of Saint Paul, who had coveted no man's riches, [131] and thus avoided the moral dangers which Oresme considered inherent in mendicancy.

It is not surprising that Oresme made more use of the Bible than of Aristotle when making ethical arguments against the friars. The desire of the mendicant orders, especially the Franciscans, to base their practice upon example rather than upon first principles or universal custom, and the extraordinary legal tangles and evasions which arose out of the imitation of lives spent in simplicity, were perhaps more foreign to the conceptions of Aristotle than were the theories of papal absolutism. Oresme was able to use the *Politics* for his practical arguments, displaying the realism which we have already seen in his discussion of the empire. Aristotle supplied common sense — but the defenders of the mendicants might have argued that common sense was not to the point in this matter.

There was perhaps no good way for the medieval thinker to bridge the gap between Athens and Jerusalem. The city-state and the universal church were not to be reconciled. Thus a medieval theorist with the *Politics* before him had set himself a difficult task. This task could be approached by exclusion or by combination.

First, the excluding writer could comment on the text of the *Politics* and ignore the church. This, as we have seen, was what was done in the earliest commentaries. This choice looks sensible to us but it suited only the limited

---

[128] Ibid., fol. 41b, p. 84a–b. Menut's reference for Walafrid Strabo is *Glossa ordinaria* on 2 Corinthians 8:2 (Migne, *PL*, 114: 562), where the phrase about "goodness of mind" is not however to be found.

[129] Fol. 41a, p. 83b.

[130] The text of Walafrid Strabo, cited by Oresme in fol. 41a, pp. 83b–84a, is found in Migne, *PL*, 114: 624.

[131] In fol. 41b, p. 84a, Oresme cites Acts 20:34, 33.

compass of an explication of Aristotle's text. It did not provide a properly comprehensive theory for the thirteenth and fourteenth centuries. Second, a writer who did choose to write about the church could ignore Aristotle. But this too would have been an inadequate and uncongenial solution. It was indeed hard to make Aristotle at home in the Middle Ages, or to make the Middle Ages at home in Aristotle, yet it was equally hard for writers in search of order and authority to resist him.

The writer could try to meet both Aristotle and the church head-on. Such an attempt occurs in the *Defensor Pacis*, with a double standard in use. In his first discourse Marsilius treated the state (and by implication the pretensions of the church) as an Aristotelian, in a naturalistic and rationalistic manner. In the second discourse he spoke directly of the church, and wrote as an interpreter of scripture. Here Aristotle seldom appears. Marsilius did not give much space to the perennial medieval question, the relative superiority of the ends of the secular and ecclesiastical organizations.[132] Nor did Oresme, although his approach to the problem of Aristotle and the church was based more on a single standard. He hesitated and made obeisance before the guardians of things spiritual, then went on to consider the church as a political organization which stood in need of Aristotle's advice, just as much as did the kingdom of France. Whatever was said in the *Politics* about good government, lawmaking or the distribution of goods could be applied to the ecclesiastical polity. If the theory and practice of the mendicant orders looked absurd and impractical when viewed through the eyes of Aristotle, so be it. The problems of church and state could also be dealt with in this way.

---

[132] Alan Gewirth, *Marsilius of Padua. The Defender of Peace*, 2 vols. (New York, 1951–1956), 2: lii.

VI. ARISTOTLE, ORESME, AND GALLICANISM

In the background of Oresme's glosses on church and state Gallicanism is the predominant (if indistinct) feature. Perhaps Gallicanism is in the distance, for as Victor Martin has said, one cannot speak of this doctrine in its proper sense before the end of the fourteenth century.[1] Therefore what we must look for in the *Livre de Politiques* are the ideas which would become characteristic of Gallicanism. These are clearly present.

According to Martin the central principles of Gallicanism are these: the king of France is independent of the papacy in temporal matters; the General Council is superior to the pope; and the clergy and king are to cooperate to preserve the ancient liberties of the French church.[2] The quarrel between Philip the Fair and Boniface VIII, and the literature inspired by this conflict, provide an example of the practice and theory of the first principle: we may remember also the related actions of Philip against the Templars. The support of the faculty of the University of Paris for the prerogatives of the General Council provides an example of the second principle.[3] The dispute over the privileges of the mendicant orders at the same university was, as Schleyer has shown,[4] part of the development of Gallican theories about the relation between the papacy and the French nation, even as it raised serious questions about authority within the church itself.

A further characteristic of Gallicanism is nearly as important as these

---

[1] *Les origines du Gallicanisme,* 2 vols. in one (Paris, 1939), 1: 34–35. See also Georges de Lagarde, "Le 'Songe du Verger' et les origines du gallicanisme," *Revue des sciences religieuses* 14 (1934): 1–33, 219–237, and Kurt Schleyer, *Anfänge des Gallikanismus im 13. Jahrhundert. Der Widerstand des französischen Klerus gegen die Privilegierung der Bettelorden* (Berlin, 1937). For more general material, see n. 16 of the preceding chapter, with special attention to be given to the works of Ladner and Lagarde. Other useful works on church and state include: Nöel Valois, *La France et le grand schisme d'occident,* 4 vols. (Paris, 1896–1902); Jean Rivière, *Le problème de l'église et de l'état au temps de Philippe de Bel: étude de théologie positive* (Paris, 1926) and Georges Digard, *Philippe le Bel et le Saint-Siège de 1285 à 1304,* 2 vols. (Paris, 1936).

For the use of Aristotle in the formulation of doctrine on this question, see Martin Grabmann, "Studien über den Einfluss der aristotelischen Philosophie auf die mittelalterlichen Theorien über das Verhältnis von Kirche und Staat," *Sitzungsberichte der Bayerischen Akademie der Wissenschaften zu München, Philosophisch-Historische Abteilung,* 1934, part 2: 3–163; the review of this work by Georges de Lagarde, in *Revue historique de droit français et étranger,* 4th ser. 15 (1936): 360–364; and Werner Gebauer, "Die Aufnahme der Politik des Aristoteles und die naturrechtlich Begründung des Staates durch Thomas von Aquino," *Vierteljahrschrift für Sozial-und Wirtschaftsgeschichte* 29 (1936): 137–160.

[2] *Les origines du Gallicanisme,* 1: 7.

[3] Lagarde, "Le 'Songe du Verger,'" 227–228, with reference to Victor Martin, *Le Gallicanisme politique et le clergé de France* (Paris, 1929), 25–40.

[4] See the citation in n. 1; see also P. Glorieux, "Prélats français contre Religieux mendiants. Autour du bulle 'Ad fructus uberes' (1281–1290)," *Revue d'histoire de l'église en France* 11(1925): 309–331; 471–475, and Alan E. Bernstein, "Magisterium and License: Corporate Autonomy against Papal Authority in the Medieval University of Paris," *Viator* 9 (1978): 291, 300–307.

principles. This is its confinement to France.[5] Gallican writers used arguments about the relative superiority of temporal and spiritual government, but they did not wish to create a general theory of church and state relations. The French church and kingdom were thought by these writers to have a special, even unique, status, by virtue of the qualities and privileges of their kings. The emperor, for example, was held to be quite a different thing from a French king, as regarded his connection to the pope. Gallican writers might be willing, and indeed eager, to admit that the emperor received his powers through his coronation by the pope. But this derivation, which provided the papacy with much ammunition against insubordinate emperors, was quite unlike the derivation of the authority of the French king, which was proposed by Gallicanism.[6]

As they sought independence from the papacy the French kings could draw with great profit upon their own religious traditions. The long association of the French monarchy with the papacy, the special signs of divine favor, such as the *sainte ampoule* and the royal touch, and the personal sanctity of Louis IX, were among the proofs of the holiness of France, her kings, and her people.[7] These characteristics gave the kings a weapon to be used against all their opponents: the empire, the papacy, the rulers of less favored countries,[8] and mere unconsecrated nobles. As the royal government gained an effectiveness which was difficult to resist, its authority gained a sanctification which was dangerous to deny.[9] Philip IV's minister

[5] Martin, *Les origines du Gallicanisme*, 1: 39, 224.

[6] See Charles T. Wood, "Queens, Queans, and Kingship: An Inquiry into Theories of Royal Legitimacy in Late Medieval England and France," in William C. Jordan, Bruce McNab and Teofilo F. Ruiz, eds., *Order and Innovation in the Middle Ages* (Princeton, 1976), 395, 565, citing Fritz Kern, *Kingship and Law in the Middle Ages* (New York, 1956), 20, n. 11. The papacy was not of course inclined to allow mere *reguli* or kinglets to slip through its fingers. Innocent IV, for example, admitted that only in the case of the empire did a special relationship between pope and ruler allow the pope as feudal overlord to assume governmental rights in case of vacancy. But, he added, the pope could succeed to the jurisdiction of other rulers as a result of his plenitude of power (see R. W. Carlyle and A. J. Carlyle, *A History of Mediaeval Political Thought*, 6 vols. [Edinburgh and London, 1903–1936], 5: 322, n. 1, from Inn. IV on *Decretales*, 2. 2. 10. *Licet*[c. 1250] No. 79, *Commentaria*). See also Jean-Pierre Royer, *L'Église et le royaume de France au XIVᵉ siècle d'après le "Songe du Vergier" et la jurisprudence du Parlement* (Paris, 1969), 137.

[7] Martin, *Les origines du Gallicanisme*, 1: 71. See also Marc Bloch, *Les rois thaumaturges. Étude sur le caractère surnaturel attribué à la puissance royale, particulièrement en France et en Angleterre* (Strasbourg and Paris, 1924); Ernst Kantorowicz, *The King's Two Bodies* (Princeton, 1957); and Joseph R. Strayer, "France: The Holy Land, the Chosen People, and the Most Christian King," in T. K. Rabb and J. E. Seigal, eds., *Action and Conviction in Early Modern Europe* (Princeton, 1969): 3–16; also in Strayer's *Medieval Statecraft and the Perspectives of History* (Princeton, 1971): 300–314.

[8] Where royal traditions were shared by more than one monarchy, their application could have unexpected effects. A man was imprisoned in Normandy from 1347 to 1353 for asserting that Edward III was the best king for France because his healing power was the best (P. S. Lewis, *Later Medieval France* [London, 1968], 62, from Raymond Cazelles, *La Société politique et la crise de la royauté sous Philippe de Valois* [Paris, 1958], 204). See also Wood, as cited above in n. 6, pp. 398, 566, on the thirteenth-century poet Richier, who derided kings who must buy the oil used for their coronations, rather than receive it from heaven (citing Bloch, *Les rois thaumaturges*, 229).

[9] Strayer, "France: The Holy Land" (from *Medieval Statecraft*), 307, mentions the patriotic sermons of the Dominican Guillaume de Sauqueville (ca. 1300), who compared the king of

Nogaret even attempted to make of his master's assault on Boniface VIII, a defense of the church, for France was too essential a part of the church to allow itself to be harmed.[10] Whatever their relations with the papacy, or their treatment of individual popes, the most Christian kings of France avoided heresy and schism, and thus retained their claim to preeminence.

Charles V continued the traditions of the royal religion, and added flourishes of his own.[11] Christine de Pisan described the careful attention given by the king to ceremonies which would impress his subjects.[12] Charles spoke of his ancestor Louis IX, whose memory would be blessed until the end of time.[13] Royal titles with religious significance were frequently used: "king by the grace of God"[14] and the more specific "most Catholic" or "most Christian" king.[15] The old legends were enhanced, for example those of the fleur-de-lis[16] and the oriflamme, which acquired a supernatural significance.[17]

France to Christ. As Strayer says, "If the king of France is a type of Christ and if, as Guillaume implies, the kingdom of France is a type of the heavenly kingdom, then resistance to the king and attacks on the kingdom are obviously sinful."

[10] Ibid., pp. 309–310. See Pierre Dupuy, *Histoire du différend d'entre le pape Boniface VIII et Philippes le Bel* (Paris, 1655), 243, where we see Nogaret speaking of the defense of France: "Item quod cum ad conservationem et defensionem corporis universi Catholicae Ecclesiae, necessaria sit conservatio, ac defensio partium corporis ipsius, et maxime tam magnae partis, tam egregiae, corporis ipsius Ecclesiae, ut est regnum Francie, cum ipsa Ecclesia in partibus suis consistat." See Ernst Kantorowicz, "*Pro Patria Mori* in Medieval Political Thought," *American Historical Review* 56 (1950–1951): 483–484, for reference to an anonymous sermon from the time of Philip IV, in which war against the king of France is equated with war against the whole church. (This is cited from Jean Leclerq, "Un sermon prononcé pendant la guerre de Flandre sous Philippe le Bel," *Revue du moyen âge latin* 1 [1945]: 165–172.)

[11] Bloch, *Les rois thaumaturges*, 136, 137, 138. See also Gaston Dodu, "Les idées de Charles V en matière de gouvernement," *Revue des questions historiques*, 3rd ser. 14 (1929): 26, and Gaston Zeller, "Les rois de France candidats à l'empire; Essai sur l'idéologie impériale," *Revue historique* 173 (1934): 304. Kantorowicz (*The King's Two Bodies*, 218) speaks of the "mysticism of French kingship, which reached its first growth in and after the times of Charles V." François Avril (*Manuscript Painting at the Court of France. The Fourteenth Century [1310–1380]*, trans. Ursule Molinaro, Bruce Benderson [New York, 1978], 112) says of an illustration in the breviary of Charles: "The thoroughly audacious idea expressed in this image, which stresses the privileged relationship between God and his foremost chosen one, the King of France, agrees perfectly with Charles V's theocratic concept of royal power."

[12] *Le Livre des fais et bonnes meurs du sage roy Charles V*, 2 vols., edited by S. Solente (Paris, 1936–1940), 1: 51, chap. 1. 18.

[13] Lewis, *Later Medieval France*, 83–84, from François André Isambert, *Recueil général des anciennes lois françaises, depuis l'an 420 jusqu'à la révolution de 1789*, 29 vols. (Paris, 1821–1833), 5: 419: ". . . cujus memoria in benedictione est, et non derelinquetur in secula . . . ." Jean Golein spoke of Charles's "sainte et sacrée lignie" (Bloch, *Les rois thaumaturges*, 243).

[14] Dodu, "Les idées de Charles V," 26, mentions the many ordinances given by "Charles, par la grâce de Dieu, roi de France" or "Karolus Dei gratia Francorum rex."

[15] Zeller, "Les rois de France candidats à l'empire," 306. Charles is described in the prologue to Raoul de Presles's translation of *The City of God* as "le plus grand, le plus hault, et le plus catholique et le plus puissant roy chrestien" (fols. 1–2 of the 1531 edition). See also Lewis, *Later Medieval France*, 82. For examples of this usage in the translations of Oresme, see above, chapter 3, n. 166.

[16] Lewis, *Later Medieval France*, 83. It had adorned the arms of France since Philip Augustus. For the fleur-de-lis in the *Livre de Politiques*, see above, chapter 3, n. 173.

[17] Lewis, *Later Medieval France*, 83.

At the center of Charles's political theology were his priestly or priest-like attributes.[18] The role of a Melchizedek was suited to this sickly king, who was unable physically (and perhaps by temperament) to be a warrior. For this role the coronation and unction were especially significant. In order to make the coronation resemble an episcopal ordination, Charles wore gloves like those of bishops,[19] and took from the latter ceremony the benediction of the ring.[20] He was also careful to diminish the effect of those religious prerogatives which he was unable to emulate. His imperial uncle Charles IV was entitled to say matins, but he was not allowed to do so during his visit to France in 1378.[21]

The most dramatic claim made for the French king (certainly some consolation for the matins) was that of the royal touch. The idea that a king, by virtue of his anointing with the sainte ampoule, had the ability to cure scrofula was not invented during the reign of Charles V, but the claim was first made explicitly in one of his charters for 1380.[22] Charles's publicists did not fail to exploit this claim: the enthusiastic Raoul de Presles congratulated the king upon his ability to perform miracles during his lifetime.[23]

The royal religion, like the imperial coronation, could actually work to the disadvantage of the monarch if it made him subordinate to the church. Royal supporters must demonstrate that the king's attributes did not depend upon clerical intervention. The author of the *Songe du Vergier* denied that the special grace given by God to the king came from unction. If it did, he said, all anointed kings would possess the blessings enjoyed by the French king.[24] The coronation, consecration, and unction were to be considered mere human inventions,[25] by which the church sanctioned powers already possessed.[26]

---

[18] See Marcel David, *La souveraineté et les limites juridiques du pouvoir monarchique du IXᵉ au XVᵉ siècle* (Paris, 1954), 228, and Lewis, *Later Medieval France*, 81–82.

[19] Bloch, *Les rois thaumaturges*, 204.

[20] Kantorowicz, *The King's Two Bodies*, 222 and n. 84. See above, chapter 4, n. 10, for the connection between this benediction and the inalienability of sovereignty.

[21] Bloch, *Les rois thaumaturges*, 204.

[22] Cited ibid., 135, n. 1, from a charter in favor of a chapter at Reims, from Guillaume Marlot, *Historia ecclesie Remensis*, 4 vols. (Reims, 1843–1846), 2: 660.

[23] Ibid., 136, from Presles's preface to his translation of the *City of God* (Paris, 1531), fol. a3ᵛᵒ:". . . vous faictes miracles en vostre vie telles, si grandes et si apertes que vous garissiez d'une tres horrible maladie qui s'appelle les escroelles de laquelle nul autre prince terrien ne peut garir fors vous." Jean Golein, on the other hand, denied that any but God could make a miracle (Bloch, pp. 140 and 488, citing his *Traité du sacre* [MS. Paris, B. N. fr. 437, fol. 54 and vᵒ]). The royal touch does not seem to be mentioned in the *Livre de Politiques* (see above, chapter 3, n. 167).

[24] Bloch, *Les rois thaumaturges*, 222. The *Songe* appears in an edition by Jean Louis Brunet, in vol. 2 of Pierre Dupuy, *Traitez des droits et libertez de l'église gallicane*, rev. ed., 4 vols. (Paris, 1731–1751). For this reference, see 1. 80. (p. 82).

[25] Dodu, "Les idées de Charles V," 45, from *Songe* 1. 74. (pp. 75–76); 1. 76. (pp. 77–78).

[26] *Songe* 1. 76. (p. 78). See also Bloch, *Les rois thaumaturges*, 222, and David, *La souveraineté*, 242, who says that these ceremonies were thought to have a "portée déclarative," rather than a constructive significance. The author of the *Songe* also says that kings, having existed before popes, are independent of them (1. 100. [p. 107], as cited in Dodu, "Les idées de Charles V," p. 45). He also denied that Christ ever exercised temporal jurisdiction (2. 1. [p. 1]; for such a denial in the *Livre de Politiques*, see 3. 23. [fol. 116b–c, p. 156a]), and remarked that Saint Peter had not been made a *chevalier* (1. 7. [p. 17]).

By the time of Charles V, the king, according to political writers, enjoyed an independence from the papacy similar to his independence from the empire.[27] Here again, many writers (John of Paris was an exception) had concerned themselves primarily with the independence of France and her most Christian king, rather than with general theories of church and state relations. The supposed liberties of the Gallican church were also defended in practice by French kings. If the defense of these by Philip IV became violent, while that by Louis IX was merely vigilant, both were determined to resist papal interference in the affairs of the French church.[28] By the time of Charles V, the papacy had moved to Avignon, where its interests were often those of its royal protector.[29] The popes were not hindered in their regulation of the internal affairs of the church, but they could assert only a certain independence, rather than a right to intervene.[30] Charles obtained some advantages, and presided over a rapprochement between the French monarchy and clergy which bore "the mark of Gallicanism."[31]

Aristotle and Gallicanism: The Predecessors of Oresme

If there was an incipient Gallicanism in France during the reign of Charles V, would Oresme (or could Oresme) use the *Politics* to support it? Certainly he had before him a varied tradition of the use of Aristotle in discussions of church and state.

Aristotle had been widely used in these discussions despite difficulties both obvious and formidable. As Gordon Leff has said:

---

[27] See Friedrich Merzbacher, "Das Somnium viridarii von 1376 als Spiegel des gallikanischen Staatskirchenrechts," *Zeitschrift der Savigny-Stiftung für Rechtsgeschichte, kan. Abt.* 42 (1956), p. 68, and Royer, *L'Église et le royaume de France,* as cited above in n. 6, p. 309. Many of the same writers defended the king's independence from the emperor (see above, chap. 3, nn. 11, 13–15), and from the papacy. Among these writers were John of Paris and the anonymous authors of the *Rex pacificus,* the gloss on *Unam Sanctam,* the *Quaestio in utramque partem,* and of course the *Songe du Vergier.* For summaries of their arguments, see Martin, *Les origines du Gallicanisme,* 1: 214–239; bibliographical information will be found in the notes mentioned above, from chapter 3. Charles V ordered from Raoul des Presles French translations of the *Rex pacificus* and the *Quaestio in utramque partem* (Martin, 1: 220, n. 4).

[28] As we are reminded by Charles Petit-Dutaillis, it was Saint Louis and not his grandson who said that the king could take all the treasures and goods of the churches to meet the necessities of the monarchy and the kingdom (*La monarchie féodale en France et en Angleterre, X^e–XIIIe siècle* [Paris, 1933], 293, n. 6, from a memorandum published in Matthew de Paris, *Chronica majora,* ed. H. R. Luard, 7 vols. [London, 1872–1883, Royal Society 57], 6 [add.]: 99–112).

[29] See Guillaume Mollat, *Les papes d'Avignon* (Paris, 1924), 266–267. As part of his campaign to keep the popes at Avignon, Charles sent one Ancel Choquart in 1367 to deliver a florid speech which was later attributed to Oresme, none to his credit as a writer (Francis Meunier, *Essai sur la vie et les ouvrages de Nicole Oresme* [Paris, 1857], 28–29; Roland Delachenal, *Histoire de Charles V,* 5 vols. [Paris, 1909–1931], 3: 516–519; Mollat, *Les papes d'Avignon,* 111; and Menut, introduction to Oresme's *Livre de Ethiques* [New York, 1940], 14–15). Émile Bridrey, *La Théorie de la monnaie au XIVe siècle. Nicole Oresme. Étude d'histoire des doctrines et des faits économiques* (Paris, 1906), 449–450 and n. 3, thought that Oresme did give this sermon.

Mollat says (p. 264) that the financial aid given by the Avignon popes to the French kings surpassed in variety and quantity that given to other monarchs. See also Martin, *Les origines du Gallicanisme,* 1: 256.

[30] Mollat, *Les papes d'Avignon,* 269–270.

[31] Royer, *L'Église et le royaume de France,* 312.

In a dualist society, which regarded spiritual and temporal authority in one form or another as both equally indispensable, naturalism — Aristotle's or any other — was a half-doctrine: it could not go beyond providing a natural justification for a certain kind of political order, where the problem was to justify it *supernaturally*.[32]

Medieval writers sometimes compensated for this insufficiency by importing ideas from other parts of Aristotle's philosophy, especially his metaphysics.[33] The finalism of his hierarchy of ends was of obvious use to those who argued that the church with its spiritual ends should predominate over the state with its temporal ends.[34] Supporters of ecclesiastical power used Aristotelian principles to describe the power of the pope.[35]

---

[32] "The Apostolic Ideal in Later Medieval Ecclesiology," *Journal of Theological Studies* 18 (1967): 66.

[33] In "Studien über den Einfluss der aristotelischen Philosophie" (see n. 1 above), pp. 6–7, Martin Grabmann describes three approaches toward the use of Aristotelian philosophy in discussions of church and state. The first was a moderate, synthetic approach, a *fides quaerens intellectum* seen in the work of Albertus Magnus and Thomas Aquinas. Aristotelian principles, especially metaphysical principles, were used to produce theories of indirect papal power. The second approach was that of the Latin Averroists, who saw philosophy and natural science as ends in themselves and wished to use Aristotle not to set up two complementary spheres of power, but to establish a monist distribution of power in which the clergy would be subordinate. Marsilius of Padua was the most prominent representative of this group. The third approach was that of the Augustinian hierocrats, who used Aristotelian teleology and ethics to just the opposite effect, to support the direct power of the papacy in temporals. Here outstanding representatives were Bonaventure and Augustinus Triumphus. For criticism of this view, see Alan Gewirth, "Philosophy and Political Thought in the Fourteenth Century," in Francis Lee Utley, ed., *The Forward Movement of the Fourteenth Century* (Columbus, Ohio, 1961): 125–164.

[34] John of Paris mentions such an argument and refutes it (*De regia potestate et papali* 11. [ed. Fritz Bleienstein (Stuttgart, 1969), 121]). The refutation is in 17. (Bleienstein, 159–160), where he denies that the precedence of the higher over the lower is absolute.
    One frequently used example of Aristotelian finalism, mentioned by Grabmann in connection with the Augustinian hierocrats, came not from the *Metaphysics* but from the *Ethics*. This was the evaluation of arts and sciences according to their ends (*Ethics* 1. 1. 1094a). Several supporters of the papacy used this sort of argument. In *De regimine christiano* 2. 7. (ed. H.-X. Arquillière [Paris, 1926], 231), James of Viterbo said: ". . . finis temporalis, qui est felicitas naturalis, ordinatur ad finem spiritualis, qui est beatitudo supernaturalis . . . ." See also Giles of Rome, *De ecclesiastica potestate* 2. 6. (ed. Richard Scholz, [Weimar, 1929], p. 68): "Sicut ergo frenifactiva, imponens frenum equo, preparat equum militi, ut ei liberius famuletur, sic potestas terrena, imponens frenum laicis, ne forefaciant in ecclesiam nec in se ipsos, disponit eos, ut potestati ecclesiastice liberius sint subiecti"; and Aquinas, *De Regimine Principum* 1. 14. (ed. Joseph Mathis [Turin, 1924], p. 21): "Sic enim ei [i. e. Romano Pontifici], ad quem finis ultimi cura pertinet, subdi debent illi, ad quos pertinet cura antecedentium finium, et ejus imperio dirigi." Thus the use of this principle was not limited to the strict hierocrats. But we are not surprised to find it used in Augustinus Triumphus (*Summa de ecclesiastica potestate* 35. ad. 1. [Rome, 1479, p. 119]): "Sicut ars militaris cuius finis est victoria, habet eligere equestrem et frenefactivam secundum quod videlicet expediri fini intentio sic ut dicitur primo ethicorum unde puto quod papa qui universos fideles in presenti ecclesia ad pacem habet ordinare: et ad supernaturalem finem consequendum dirigere et destinare . . . ." For further references, see Alan Gewirth, *Marsilius of Padua. The Defender of Peace*, 2 vols. (New York, 1951–1956), 1: 105, n. 88.

[35] A teleological principle, again from the *Ethics*, was used by Augustinus Triumphus to show that the pope best understood the ends of government. In *Ethics* 2. 1. 1103b (Rackham, p. 73), Aristotle said: ". . . lawgivers make the citizens good by training them in habits of right action." Augustinus Triumphus said (*Summa de ecclesiastica potestate* 44. 1. [Rome, 1479, p. 139]): "preterea ad primum dicit philosophus secundo ethicorum quod intentio legislatoris

But what could be done with the *Politics*? We have seen in the previous chapter that the church was sometimes described as a communitas perfecta on the Aristotelian model. This conception, emphasizing as it did the ends of ecclesiastical government (spiritual, and thus one might say, superior ends) affected theories of church and state as well as it did theories about the structure of the church itself.[36] The finalism of the hierarchy of communities and the communitas perfecta had much the same effect as the finalism of the hierarchy of ends.

Among those who wrote commentaries on the *Politics*, some spoke of the state conceived "in the role which it would fulfil if there were no church,"[37] but rather a priesthood of retired men "already weary with years."[38] Albertus Magnus (in his commentary on the *Ethics*) agreed with Aristotle that the ruler alone could appoint the sites for temples and the times for the performance of religious rites.[39] On the other hand, in the commentary of Walter Burley one finds the "most specific statement of the superiority of the ecclesiastical power over the secular."[40]

---

semper est ut homines ad virtutem inducat." Later (p. 143), he concluded that, as the "spiritualis homo omnia iudicat," the pope is the best leader. Peter de Lutra said in *Liga fratrum* 7. (ed. Richard Scholz, *Unbekannte kirchenpolitische Streitschriften aus der Zeit Ludwigs des Bayern* . . . , 2 vols. [Rome, 1911–1914], 2: 59): "Quia secundum philosophum II. Ethic. intencio legislatoris est cives facere bonos, et dominus papa in ordine ad finem supernaturalem eterne beatitudinis est universalis legislator tocius ecclesiastice multitudinis . . . ipse tenetur menbra tocius ecclesie in ordine ad finem . . . ."

[36] See, for example, chap. 5, nn. 20, 26, for other material with an obvious bearing on theories of church and state.

[37] Conor Martin, "Some Medieval Commentaries on Aristotle's *Politics*," *History* 36 (1951): 36, speaking of Peter of Auvergne. As for Buridan, Mario Grignaschi says "inutile de rechercher dans ses 'Quaestiones' les opinions de Buridan sur les rapports entre l'Église et l'État" ("Un commentaire nominaliste de la Politique d'Aristote: Jean Buridan," *Anciens pays et assemblées d'états* 19 [1960]: 127).

[38] *Politics* 7. 9. 1329a (Barker, 303).

[39] Jean Dunbabin, "Aristotle in the Schools," in Beryl Smalley, ed., *Trends in Medieval Political Thought* (Oxford, 1965), 81. The first course of his commentary on the *Ethics* is cited here from the Cambridge MS. Gonville and Caius 510 (338), fol. 125vb (cited on p. 85, n. 68). Generally, says Dunbabin (p. 81): "[t]he commentators on the *Ethics* and *Politics* deal simply with natural religion, making no attempt whatsoever to infiltrate Christian ideas into the text." Of course these commentators were tied to the text of Aristotle, and were at first fully occupied with the literal exposition of the text. Modern commentators take Aristotle simply as Aristotle; perhaps these medieval commentators did the same, and saved their opinions on the church for more congenial occasions.

[40] Ferdinand E. Cranz, "Aristotelianism in Medieval Political Theory" (Ph.D. dissertation, Harvard University, 1938), p. 203. Lowrie J. Daly, "The Conclusions of Walter Burley's Commentary on the *Politics*, Books V and VI," *Manuscripta* 13 (1969): 149, describes the argument as it appears in a *notandum* from Book 6. Here Burley referred to a section of the *Politics* (6. 8. 1322b) where Aristotle spoke of those who were to care for temples and religious revenues. Peter of Auvergne, as Daly says, simply explicated this section (see R. Spiazzi's edition of the *In libros politicorum Aristotelis expositio* of Aquinas [Rome, 1951], p. 336). For Albertus Magnus, see his *Politics* commentary in *Opera omnia*, 38 vols. (Paris, 1890–1899), 8 (1891): 613, and the previous note. Burley on the other hand said that the spiritual office is unlike the political, and "divina super omnia alia sunt et per consequens" (text from Cranz, 203) the divine office is above the others. There must be order and subordination in the state, but the religious offices cannot be subordinated to the temporal offices with their lower ends. See also Martin, "Some Medieval Commentaries," 40.

We must also consider the effect of Aristotle's naturalism. His description of the origin of the state is thought to have had a tremendous effect on medieval estimations of the worth and independence of secular government. Walter Ullmann has said:

The concept with which the medieval period before the thirteenth century was not familiar was that of the State, understood as an independent, self-sufficient, autonomous body of citizens which lived, so to speak, on its own substance and on its own laws. This concept came about in the thirteenth century as a result of the influence of the Greek philosopher, Aristotle.[41]

If a supporter of ecclesiastical supremacy could follow Augustine in declaring that temporal government was merely a remedy for sin, or use Aristotle's hierarchy of ends and of communities to demonstrate the superiority of the church, a supporter of the secular state, it is said, could find his own justification in the *Politics*. The state could be seen, following Aristotle, as an association arising naturally among men, with its own ethical purpose, the attainment of the good life. Thus a new and powerful weapon could be directed against the pretensions of the church.

Several objections may be raised against the view of the *Politics* as the great prop of secularism. One objection, set forth at length in the work of Gaines Post, is that Aristotle was neither the first nor the only source of medieval political naturalism. We may contrast his view with that of Ullmann: "Long before the recovery of Aristotle's *Politics*, the naturalness of living in politically and legally organized communities of corporate guilds, chapters, town and States was recognized both in practice and in legal thought."[42]

After reading his evidence, especially the evidence from legal sources, it would be rash to ascribe all enthusiasm for the state to an Aristotelian revolution. A broader objection is that naturalism, whatever its source, was not likely to make an overwhelming change. We have noted the opinion of Gordon Leff, that the *Politics* could not provide an adequate basis for theories about church and state. We may also ask whether the acceptance of a naturalistic account of the origin of society must have a predetermined and specific effect upon theories about the merits of spiritual and temporal power. After all, both Augustine and Aquinas said that political life represents the highest human good, but denied that human good is the highest of goods.[43]

---

[41] *A History of Political Thought: The Middle Ages* (Baltimore, 1965), 17. See also Michael Wilks on an Aristotelian "revolution" (*The Problem of Sovereignty in the Later Middle Ages* [Cambridge, 1963], 84).

[42] From the introduction to Post's *Studies in Medieval Legal Thought* (Princeton, 1964), 3. See also the section of this book entitled "The Naturalness of Society and the State."

[43] Augustine made statements which approach the conception of the social animal. In *De civitate Dei* 12. 22. (4: 110 in the Loeb edition of 7 vols. [Cambridge, Mass., and London, 1957–1972], this vol. [1966] with trans. by Philip Levine), he said: ". . . unum ac singulum creavit [Deus], non utique solum sine humana societate deserendum, sed ut eo modo vehementius ei commendaretur ipsius societatis unitas vinculumque concordiae, si non tantum

It is most unlikely that the reintroduction of the *Politics* caused a transformation in thought about the value of temporal government. Acceptance of the natural state of the *Politics* was compatible with the suggestion of a divine sanction for secular government.[44] One could, like Hervaeus Natalis, make an indirectly Aristotelian argument by saying that secular government arose from a social instinct implanted by God.[45] However, a simple distinction between Augustinian hierocrats and Aristotelian secularists cannot be made.

Church and State in the *Livre de Politiques*

In his glosses on the *Politics* Oresme did not make full use of the few opportunities provided by Aristotle for a discussion of spiritual and temporal authority. His glosses for the first chapter of his text are straightforward and describe the development of the political community without making any special claims for it. He did not object to Aristotle's description of the state as arising from nature. Only later, in a gloss on another subject, is it stated that spiritual government comes from God by grace, while temporal government comes from God "through another means and in another manner."[46] The means and manner may well be natural, but Oresme does

---

inter se naturae similitudine verum etiam cognationis affectu homines necterentur . . . ." See also 15. 4. (4: 422, 424, 426). In 19. 13. (6: 178, 180, this vol. having a translation by William Chase Greene [1960]), he spoke of the God-given "bona huic vitae congrua," that is, temporal peace and the things necessary to it, which, if rightly used, will lead to "inmortalitatis pacem." The temporal peace of the people, "quandam pacem suam non inprobandam," is also mentioned in 19. 26. (6: 236), where he said that there was profit in the peace of Babylon, and recalled that Paul had recommended prayers "pro regibus . . . atque sublimibus [1 Timothy 2:2]," and that Jeremiah had asked his people to pray for Babylon (Jeremiah 29:7).

Aquinas said in his *Sententia libri ethicorum* 1. 2. (1094b) (*Opera omnia* [Rome, 1882-], 47: 1 [1969]: 9)". . . unde concludit quod hic, scilicet finis politicae, est humanum bonum, id est optimum in rebus humanis. . . . Dicit autem ad politicam pertinere considerationem ultimi finis humanae vitae . . . ." In the *De regimine principum* 1. 14. (ed. Mathis, p. 21) he said: "Non est ergo ultimus finis multitudinis congregatae vivere secundum virtutem, sed per virtuosam vitam pervenire ad fruitionem divinam."

For a denial that Augustine and Aquinas were "as far apart on their treatment of this question as some scholars would have us believe," see Kimon Giocarinis, "Speculation on the Origins of Lordship: Francesco Suarez in his *De Legibus*," *Studia Gratiana* 15 (1972): 335–361, with the above phrase on p. 343.

[44] For example John of Paris, *De reg. pot. et pap.* 10. (ed. Bleienstein, 113): ". . . potestas regia nec secundum se nec quantum ad executionem est a papa, sed est a Deo et a populo regem eligente in persona vel in domo, sicut ante." For a similar argument from Guido Vernani, found in his *De potestate papae* 14., see Grabmann, "Studien über den Einfluss der aristotelischen Philosophie," 98–99.

[45] Grabmann, "Studien über den Einfluss der aristotelischen Philosophie," 35, gives this text, from *De potestate papae, de jurisdictione ecclesiastica et de exemptione*: ". . . alii principes (sc. saeculares) non sunt vicarii Dei expresse et explicite per institutionem expressam et explicitam nisi aliqui reges fuerint instituti revelatione divina. Possunt tamen principes dici vicarii Dei implicite, inquantum Deus dedit naturae humanae rationem naturalem . . . ."

[46] This occurs in his long gloss on universal government, where Oresme wishes to exempt the papal monarchy from his criticisms of such government, and says (in a passage cited above in chapter 3, n. 108): ". . . celle monarchie esperituele vient de Dieu par grace especial. . . . Et donques a ceste policie ne est pas semblable la policie temporele, laquelle vient de Dieu par autre influence et par autre maniere" (7. 10. [fol. 251c, p. 293a]). For a similar but more specific statement from Buridan's treatment of universal government, see above, chapter 3, n. 133.

not tell us. He did not show much interest in the origin of authority. He does not make the type of metaphysical arguments described in the preceding pages.[47] For the most part he spoke of the necessities of political power and administration as they concern the clergy, and of the proper role of the clergy as it can be seen in scripture and history.

The views of Oresme on issues of church and state conform to the Gallican principles described by Victor Martin.[48] We have seen that Oresme's glosses reflect the special religious position of the French king and French nation, that he referred to Charles as king by the grace of God and defender of the church, and mentioned the fleur-de-lis, a national symbol with a religious significance. He also made a rather pointed reference to the residence of the popes at Avignon.[49]

We have seen Oresme as a critic of the papal prerogative. We see him now as a defender of the French church, but we must not imagine him to be a successor of Nogaret. Oresme is more to be compared with John of Paris, a moderate figure of the time of Philip the Fair. John of Paris, who wished to avoid the errors of Herod and of the Waldensians, is taken as one of the most prominent among the representatives of the *via media* in questions of church and state.[50] These writers wished to avoid, on the one hand, the theocracy which claimed temporal sovereignty for the church, and, on the other, the unitary statism seen in Marsilius of Padua, in favor of theory based in political reality[51] and founded upon the harmony between two divinely ordained powers with distinct spheres of interest.[52] They included

---

[47] He did introduce a teleological argument based on the architectonic quality of political science, but this he rejected, as John of Paris had rejected the teleological argument he introduced (see above, n. 34; for Oresme, see below, nn. 84–87).

[48] Jeannine Quillet, whose book *La philosophie politique du Songe du Vergier* (1378). *Sources doctrinales. L'Église et l'État au moyen âge* 15 (Paris, 1977), contains much discussion of the *Livre de Politiques*, has said that in this work "un pas de plus est fait dans la direction du gallicanisme . . ." (p. 137). See also 166–167.

[49] Speaking of the different definitions of the word *city*, he said: "Et recite Lucan comment Pompeius disoit as senateurs que en quelconques lieu il estoient, illeques estoit Rome; jouxte ce que l'en seult dire: Ubi papa, ibi Roma. Combien que Pape Innocent tiers en un sermon de Saint Pierre et Saint Pol veille dire, ce semble, que le pape ne doit onques demourer ailleurs que ou lieu de Rome" (3. 3. [fol. 78b–c, p. 119b]). It seems that it was Lentulus and not Pompey who made the speech to which Oresme refers (*De Bello Civili* 5. 15–34 [pp. 238, 240 in the Loeb edition with trans. by J. D. Duff (London and New York, 1928)]). The phrase "Ubi senatus, ibi Roma" does not itself appear in this speech. For the remark of Innocent III, see Migne, *PL*, 217: 556–557, from Sermon 22. On the origins of the phrase "Ubi papa, ibi Roma," see E. Dupré-Theseider, *I papi di Avignone e la questione romana* (Florence, 1939), xxii. See also above, chap. 5. n. 62.

[50] See Rivière, *Le problème de l'église et de l'état*, as cited above in n. 1, esp. pp. 272–340; Royer, *L'Église et le royaume de France*, as cited in n. 6; also Marcel Pacaut, *La Théocratie. L'église et le pouvoir au Moyen Age* (Paris, 1957); idem, "La permanence d'une 'Via Media' dans les doctrines politiques de l'Église Médiévale," *Cahiers d'Histoire publiés par les Universités de Clermont-Lyon-Grenoble* 3.4 (1958): 327–357; and G. H. M. Posthumus Meyjes, *Jean Gerson et L'Assemblée de Vincennes* (1329). *Ses conceptions de la juridiction temporelle de l'Église* (Leiden, 1978).

[51] Pacaut, "La permanence," 331.

[52] Royer, *L'Église et le royaume de France*, 129. Pope Gelasius may be said to be the ancestor of these thinkers.

the authors of the *Quaestio in utramque partem*,[53] the gloss on *Unam Sanctam*,[54] the *Somnium viridarii*[55] and the less moderate[56] *Songe du Vergier*,[57] and Jean Gerson.[58] It is no coincidence, as Meyjes says, that the adherents of the via media, a theory congenial to a restrained Gallicanism, were French.[59]

Nor will it be a surprise, after this introduction, to learn that Oresme, a Frenchman, courtier and prelate by circumstance and a realist by temperament, is to be included in this group. The *Songe du Vergier*, a work undoubtedly to be associated with and compared with the work of Oresme, if not to be ascribed to him, is noted for its Gallican leanings[60] as well as for its attempt to "preserve the independence of the temporal without contesting the existence or organization of the Church," to weaken the church without annihilating it.[61] It will become clear that Oresme shared this first goal. He did not go so far toward the second; in fact, he is unusual among those of the moderate or Gallican persuasion in making a strong defense of the property and jurisdiction of the clergy.

Oresme could defend the right of the French king to independence in temporal matters by speaking of his special spiritual qualities, and by asserting the incompetence of the church in worldly matters. In a gloss on the qualities of good rulers, Oresme used scriptural and patristic sources to demonstrate that worldly lordship is forbidden to the clergy. The virtue of contemplation, he said, is not the virtue which makes men good rulers.

And [this] is because those who are superior in this virtue would not wish to be, and should not be, temporal rulers, as appears clearly from what was said in *Ethics* 10. 16. And for this reason Our Lord Jesus Christ . . . [said]: "The kings of the Gentiles lord it over them, etc. But you not so . . ." [Luke 22:25, 26; Douay Version]. . . . [This] is interpreted with a bearing on the present matter by the doctors Augustine, Chrysostom, Origen, Basil, and Bernard, who said: "It is clear that all [worldly] lordship is forbidden to the apostles." And Our Lord himself said: "My kingdom is not of this world . . ." [John 18:36; Douay Version].[62]

---

[53] Rivière, *Le problème*, 274–281; Pacaut, *La Théocratie*, 193; J. Watt, "The 'Quaestio in utramque partem' reconsidered," *Collectanea Stephan Kuttner. Studia Gratiana* 13 (1967): 443, 451.

[54] Rivière, *Le problème*, 300–307; Royer, *L'Église et le royaume de France*, 130.

[55] Ibid., 129, where the *Somnium* is called "le véritable aboutissement des thèses moyennes émises au cours du Moyen Age."

[56] Ibid., 169.

[57] Ibid., 124.

[58] Meyjes, *Jean Gerson et L'Assemblée de Vincennes*, 77–79.

[59] Ibid., 114.

[60] See Lagarde, "Le 'Songe du Verger,'" as cited above in n. 1; Royer, *L'Église et le royaume de France*, p. 84; and Jeannine Quillet, *La philosophie politique*, as cited above in n. 48; 60.

[61] Royer, *L'Église et le royaume de France*, 59, 63.

[62] 3. 19. (fol. 105b, p. 145b). Oresme's "*Ethics* 10.16." corresponds to *Ethics* 10. 8.1178b–1179a, but neither in his translation nor in his glosses on this section do I find this remark. For Bernard, see *De consideratione* 2. 6. (Migne, PL, 182: 748): "Planum est: Apostolis interdicitur dominatus." For this passage as used by John of Paris, see *De reg. pot. et pap.* 10. (ed. Bleienstein, p. 110), 13. (p. 135), and 19. (p. 176). For its use in the *Defensor Pacis*, see 2. 4. 13. (ed. Scholz, p. 177) and 2. 24. 8. (ed. Scholz, p. 457). For its use by Conrad of Megenberg and William of

In a discussion of those who properly can be called magistrates, Oresme invoked Saint Paul to the same effect:

. . . priesthood is a magistracy, and consequently priests are princes. But note that this sacerdotal magistracy is not the same as a political magistracy, that is, a secular magistracy. And this conforms to what the Apostle said: "No man, being a soldier to God, entangleth himself with secular businesses. . . " [2 Timothy 2:4; Douay Version].[63]

Oresme denied that the structure and function of the church were of the same nature as those of the secular state, although he applied the political ideas of Aristotle to the church. This was done by analogy, he suggested: priests may be called princes, and princes priests, but this does not make them the same thing. Oresme took up this matter at greater length in a gloss on the jurisdictions of spiritual and temporal offices:

For although the greatest among clergymen are called kings . . . this is done merely as a metaphor or simile. . . . And the case of secular princes who are called *sacerdotes* is similar. Thus Pliny records this inscription: "Emperor Augustus, Pontifex Maximus and son of the Divine Caesar." . . . according to Aristotle, the office of a king and that of a prelate are two different things, and are distinct one from the other.[64]

He then introduced examples from the Old Testament:

This conforms to what a prophet said to a king of Jerusalem: "It doth not belong to thee, Ozias, to burn incense to the Lord, but to the priests. . ." [2 Paralipomenon/2 Chronicles 26: 18; Douay Version] . . . the office [of the clergy] is more contempla-

---

Ockham, see Scholz, *Unbekannte kirchenpolitische Streitschriften,* 2: 326, 344, and 463. See also Rivière as cited above in n. 1, 405–423, especially 411 and 414.

[63] 4. 21. (fol. 157a, p. 196a). Here Oresme managed to approximate the meaning of Aristotle after giving a partially mistaken translation of his text. The passage from *Politics* 4. 15. 1299a (Barker, 194–195) which inspired this gloss is: "We cannot, therefore, reckon as magistrates all the persons appointed-by election or lot-to any office. We can hardly include, for example, the priests of the public cults, whose office must be reckoned as something different from the political magistracies." Moerbeke has this as: ". . . quidem omnes neque electos neque sortiales ponendum principes, puta sacerdotes primo (hoc enim alterum aliquid praeter politicos principatus ponendum)" (ed. Susemihl, p. 440, lines 10–12). Oresme's translation (fols. 156d–157a, p. 196a) is: ". . . l'en ne doit pas mettre ne ordener que tous les princes soient faiz par election ne tous par sort, si comme les prestres premierement. Et ce princey est a mettre autre que ne sunt princeys politiques, et est aucune chose hors telz princeys."

Oresme also cited 2 Timothy 2:4 in 7. 21. in another discussion of the proper jurisdiction of the clergy (fol. 270d, p. 312b). In this case, as we shall see, Oresme accepted the injunction as it referred to temporal matters but denied that it referred to the jurisdiction of the church over its own affairs.

[64] 7. 21. (fol. 269d, p. 311b). In this section Oresme refers to *Politics* 6. 8. 1322b (Barker, 277), where Aristotle said that those who manage public sacrifices "not legally assigned to the priests" are "in some states called archon, in others king, and in others prytaneis." Moerbeke translated the latter part of this as ". . . vocant autem hii quidem principes hos, hii autem reges, hii vero prytanees . . ." (ed. Susemihl, 493, lines 4–5). Oresme had this as ". . . les uns les appellent *princes*. . . . Et autres les appellent *roys*. . . . Et autres les nomment *prytanees*" (6. 13. [fol. 232d, p. 275a–b]). For the inscription from Pliny, see *Naturalis Historia* 3. 20. 136. (2: 100 in the Loeb edition of 10 vols. [Cambridge, Mass., and London, 1938–1962], this vol. [1942] with trans. by H. Rackham): "*Imp. Caesari divi filio Aug. pont. max., imp.* . . ."

tive than active, while that of the king is more active. And therefore the two offices cannot be combined in one person except by divine dispensation, as it was said of Melchizedek [Genesis 14:18]. But this matter transcends this science.[65]

The example of Melchizedek had in fact been used by Innocent IV to defend papal intervention, for if Christ was a Melchizedek who united kingship and priesthood in his person, his vicar must have the same quality.[66] Oresme apparently did not recognize this dispensation.

Later in the same gloss, Oresme seemed to reverse his position, saying that the clergy must have jurisdiction over their members and posessions, for they are often called princes and kings, and cannot be princes if they lack this jurisdiction.

. . . clergymen should have a restful life [and liberty] . . . if they and their persons and their goods were under another's jurisdiction, they would not have liberty, or a restful life without harassment. In addition, as has been said several times, they are called princes and kings, and though this is done [principally] to honor the worth of their position, it follows from this that it is fitting for them to have jurisdiction over their persons and their goods . . . for otherwise they would not be princes.[67]

Oresme insisted that the clergy must have direct ownership and jurisdiction over their possessions in order to retain their separate, contemplative way of life, to save them perhaps from becoming hostages to secular overseers.[68] Modest possessions held in security do not push the clergy into worldly affairs, but save the clergy from them.

Thus Oresme was not inconsistent. He thought that the clergy were princes in so far as they possessed jurisdiction. This jurisdiction was both necessary and real but it was not the same as the political power of secular princes. The two powers were not to compete with each other, nor could one be measured in terms of the other, although, as we have seen, the church

---

[65] Fols. 269d–270a, p. 311b.

[66] See Walter Ullmann, "Frederick II's opponent, Innocent IV, as Melchisedek," *Atti del Convegno Internazionale di Studi Federiciana* (Palermo, 1952): 53–81. According to Ullmann, whereas Gelasius had said that Christ was the last Melchizedek, by the time of Nicholas I, the pope as vicar of Christ "automatically assumes the role of Christ on earth; by virtue of his vicariate the pope becomes also Melchisedek" (75).

[67] Fols. 270d–271a, p. 312b. Oresme had already associated princes, priests and possessions in a gloss on *Politics* 6. 8. 1322b, where Aristotle spoke of the religious officials called variously archons, kings and prytaneis (see above, n. 64). Oresme had little to say about the archons and prytaneis but of the kings he said: "Jouxte ce que dit Saint Pere: Vos autem estis genus electum, regale sacerdocium [1 Peter 2:9]. Et par ce, aucun pourroit dire que il ont en leur possessions la souvereinté" (6. 13. [fol. 232d, p. 275b]). (This association also turned up in Oresme's criticism of apostolic poverty: "Et dire que princes et roys en leur estate fussent mendians, ce est grande absurdité" [7. 19. (fol. 266b, p. 307b)]).

[68] The knight in the *Disputatio inter clericum et militem*, for example, denied that the clergy had a right to property, and thought that laymen should provide for the needs of priests (Martin, *Les origines du Gallicanisme*, 1: 213). See the edition by Norma N. Erickson, "A Dispute between a Priest and a Knight," *Proceedings of the American Philosophical Society* 111 (1967): 297–298 (for the Latin text) and 305–306 (for an English translation). Marsilius of Padua said that ownership was not compatible with the perfection of the preacher, and spoke of "patrons" who should assume ownership of the materials necessary to the support of the clergy (*Defensor pacis* 2. 14. 8.; p. 307 in the edition of Scholz). See above, chap. 5, n. 93.

could serve as an example to temporal government. Later we will take a more positive and detailed look at Oresme's ideas on the jurisdiction of the church.

It appears from these examples that Oresme supported the first principle of Gallicanism, the independence of the French king in temporal affairs. He upheld this principle by denying that the functions of king and priest could be united in one person, and by demonstrating that in the earliest records of the church clergymen were forbidden to become involved in secular matters. At the same time Oresme gave positive support to the king by emphasizing the special religious status of the French monarchy and people.

Oresme accepted the second principle of Gallicanism, the superiority of the council over the pope (or at least, the denial of the superiority of the pope over the council).[69] He made several references to the role of the king in convoking councils. The Synod of Toledo, he said, had been brought about through "the devotion of the king and by his commandment":[70] this was one of many councils convoked by, and attended by, kings. The presence of laymen was especially appropriate, according to Oresme, when political as well as religious matters were to be discussed.[71] He ended this gloss with a reminder of the duties of kings in the matter of councils, praising the French monarchy in general and Charles V in particular.[72]

The third principle of Gallicanism, the union of the French clergy and king for the preservation of the liberties of their church, was to be upheld at the expense of the pope. When Oresme defended the preeminence of the French king within the French church, and called for regular councils which might well be convoked by this king, he favored such autonomy. This was also true of his criticism of the pope as distributor of benefices: if those who

---

[69] See above, chap. 5, nn. 69–79. While this was certainly a Gallican principle, Martin reminds us that "ses origines n'ont rien de spécifiquement français" (*Les origines du Gallicanisme*, 2: 70).

[70] 3. 24. (fol. 124b, p. 161a).

[71] Ibid., fol. 124d, p. 161a. John of Paris, who had anticipated some of the principles of Gallicanism, supported the use of general councils, and the involvement of the prince, in the deposition of improper popes. In *De reg. pot. et pap.* 24 (Bleienstein, 201–202), he said that, while the college of cardinals was qualified to judge in the case of abdication, the general council was required for deposition. He suggested that the cardinals could call in a secular ruler (the emperor alone being named) in order indirectly to depose a scandalous pope (chap. 13; Bleienstein, 138). In the same chapter (Bleienstein, 140) he spoke of invoking the secular arm, as the church could not use the "gladium saecularem." For a description of the work of John of Paris as "by far the most consistent and complete formulation of conciliar doctrine before the outbreak of the Great Schism," see Brian Tierney, *Foundations of the Conciliar Theory. The Contribution of the Medieval Canonists from Gratian to the Great Schism* (Cambridge, 1955), 177, and see the introduction of Bleienstein, 36, who says that John of Paris points the way to Gallicanism as well as conciliarism.

Marsilius of Padua said that only the *humana legislator fidelis* or its representative, the *princeps*, could convoke a general council (*Defensor Pacis* 2. 21. 1.).

[72] 3. 24. (fol. 125a, p. 161b). Philip IV had been advised by Nogaret to convoke a General Council to judge and depose Boniface VIII, and the king did send out a summons around the time of the attack at Anagni (Jean Rivière, *Le problème de l'église et de l'état*, 109–115; Martin, *Les origines du Gallicanisme*, 1: 198–199; and H.-X. Arquillière, "L'appel au concile sous Philippe le Bel et la genèse des théories conciliares," *Revue des questions historiques*, n. s. 45 [1911]: 23–55).

make appointments should know the characters of candidates, as Aristotle had said, surely Frenchmen could make the best appointments for the French church. When Oresme described with apparent approval the custom of choosing prelates by election and by the acclaim of the people, he was speaking of a method which could be practiced only at the local level. It is true that Oresme's criticism of the mendicant orders did not touch upon their relationship with the papacy, a question which had provoked the French clergy to make objections foreshadowing Gallicanism. His attitudes toward France and the papacy are nevertheless made sufficiently clear to justify the study of the *Livre de Politiques* as part of the history of Gallican ideas.

Did Oresme leave the French church entirely subordinated to the king, in effect forcing it to exchange one master for another? It is clear that he did not. The church, according to Oresme's glosses, was to be independent but not interventionist. Like the secular state, it was to have its own jurisdiction and prerogatives.[73]

Of course it was in the care of souls that the clergy was to find its principal independence, for this was the duty established for it by Christ.[74] But the independence of the church required more than this. The gloss from the *Livre de Politiques* 7. 21., in which Oresme said that clergymen as princes must have jurisdiction[75] over their persons and their possessions, has been mentioned. It was one of several claims of jurisdiction made for the church by Oresme.

In his discussion of the forms of kingship described by Aristotle, Oresme spoke approvingly of the kingship of the Heroic Age, in which (as it seemed to Oresme) the kings had had lordship "over all goods and possessions whatsoever which did not belong to the priests."[76] Unfortunately, his interpretation of this passage, which he used for support on at least three occasions, was based upon a faulty translation by Moerbeke.[77]

---

[73] The similarity between Oresme's moderation and the attempt of John of Paris to mediate between those the latter called Waldensians and those he identified with Herod is apparent here as it is in the question of ecclesiastical property (see chap. 5, n. 120). As Pacaut says ("La permanence d'une 'Via Media,'" p. 329) one principle of the *via media* is that the church is "une société réelle" which has its own title to administer individuals, institutions and property pertaining to it, even when these things are not essentially spiritual.

[74] Oresme's denial of the propriety of clerical involvement in worldly affairs (see n. 63 above) was followed by the statement that "determiner les questions du divin cultivement appartient a la gent sacerdotal" (7. 21. [fol. 270d, p. 312b]). In 3. 21. (fol. 108b, p. 148b), he said of Aristotle's description of the kingship of the Heroic Age, in which the king acted "as general and judge and the head of religious observances" (*Politics* 3. 14. 1285b; Barker, 139), "Mes ce estoit quant a l'administration et yconomie ou dispensation des biens; car quant as ordres ou caras de l'ame, Nostre Sire Jhesu Crist les donne sans moyen, combien que de divine ordenance a ce soit requis certain mistere, qui ne peut estre fait fors par evesques."

[75] He defined jurisdiction as "la garde de justice," and divided it "selon ce qu'il appert en le .viii.ᵉ chapitre du quint d'*Ethiques*" into distributive and commutative (7. 21. [fol. 269c, p. 311b]). See *Ethics* 5. 2.–4. 1130a–1132b.

[76] 3. 20. (fol. 107c–d, p. 148a).

[77] (See above, chapter 5, n. 116, for a brief reference to this confusion caused by a single improperly rendered word.) Aristotle had said (*Politics* 3. 14. 1285b; Barker, 139) that these kings ". . . were commanders in war; [and] they had the religious function of offering such

One of the places where Oresme exhibited the kings of the Heroic Age was his gloss concerning priests as magistrates, from 4. 21. After explaining why the magistracy of priests is unlike that of secular rulers, and citing 2 Timothy 2:4, Oresme turned to the explications of the earlier commentaries:

Moreover, one expositor says that what Aristotle means by "something different from the political magistracies" is that priests are not subject to the political order, that is, [that they are not subject] to temporal rulers. And concerning this it was said in 3. 20. that the kings of the good old days had no jurisdiction over the goods of the priesthood. Besides, the priests or clergymen have their own polity. . . . And the rulers of such polities were formerly called *principes sacerdotum*.[78]

The independent priesthood of the Heroic Age was mentioned again in a gloss from 6. 13. Here Oresme discussed the managers of public sacrifices, who were sometimes called kings. From this designation he deduced that they had sovereignty over their possessions. He continued:

. . . in the good old days there was a sort of kingship in which the kings had no lordship over the possessions of the priesthood, while [having lordship] over all other [goods], even though, as appears in 3. 21., they did ordain priests and regulate whatever things pertained to the gods. And perhaps more will be said about this in book 7.[79]

---

sacrifices as did not require a priest." Soon after this he said that this sort of king was "general and judge and the head of religious observances," a recapitulation of his earlier remarks and of course consistent with them. But Moerbeke translated the first of these passages as ". . . erant praesulatus secundum bellum et substantiarum, quaecunque non sacerdotales . . . ." (ed. Susemihl, 217, lines 8-9), and the second as ". . . dux enim exercitus et iudex erat rex et eorum quae ad deos dominus" (218, lines 8-9). In the first text Moerbeke, by speaking of substances rather than sacrifices, managed completely to alter the meaning of Aristotle. Instead of kings who directed religious observances, he presented kings whose competence excluded religious matters or at least religious goods. This translation was also inconsistent with his (correct) translation of the second text.

We see the same in Oresme's translation from Moerbeke. His version of the first text (from which comes the citation in the text above) is seen at n. 76 above; his version of the second is: ". . . estoit duc et seigneur de l'ost et estoit juge des causes et estoit seigneur des choses appartenantes au cultivement dez diex" (fol. 108a, p. 148a). Thus Oresme like Moerbeke was left with a contradiction between the misinterpreted purely secular kings and the correctly interpreted heads of religious observances. He tried to resolve this contradiction in his gloss: "Ce est assavoir de instituer les prestres et de teles choses, si comme il fu dit de l'espece de royalme qui est mise la premiere ou chapitre precedent. Et toutesvoies, selon ceste policie les roys ne avoient pas seigneurie sus les possessions des prestres, si comme il appert ou chapitre precedent. Et par ce semble que les possessions des prestres estoient toutes determinees et que il en estoient souverains seigneurs. Et les roys instituoient ou elisoient les prestres" (fol. 108a, p. 148a-b). (He denied that this was done in Christendom.)

Oresme was not alone in his confusion. Albertus Magnus (*Opera omnia*, 8: 289) spoke of "substantiarum, id est, facultatum facti sunt domini, quaecumque, scilicet substantiae, non sacerdotales, supple, erant," and in the summary said "*erat Rex, et eorum quae ad Deos, dominus, sicut paulo ante dictum est*" (p. 290: 3. 9. in the commentary). Peter of Auvergne spoke in the first case of "substantiarum quae non erant sacerdotales," and, in the summary, of kings who controlled "eorum quae pertinebant ad cultum divinum" (ed. Spiazzi, p. 171: 3. 13.- # 483, 485).

[78] Fol. 157a, p. 196a. The expositor mentioned by Oresme is not Peter of Auvergne (*In Libros Politicorum Aristotelis Expositio* 4. 13. #683 [ed. Spiazzi, p. 235]). This must be Albertus 4. 12. (*Opera omnia*, 8: 405): ". . . *praeter politicos principatus, ponendum.* Et hujus causa est, quia sacerdotes circa sacra occupabantur, et ideo politicae ordinationi non subjacebant."

[79] Fol. 232d, p. 275b. Here again Oresme had trouble with the contradictions in the version of Moerbeke.

Oresme had a great deal more to say in the seventh book. In a gloss covering over three folios, and organized after the manner of a formal quaestio, he discussed the property and jurisdiction of the church. This gloss arises from a chapter in which Aristotle describes the distribution of land in his ideal city, and says that "one section of the public property should be allocated to the service of the gods."[80] This led Oresme to ask two questions, "In what manner the clergy of a good polity should have lordship over their possessions and their persons" and "whether they should have jurisdiction, and what sort of jurisdiction."[81] In accordance with the scruples he so often expressed, Oresme declared that he would treat this question "comme pur philisophe," and subjected his opinions to all worthy correction. He then presented arguments in favor of the distribution of sacerdotal honors by the secular ruler. He noted that, as Aristotle says, the clergy is a part of the city.[82] The unity of the city may be said to demand that the prince have the sovereign power to distribute honors and offices to its members.[83] Oresme then explained why, although prelates are sometimes called kings, they cannot be said to have the same sort of office as secular rulers. Another argument taken from Aristotle was based on the preeminence of politics, the architectonic science, over all sciences.[84] If politics orders the other sciences, then the political leader should order the other elements in the state.[85] Similarly, the virtue proper to princes, political prudence, orders the other virtues, including wisdom, the virtue of prelates.

Here Oresme objected. Wisdom, he said, is better than prudence, as Aristotle himself said in the *Metaphysics* 1. 1. 981b. Furthermore, Aristotle said in the *Ethics* that if prudence orders wisdom that does not mean that prudence is superior to wisdom, and furthermore, he said that if political prudence orders all that pertains to the worship of the gods in the city, that does not mean that the rulers have sovereignty over the gods.[86] The question of sovereignty, said Oresme, has two aspects. Wisdom has sovereignty over prudence according to its worth, or, as Oresme puts it, in "excellence de dignité." Prudence has sovereignty over wisdom in the ordering and appointing of persons, but not over the objects of contemplation.[87] Oresme admitted that in several cases pagan and even Christian princes had made appointments to sacerdotal offices, and that this may have been done with divine approval, either implicit or explicit, just as similar appointments of secular rulers had been made by clergymen.[88] These examples did not dissuade him from his general conclusion.

Next Oresme considered the commutative jursidiction of the clergy. To

---

[80] *Politics* 7. 10. 1330a (Barker, 305).
[81] 7. 21. (fol. 269b, p. 311a).
[82] Fol. 269d, p. 311b, from *Politics* 7. 9. 1329a (*Le Livre de Politiques* 7. 19. [fol. 264d, p. 306b]).
[83] Fol. 269d, p. 311b.
[84] *Ethics* 1. 2. 1094b.
[85] Fol. 270a, p. 311b.
[86] *Ethics* 6. 13. 1144b–1145a.
[87] Fol. 270a–b, p. 312a.
[88] "Mes l'en pourroit dire que teles choses ont esté faites en nostre lay selon la forme du

deny (for the sake of discussion) that the clergy should have this sort of jurisdiction, he pointed to the organization of Aristotle's city, where the priesthood and the judges were two separate groups. Older men were to become priests only after ending their careers as soldiers or judges.[89] A similar argument was made from a Christian point of view: the clergy was established for worship and contemplation, whereas civil and political cases are worldly and practical matters, such as Saint Paul forbade believers to treat. An Old Testament example was added in the person of King Josaphat, who established priests as well as Levites.[90]

Then it was time for Oresme to "demonstrate the contrary." First, Aristotle said that the clergy should have leisure and rest.[91] But how can they have rest if their persons and possessions are under the jurisdiction of another? Here the reasoning is similar to that used by Oresme against the Franciscans. A moderate involvement in worldly matters, be it jurisdiction or possessions or both, does not so much draw the clergy into worldliness as it frees them from care and dependence on others, and allows them to pursue their spiritual goals. Oresme's second point is quite familiar. If priests are called kings and princes, they must have lordship over their own persons and goods. His third argument is also familiar, for it features the paradoxical kings of the Heroic Age.[92] It is just and proper, one might say natural, for the clergy to be independent, for according to Aristotle this was the custom in the "good old days."

Then Oresme turned to recorded history. He recalled the injunction of Paul in 1 Corinthians (6:4): "If therefore you have judgments of things pertaining to this world, set them to judge who are most despised in the church." This is not a very strong endorsement of the worldly jurisdiction of the church, but it shows that such jurisdiction had existed even in the

---

legislateur humain, et le divin legislateur les souffroit ou octroioit estre ainsi faictes de grace ou approvoit expressement ou taisiblement. . . . Et encor ovecques ce, en la lay de Moÿse et en nostre lay de grace pluseurs roys et emperieres ont esté institués par la gent sacerdotal" (fol. 270c, p. 312a). Here Oresme managed to dispose of historical examples by speaking of divine intervention, thus leaving intact the principle that the clergy should be allowed to make its own appointments.

In another place, however, he treated such examples differently. In a gloss from 3. 21. (fol. 108a–b, p. 148b) speaking once again of the kings of the Heroic Age he described church appointments by laymen as exceptions but he did not mention divine intervention. Rather he suggested that these appointments left the most basic function of the church, the care of souls, untouched. But we shall see that he did not consider the jurisdiction of the church to be limited to care of souls. Perhaps this apparent contradiction resulted from Oresme's confusion over the inconsistencies in Moerbeke's version.

[89] Fol. 270c–d, p. 312b. For the use of older men as priests, see *Politics* 7. 9. 1329a.

[90] Oresme cited 2 Paralipomenon/2 Chronicles 19:8, which reads in full: "In Ierusalem quoque constituit Iosaphat Levitas, et Sacerdotes, et Principes familiarum ex Israel, ut iudicium et causam Domini iudicarent habitatoribus eius." This appears in fol. 270d, p. 312b, in the gloss.

[91] *Politics* 7. 9. 1329a, and see above, n. 67.

[92] "Et puisque ainsi estoit en cel temps, il semble que ce estoit chose juste et aussi comme naturele a bonne communication humaine" (fol. 271a, p. 312b). Here he actually avoided the paradox of these kings, for he spoke only of the (mistranslated) first passage.

earliest Christian times.[93] Here, like Marsilius of Padua, Oresme was "treating the Bible not just as authority but also as historical evidence."[94] Another appeal to precedent came from the history of France. Oresme made a leap, in which one must suppose he saw nothing incongruous, from Paul and the Corinthians to Julius Caesar and the Druids. He described the enviable prerogatives of these predecessors of the Gallican clergy:

> . . . those who had charge of sacrifices and divine worship, who were called *druids*, had cognizance of almost all matters, including homicides and [other] crimes and [disputes over] inheritances and boundaries. . . . And if any private person or persons or faction failed to hold and obey their judgments and decrees, they put them [under interdict]. . . . this was considered a very severe penalty. . . . [Thus] it appears that at the time of Julius Caesar the clergy of the country of France had a broader jurisdiction than they now have. And perhaps this is because there were only two honorable estates or classes, that is soldiers and priests, according to [Caesar]. And all others were simply serfs. *Nota:* this was not a good constitution.[95]

Then he described other practices and prerogatives of the priesthood of Gaul, which were also claimed by the clergy of the medieval church, including exemption from military service and from payment of taxes.[96] This lengthy treatment of the Druids might seem to be based on nothing more than geographical coincidence. One could ask, what has Gaul to do with Jerusalem, and the answer might be that when a collection of historical examples approaches unanimity it seems to reflect human nature itself. And then, what is natural may be associated with what is divine. This was one of Oresme's arguments for clerical property,[97] which could also serve in the matter of clerical jurisdiction.

Similarly, Oresme noted that property transferred from pagan to Christian hands at the time of conversion had remained in the possession of the church for so long that this condition, like the jurisdiction of the Druids or the independence of the priesthood of the Heroic Age, must have something natural in it.

> . . . the goods and temples formerly devoted to the worship of the false gods were given and consecrated to the true divine worship. . . . these conditions have

---

[93] Fol. 271a, p. 312b. The gloss mentioned does not much resemble that of Walafrid Strabo, the *Glossa ordinaria* (Migne, *PL*, 114: 528).

[94] Gordon Leff, "The Apostolic Ideal in Later Medieval Ecclesiology," *Journal of Theological Studies* 18 (1967): 67. Of course the result of Marsilius's use of the records of the primitive church was quite different from the result of Oresme's use of these records. Marsilius, in order to make the church conform to the apostolic model, allowed the clergy neither jurisdiction nor possessions (Leff, p. 71; *Defensor Pacis* 2. 10. 8.; 2. 14. 14–15).

[95] Fol. 271b, p. 313a. For Caesar, see *De Bello Gallico* 6. 13. (pp. 334–336 in the Loeb edition with trans. by H. J. Edwards [London and Cambridge, Mass., 1917]). The Druids also turn up (on p. 102) in the memorandum mentioned above in n. 28.

[96] "Item, que il avoient coustume de non estre es guerres et ne payoient treu ne taille comme funt autres gens. Et que il avoient repos et vacation et franchise ou immunité de toutes choses, et estoient docteurs. Et il est certain que toutes teles choses ont esté en l'estat sacerdotal de nostre lay de grace" (fol. 271c, p. 313a).

[97] See above, chapter 5, n. 110, with the citation from Cicero.

been . . . maintained for a long time. . . . and, passing from one law to another, have for the most part been unchanged even in form. For this reason it seems to me that these conditions are like a natural part of human society, and that they are proper, and conducive to good government. And as the jurisdiction [of the clergy] was one of the principal matters [involved in this transfer of authority], it seems that it must follow by natural reason that the clergy should have their own jurisdiction.[98]

In this discussion Oresme united several themes from earlier glosses to present an ordered argument for the independence and jurisdiction of the church.[99] In doing this he was able to use material from the *Politics*, some of which was distorted, and some simply inaccurate, for example the tale of the kings of the good old days. To this he added precepts from the Old and New Testaments and historical examples meant to suggest the naturalness of clerical independence.

Oresme used this amalgam of sources to defend principles which were to become characteristic of Gallicanism. He did not defend these principles by relying on Aristotle's metaphysics or upon his naturalism, as had other medieval writers. Nor did he, like Marsilius of Padua, subject the church according to the New Testament to the state according to Aristotle. Instead, Oresme, while recognizing the moral worth of political organization, insisted that the church must be autonomous in order to fulfill its particular and necessary ends. Though he opposed papal omnicompetence, and argued, with support from the *Politics*, that appointments would best be made on a local level, he did not advocate intervention by secular rulers except when emergency demanded the convocation of a General Council. His description of the role of the church was moderate and balanced, a worthy successor to the writings of John of Paris, and a notable contribution to the tradition of the via media. In this matter as in others, Oresme presented a series of opinions rather than an original synthesis, defending the rights of the clergy as a political institution in a reasonable manner quite in keeping with the temper of Aristotle.

---

[98] Fol. 271c–d, p. 313a–b.

[99] Oresme completed the scholastic form of his gloss with responses to the objections he had made to his arguments for the jurisdiction of the clergy (fols. 271d–272a, p. 313b). To the objection that Aristotle established different groups to serve worship and justice, he said that the jurisdiction of the clergy should still extend to its own members. To the objection that secular matters were forbidden to the clergy, he said that there are several orders and offices among the clergy, and that some, as Paul said in 1 Corinthians 6:4, are suited to deal with such matters. To the objection based upon Josaphat's separate institution of priests and Levites, he said that Josaphat did not forbid the clergy to have cognizance over their members and property. And, added Oresme, if the jurisdiction of the Christian clergy be great, "ce ne est pas merveille, si comme je ay dit devant, consideré ce que il sunt institués de Dieu et qu'il ont le gouvernement de la cure des ames" (fols. 271d–272a, p. 313b).

CONCLUSION

Nicole Oresme's version of the *Politics* claims our attention as a crossroads of thought and action. Oresme the scientist has been hailed as a genius and precursor. It is unlikely that a new Duhem will arise to champion Oresme the political writer, for in this field he was clearly neither an inspirer of later thinkers, as were the Constance conciliarists, nor a figure of originality, like Pierre Dubois. His translation of the *Politics* was admirable, but not as influential as that of Moerbeke. His glosses were useful, but never had the authority of those of Albertus Magnus and Aquinas/Auvergne, or the popularity of those of Walter Burley, while his text explication was more a redistribution of error than a reconciliation and rectification of his predecessors. Oresme wrote many long and carefully argued glosses on contemporary subjects, but did not produce a synthesis like those of John of Paris or Marsilius of Padua. This does not mean that he added nothing to the tradition of the *Politics*.

The *Livre de Politiques* was composed at the center of French political life. It was part of the university commentary tradition but it was at the same time a guidebook for a conscientious and self-conscious king. One can compare the lively and topical glosses of Oresme with the rigid, detached, and rather stupefying *Quaestiones* of Jean Buridan, which not only avoid fourteenth-century politics but seem hardly to be about politics (or the *Politics*) at all, to see a contrast which is the result of differing circumstances as well as differing temperaments. Similarly, the earliest commentaries are of value as text-explication, and for the sake of their authors, but tell us little of what the *Politics* meant to medieval political life. Albertus, Aquinas, and Peter of Auvergne chose literal exposition over contemporary application. Perhaps it was their preference to be academic; but at the start simply making sense of the Moerbeke version was a great task. Walter Burley was not in the first generation of commentators, and might have built theory upon their foundations. But he confined himself to a methodical maze, modestly declining (unlike Oresme) even to explain the elements of Greek etymology and history, of which he was thoroughly ignorant.

Oresme was like his predecessors a university man, but he was also the king's man, and wrote the first commentary meant largely for laymen. Thus his glosses, though neither brilliant nor influential, are outstanding in their application to contemporary life. While earlier commentators avoided the ungrateful task of applying Aristotle to the church, Oresme made over one hundred and fifty references to Christian institutions, some of them part of extended discussions. He also took up the conceptions of the hierarchy of communities and the preeminence of the common good, which had been

147

adopted, at least superficially, by almost every political writer, and combined them with religious and legal notions to defend the sovereignty of the national state and its corporate or public government.

Oresme like other writers saw that the communitas perfecta, the culmination of Aristotle's hierarchy of communities, could be identified with the sovereign national state, which subordinates merely local communities while refusing interference from larger powers like the papacy and the empire. In his *Ethics* commentary Oresme linked national sovereignty with the hierarchy of communities; in his glosses for the *Politics* itself he showed that he appreciated the special qualities of the communitas perfecta which for Aristotle made it the source of the good life and the completion of human society. It is true that the French nation surpassed the boundaries of Aristotle's surveyable polis. Oresme like others extended and distorted the hierarchy of communities by topping it off with a kingdom, but he returned to Aristotelian principles and arguments when he wrote his long gloss against the claims of the empire. And beyond his treatment of Aristotle, he used terms like souverain and souveraineté as was done in contemporary political life, in ways that show he considered the political community to be qualitatively superior to other human associations.

The public character of the sovereign state, and the obligation of the government to serve the needs of the community, could be demonstrated by invoking the principle of the common good. The importance of the good of the whole was made apparent from the first chapters of the *Politics*, where Aristotle spoke of communities before speaking of rulers. Throughout this treatise he took this principle as the standard for judging all aspects of government, from the choice of magistrates to the making and even breaking of laws. Oresme followed Aristotle in his application of this principle, while in sanctioning the alteration of law to serve the public interest he went beyond the caution of the *Politics*, echoing instead the pragmatism of contemporary lawmakers. Oresme also used corporatist ideas to suggest the interdependence of members of the community, though failing (as it seems to us) to consider the responsibilities of subjects as well as rulers. These ideas, and his objections to the feudal or proprietary conception of kingship, appear also in his works on currency, which not only reflected practice, but affected it as well.

The *Livre de Politiques* differs most strikingly from the other commentaries in the number of its references to the church. Oresme was not the first to apply Aristotle to this subject, although his commenting predecessors generally had not tried to reconcile the aged priesthood of Aristotle with the great ecclesiastical institutions of the Middle Ages. Outside the commentaries, however, writers had shown their respect for the authority of Aristotle (and much imagination as well) in adapting to the church his metaphysical and physical, as well as his political, principles. Oresme avoided the more exotic of these devices, and followed the common practice of treating the church as a political organization like any other. Thus he could exhort its rulers to serve the common good and obey the law, complain of existing extremes of poverty and wealth in the name of Aristotle's middle-class polity, and use his praise for the (reasonable) multitude to promote the use of reforming General Councils. Aristotle's justification of private property and his criticism of Plato's communism were added to Biblical and historical elements in an attack on the proponents of apostolic poverty.

When the question was one of relations between church and state, in which the church must be considered and justified not as an ecclesiastical polity but as a divine institution, the use of Aristotle was more difficult. Here again, some writers took advantage of his metaphysical principles, for example the ordinatio ad unum. Others, like Marsilius of Padua, reduced the clergy to the role it played, now in the polis, now in the New Testament. Oresme combined the *Politics* and the Bible to produce a more moderate solution, which recalls the middle path of John of Paris, and looks forward to Gallicanism. The Bible was used to deny worldly dominion and jurisdiction to the soldiers of Christ; Aristotle, to defend, with greater force than one sees in other writings favoring the French monarchy, the church's control over its members and goods. This defense contains a striking example of the distortions suffered by classical texts at the hands of their medieval admirers, for much of Oresme's argument is based on a passage which had been turned virtually upside down when Moerbeke mistranslated one word.

The work of Oresme shows breadth or extension, if not the greatest depth, in its adaptation of the *Politics.* Oresme was able to use Aristotle as King Charles had intended, to illuminate the political life of the time, while displaying a sensible realism similar to that found in his text. The very active and selective use which Oresme, more than the earlier commentators, made of this treatise, shows that medieval writers accepted on their own terms the passive and enfeebled text of Aristotle, and made no uniform or uncritical response to the work of the Philosopher.

BIBLIOGRAPHY

The works listed here are those which have been mentioned more than a few times in the footnotes above, and those which are worth mentioning because they have appeared recently or because they have a particular bearing upon the present subject. (These categories are not of course mutually exclusive.) For further listings, please consult the first few pages of each chapter.

PRIMARY SOURCES: PRINTED EDITIONS

Albertus Magnus. *Opera omnia.* 38 vols. Paris, 1890–1899.
Aristotle. *Aristotelis Politicorum libri octo, cum vetusta translatione Guilelmi de Moerbeka.* Edited by Franz Susemihl. Leipzig, 1872.
——. *The Nicomachean Ethics.* Translated by Harris Rackham. Loeb Classical Library. New York, 1926.
——. *The Politics of Aristotle.* Translated by Ernest Barker. Oxford, 1946.
Augustine. *De civitate Dei.* 7 vols. Loeb Classical Library. Cambridge, Mass., and London, 1957–1972.
Augustinus Triumphus. *Summa de ecclesiastica potestate.* Rome, 1479.
Buridan, Jean. *Quaestiones . . . super octo libros politicorum Aristotelis.* Paris, 1513.
Dante Alighieri. *De monarchia.* Edited by L. Bertalot. Florence and Rome, 1920.
Engelbert of Admont. *De ortu et fine Romani imperii.* Edited by Melchior Goldast, in *Politica Imperialia.* Frankfurt, 1614, pp. 754–773.
Giles of Rome. *De Regimine Principum.* Rome, 1556.
James of Viterbo. *De regimine christiano.* Edited by H.-X. Arquillière: *Le plus ancien traité de l'église. Jacques de Viterbe De regimine christiano.* Paris, 1926.
John of Salisbury. *Ioannis Saresberiensis Episcopi Carnotensis Policraticus sive De Nugis Curialum.* 2 vols. Edited by Clemens C. I. Webb. Oxford, 1909.
John of Paris. *De regia potestate et papali.* Edited, with a German translation, by Fritz Bleienstein: *Über königliche und päpstliche Gewalt.* Stuttgart, 1969.
Marsilius of Padua. *Defensor Pacis.* Edited by Richard Scholz. Hanover, 1932. English translation by Alan Gewirth: *Marsilius of Padua. The Defender of Peace.* 2 vols. New York, 1951–1956.
Migne, J.-P., ed. *Patrologiae cursus completus . . . series latina.* 221 vols. Paris, 1878–1890. (Abbreviated as *PL.*)
Oresme, Nicole. *Le Livre de Ethiques d'Aristote.* Edited by Albert Douglas Menut. New York, 1940.
——. "Le Livre du ciel et du monde." Edited by Albert Douglas Menut and Alexander J. Denomy: *Mediaeval Studies* 3 (1941): 185–280; 4 (1942): 159–297; 5 (1943): 167–333. This edition has also been published separately (Madison, Wis., 1968).
——. *Le Livre de Politiques d'Aristote.* Edited by Albert Douglas Menut: *Transactions of the American Philosophical Society,* n. s. 60, pt. 6, Philadelphia, 1970.
Pisan, Christine de. *Le livre des fais et bonnes meurs du sage roy Charles V.* 2 vols. Edited by S. Solente. Paris, 1936–1940.
Somnium viridarii. Edited by Melchior Goldast, in *Monarchia s. Romani imperii.* 3 vols. Hanover, 1611–1614. 1: 58–229. Reproduced in *Revue du moyen âge latin* 22 (1966).
Le Songe du Vergier. Edited by Jean Louis Brunet as vol. 2 of Pierre Dupuy, ed., *Traitez des droits et libertez de l'église gallicane.* Rev. ed. 4 vols. Paris, 1731–1751. Reproduced in *Revue du moyen âge latin* 13 (1957) and 14 (1958).
Thomas Aquinas. *Opera omnia.* Rome, 1882–.
——. *De Regimine Principum.* Edited by Joseph Mathis. Turin, 1924.
——. *In libros politicorum Aristotelis Expositio.* Edited by Raimundo M. Spiazzi. Rome, 1951.
William of Ockham. *Dialogus.* Edited by Melchior Goldast, in *Monarchia s. Romani imperii.* 3 vols. Hanover, 1611–1614. 2: 392–957.

Collections of Documents

Delachenal, Roland, ed. *Chroniques des règnes de Jean II et de Charles V.* 4 vols. Paris, 1910–1920.

Delisle, Léopold, ed. *Mandements et actes divers de Charles V (1364–1380), recueillis dans les collections de la Bibliothèque Nationale.* Paris, 1874.

Isambert, François André, ed. *Recueil général des anciennes lois françaises, depuis l'an 420 jusqu'à la révolution de 1789.* 29 vols. Paris, 1821–1833.

Secousse, Denis François, ed. *Ordonnances des roys de France de la troisième race.* 21 vols. Paris, 1723–1849.

Teulet, Alexandre et al., eds. *Layettes du trésor des chartes (Inventaires et documents).* 5 vols. Paris, 1863–1909.

Secondary Sources

Bloch, Marc. *Les rois thaumaturges. Étude sur le caractère surnaturel attribué à la puissance royale, particulièrement en France et en Angleterre.* Strasbourg and Paris, 1924.

Bossuat, André. "La formule 'Le roi est empereur en son royaume' et son emploi au XVᵉ siècle devant le parlement de Paris." *Revue historique de droit français et étranger,* 4th ser. 39 (1961): 371–381.

Bridrey, Émile. *La théorie de la monnaie au XIVᵉ siècle. Nicole Oresme. Étude d'histoire des doctrines et des faits économiques.* Paris, 1906.

Canning, J. P. "The Corporation in the Political Thought of the Italian Jurists of the thirteenth and fourteenth centuries." *History of Political Thought* 1 (1980): 9–32.

Cazelles, Raymond. *Société politique, noblesse et couronne sous Jean le Bon et Charles V.* Geneva, 1982.

Chaplais, Pierre. "La souveraineté du roi de France et le pouvoir législatif en Guyenne au début du XIVᵉ siècle." *Le moyen âge* 69 (1963): 449–469.

Clagett, Marshall. "Nicole Oresme and Medieval Scientific Thought." *Proceedings of the American Philosophical Society* 108 (1964): 298–309.

Coopland, George. *Nicole Oresme and the Astrologers. A Study of his Livre de Divinacions.* Liverpool, 1952.

Cranz, Ferdinand Edward. "Aristotelianism in Medieval Political Theory: A Study of the Reception of the *Politics.*" Ph.D. dissertation, Harvard University, 1938.

Daly, Lowrie J. "Walter Burley and John Wyclif on some Aspects of Kingship." *Mélanges Eugène Tisserant.* 7 vols.; 4: 163–184. Vatican City, 1964.

———. "Medieval and Renaissance Commentaries on the *Politics* of Aristotle." *Duquesne Review* 13 (1968): 41–55.

———. "The Conclusions of Walter Burley's Commentary on the *Politics.*" *Manuscripta* 12 (1968): 79–92, for books 1–4; 13 (1969): 142–149, for books 5–6; 15 (1971): 13–22, for books 7–8.

———. "Some Notes on Walter Burley's Commentary on the *Politics.*" In *Essays in Medieval History Presented to Bertie Wilkinson,* edited by T. A. Sandquist and M. R. Powicke, pp. 270–281. Toronto, 1969.

David, Marcel. *La souveraineté et les limites juridiques du pouvoir monarchique du IXᵉ au XVᵉ siècle.* Paris, 1954.

Delachenal, Roland. *Histoire de Charles V.* 5 vols. Paris, 1909–1931.

Dijksterhuis, Eduard Jan. *The Mechanization of the World Picture.* Translated by H. C. Dikshoorn. Oxford, 1961.

Dodu, Gaston. "Les idées de Charles V en matière de gouvernement." *Revue des questions historiques,* 3rd ser. 14 (1929): 5–46.

Dunbabin, Jean. "Aristotle in the Schools." In *Trends in Medieval Political Thought,* edited by Beryl Smalley, pp. 65–85. Oxford, 1965.

Durand, Dana B. "Nicole Oresme and the Mediaeval Origins of Modern Science." *Speculum* 16 (1941): 167–185.

Egenter, Richard. "Gemeinnutz vor Eigennutz. Die soziale Leitidee im 'Tractatus de bono communi' des Fr. Remigius von Florenz (*1319)." *Scholastik* 9 (1934): 79–92.

Eschmann, I. Th. "A Thomistic Glossary on the Principle of the Preeminence of a Common Good." *Mediaeval Studies* 5 (1943): 123–165.

Figgis, J. N. *Studies of Political Thought from Gerson to Grotius 1414–1625.* Cambridge, 1931.

Folz, Robert. *L'Idée d'empire en occident du Vᵉ au XIVᵉ siècle.* Paris, 1953.

Gierke, Otto von. *Political Theories of the Middle Age.* Translated by F. W. Maitland. Cambridge, 1900.

Gilby, Thomas. *The Political Thought of Thomas Aquinas.* Chicago, 1958.

Grabmann, Martin. "Studien über den Einfluss der aristotelischen Philosophie auf die mittelalterlichen Theorien über das Verhältnis von Kirche und Staat." *Sitzungsberichte der Bayerischen Akademie der Wissenschaften zu München. Philosophisch-Historische Abteilung,* 1934, pt. 2.

———. "Die mittelalterlichen Kommentare zur Politik des Aristoteles." *Sitzungsberichte der Bayerischen Akademie der Wissenschaften zu München. Phil-Hist. Abt.* 1941, vol. 2, pt. 10.

Grignaschi, Mario. "Un commentaire nominaliste de la Politique d'Aristote: Jean Buridan." *Anciens pays et assemblées d'états* 19 (1960): 125–142.

———. "Nicole Oresme et son commentaire à la 'Politique' d'Aristote." *Album Helen Maud Cam.* 2 vols.; 1: 97–151. Louvain-Paris, 1960–1961.

Guenée, Bernard. "État et nation en France au moyen âge." *Revue historique* 237 (1967): 17–30.

Hertling, Georg von. "Zur Geschichte der Aristotelischen Politik im Mittelalter." *Rheinisches Museum für Philologie,* n. s. 39 (1884): 446–457.

Johnson, Charles, ed. *The De moneta of Nicholas Oresme and English Mint Documents.* London, 1956.

Jourdain, Charles, "Nicole Oresme et les astrologues de la cour de Charles V." *Excursions historiques et philosophiques à travers le moyen âge,* pp. 559–585. Paris, 1888.

Kantorowicz, Ernst. "*Pro patria mori* in Medieval Political Thought." *American Historical Review* 56 (1950–1951): 472–492.

———. *The King's Two Bodies.* Princeton, 1957.

Koht, Halvdan. "The Dawn of Nationalism in Europe." *American Historical Review* 52 (1946–1947): 25–80.

Ladner, Gerhart B. "Aspects of Mediaeval Thought on Church and State." *Review of Politics* 9 (1947): 403–422.

Lagarde, Georges de. "Le 'Songe du Verger' et les origines du gallicanisme." *Revue des sciences religieuses* 14 (1934): 1–33; 219–237.

———. *La Naissance de l'esprit laïque au déclin du moyen âge.* 6 vols. Paris, 1934–1946.

Lavisse, Ernest. "Étude sur le pouvoir royal en France au temps de Charles V." *Revue historique* 26 (1884): 223–280.

Leff, Gordon. "The Apostolic Ideal in Later Medieval Ecclesiology." *Journal of Theological Studies* 18 (1967): 58–82.

Lemosse, Maxime. "La lèse-majesté dans la monarchie franque." *Revue du moyen âge latin* 2 (1946): 5–24.

Lewis, Ewart. *Medieval Political Ideas.* 2 vols. New York, 1954.

Lewis, Peter S. *Later Medieval France.* London, 1968.

Lohr, Charles. "Medieval Latin Aristotle Commentaries." *Traditio* 23 (1967): 313–413; 24 (1968): 149–245; 26 (1970): 135–216; 27 (1971): 251–351; 28 (1972): 281–396; 29 (1973): 93–197; 30 (1974): 119–144.

McIlwain, Charles H. *The Growth of Political Thought in the West.* New York, 1932.

Martin, Conor. "Some Medieval Commentaries on Aristotle's *Politics*." *History* 36 (1951): 29–44.

Martin, Victor. *Les origines du Gallicanisme.* 2 vols. in one. Paris, 1939.

Menut, Albert Douglas. "A Provisional Bibliography of Oresme's Writings." *Mediaeval Studies* 28 (1966): 279–299, with a supplement in vol. 31 (1969): 346–347.

Meunier, Francis. *Essai sur la vie et les ouvrages de Nicole Oresme.* Paris, 1857.

Mochi Onory, Sergio. *Fonti canonistiche dell'idea moderna dello stato (imperium spirituale-iurisdictio divisa-sovranità).* Milan, 1951.

Mollat, G. *Les papes d'Avignon.* Paris, 1924.

Monfrin, Jacques. "Humanisme et traductions au Moyen Age." *Journal des savants,* July–Sept. 1963, pp. 161–190.

———. "Les Traducteurs et leur public au Moyen Age." *Journal des savants,* January–March 1964, pp. 5–20.

Pacaut, Marcel. *La Théocratie. L'église et le pouvoir au Moyen Age.* Paris, 1957.

———. "La permanence d'une 'Via Media' dans les doctrines politiques de l'Église Médiévale." *Cahiers d'Histoire publiés par les Universités de Clermont-Lyon-Grenoble* 3. 4. (1958): 327–357.

Peterman, Larry. "Dante's *Monarchia* and Aristotle's Political Thought." *Studies in Medieval and Renaissance History* 10 (1973): 1–40.

Post, Gaines. "Two Notes on Nationalism in the Middle Ages." *Traditio* 9 (1953): 281–320.
——. *Studies in Medieval Legal Thought.* Princeton, 1964.
Posthumus Meyjes, G. H. M. *Jean Gerson et L'Assemblée de Vincennes (1329). Ses conceptions de la juridiction temporelle de l'Église.* Leiden, 1978.
Quillet, Jeannine. *La Philosophie politique du songe du vergier (1378). Sources doctrinales.* Paris, 1977.
Renna, Thomas. "Aristotle and the French Monarchy, 1260–1303." *Viator* 9 (1978): 309–324.
Riesenberg, Peter N. *Inalienability of Sovereignty in Medieval Political Thought.* New York, 1956.
Rivière, Jean. *Le problème de l'église et de l'état au temps de Philippe le Bel: étude de théologie positive.* Paris, 1926.
Royer, Jean-Pierre. *L'Église et le royaume de France au XIVe siècle d'après le 'Songe du Vergier' et la jurisprudence du Parlement.* Paris, 1969.
Schramm, Percy Ernst. *Der König von Frankreich. Das Wesen der Monarchie vom 9. zum 16. Jahrhundert.* 2 vols. in one. Weimar, 1939.
Shahar, Shulamith. "Nicolas Oresme, un penseur politique indépendant de l'entourage du roi Charles V." *L'Information historique* 32 (1970): 203–209.
——. "Traduction et commentaire de la 'Cité de Dieu' par un penseur politique sous Charles V." *L'Information historique* 39 (1977): 46–51.
Sherman, Claire Richter. "Some Visual Definitions in the Illustrations of Aristotle's *Nicomachean Ethics* and *Politics* in the French Translations of Nicole Oresme." *The Art Bulletin* 59 (1977): 320–330.
——. "A Second Instruction to the Reader from Nicole Oresme, Translator of Aristotle's *Politics* and *Economics*." *The Art Bulletin* 61 (1979): 468–469.
Spiegel, Gabrielle. "The *Reditus Regni ad Stirpem Karoli Magni*: A New Look." *French Historical Studies* 7 (1971): 145–174.
——. " 'Defense of the realm': evolution of a Capetian propaganda slogan." *Journal of Medieval History* 3 (1977): 115–133.
Steenberghen, Fernand Van. *Aristotle in the West. The Origins of Latin Aristotelianism.* Translated by Leonard Johnston. Louvain, 1955.
Strayer, Joseph R. *On the Medieval Origins of the Modern State.* Princeton, 1970.
——. *Medieval Statecraft and the Perspectives of History.* Princeton, 1971.
Taylor, Robert A. "Les Néologismes chez Nicole Oresme, traducteur du XIVe siècle." *Actes du Xe Congrès International de Linguistique et de Philologie Romanes,* pt. 4, vol. 2, pp. 727–736. Paris, 1965.
Thomson, S. Harrison. "Walter Burley's Commentary on the *Politics* of Aristotle." *Mélanges Auguste Pelzer,* pp. 557–578. Louvain, 1947.
Ullmann, Walter. "The Development of the Medieval Idea of Sovereignty." *English Historical Review* 64 (1949): 1–33.
Valois, Noël. *La France et le grand schisme d'occident.* 4 vols. Paris, 1896–1902.
Wahl, J. A. "Immortality and Inalienability: Baldus de Ubaldis." *Mediaeval Studies* 32 (1970): 308–328.
——. "Baldus de Ubaldis and the Foundations of the Nation-State." *Manuscripta* 21 (1977): 80–96.
Wilks, Michael. *The Problem of Sovereignty in the Later Middle Ages.* Cambridge, 1963.
Wisman, Josette A. "L'éveil du sentiment national au Moyen Age: la pensée politique de Christine de Pisan." *Revue historique* 257 (1977): 289–297.
Wood, Charles T. "*Regnum Francie*: A Problem in Capetian Administrative Usage." *Traditio* 23 (1967): 117–147.
——. "Queens, Queans, and Kingship: An Inquiry into Theories of Royal Legitimacy in Late Medieval England and France." In *Order and Innovation in the Middle Ages. Essays in Honor of Joseph R. Strayer,* edited by William C. Jordan, Bruce McNab, and Teofilo F. Ruiz, pp. 385–400; 562–566. Princeton, 1976.
Woolf, C. N. S. *Bartolus of Sassoferrato. His Position in the History of Medieval Political Thought.* Cambridge, 1913.
Zeller, Gaston. "Les rois de France candidats à l'empire. Essai sur l'idéologie impériale." *Revue historique* 173 (1934): 273–311.

INDEX

Active and contemplative lives, 12, 78, 96n
Adam of Bocfield, 22n
Aides, 42
Alanus Anglicus, 35n
Albertus Magnus, 12, 17–20, 21n, 22–31, 104, 132n, 133, 142n, 147
Alchemy, 6
Alcibiades, 28n
Alexander the Great, 24n
Alexander III, Pope, 110n
Allemagne, 2n
Amphipolis, 28n
Anagni, 140n
Analogy, 54, 56, 57n, 119, 138
Andreas de Isernia, 35n
Angoulême, 43n
Antonius de Petra, 34n
Apanages, 70, 86
Apostudyamenos, 60n, 91
Appointments, 99
Apulia, 27
Archytas, rattle of, 30n
Aristocracy, 81
Assizes, 66n
Astrology, 6
Astynomos, 29
Athens, 18n, 27n, 28n, 111, 112, 125
Augustine, 6n, 7, 39n, 54n, 55–58, 72, 74n, 79, 80, 83n, 85n, 106, 116n, 121, 129n, 130n, 132n, 134, 135n, 137
Augustinus Triumphus, 46n, 47n, 101, 132n
Augustus, Emperor, 138
Averroës, Averroism, 14, 15n, 23, 48, 132n
Avicenna, 18, 22
Avignon, 3, 98, 99, 118, 131, 136

Babylon, 52, 135n
Babylonian Captivity, 110n
Bacon, Roger, 15n, 77n
Bailiffs, 66n
Bailliages, 11
Baldus de Ubaldis, 35n
Bambagliolo, Graziolo, 47n
Ban, 88n
Banishment, 12, 93
Bartolus of Sassoferrato, 5n, 35n
Basil the Great, Saint, 137
Bayeux, 2
Beaumanoir, Philippe de Remi, Sire de, 41, 44n, 75n
Benedict XII, Pope, 99
Bernard, Saint, 137

Bernardus Compostellanus, 35n
Bersuire, Pierre, 7n, 10n
Bible, 6, 11, 12, 103, 119, 120, 123–126, 145, 146, 149; Acts, 124, 125n; Amos, 84n; Corinthians, 83n, 96n, 117n, 118n, 124, 125n, 144, 146n; Deuteronomy, 55n; Ecclesiasticus, 84n; Ephesians, 107; Ezekiel, 80, 109, 119; Jeremiah, 55n, 135n; Job, 84n; John, 137; Kings, 55n; Luke, 124n, 137; Matthew, 125; Paralipomenon/Chronicles, 138; Peter, 139n; Proverbs, 54, 58n, 84n; Psalms, 124n; Romans, 83n; Samuel, 81n, 94n; Thessalonians, 125; Timothy, 135n, 138, 142
Bishops, 103n
Black Prince, 42
Bodin, Jean, 34, 43
Boethius, 8n, 14, 28n, 58
Bonaventure, Saint, 132n
Boniface VIII, Pope, 127, 129, 140n
Brasidas, 28n
Brétigny, Treaty of (1360), 42
Buridan, Jean, 2, 17, 20, 21, 23–26, 57n, 58, 59, 104, 133n, 135n, 147
Burley, Walter, 17, 19, 20, 23–26, 29, 104, 133, 147

Caen, 2
Calabria, 27
Cambrai, 37
Camicus, 28n
Canon law, 70, 77n, 103n, 118
Canons, 103n
Cardinals, 98, 103n, 112, 140n
Carthage, 11
Cassiodorus, 87
Celestine I, Pope, 110n, 117n, 118n
Centralization, 98
Charlemagne, vii, 36n, 38, 53
Charles IV, Emperor, 3, 37, 130
Charles V, King of France, vii, 1n, 3–9, 32, 33n, 35–37, 39, 40n, 41–44, 58n, 65, 66, 68, 70, 83n, 85n, 88n, 89, 95n, 97, 118n, 129–131, 140, 147, 149
Charles VI, King of France, 5n, 70n, 111n, 113n
Chaucer, Geoffrey, 28n
Choquart, Ancel, 131n
Christine de Pisan, 8, 37n, 39n, 67n, 129
Chrysostom, John, Saint, 137
Church, 12, 13, 21, 32, 52, 53, 77n, 88n, 93n,

154

PUBLICATIONS

OF

The American Philosophical Society

The publications of the American Philosophical Society consist of PROCEEDINGS, TRANS-ACTIONS, MEMOIRS, and YEAR BOOK.

THE PROCEEDINGS contains papers which have been read before the Society in addition to other papers which have been accepted for publication by the Committee on Publications. In accordance with the present policy one volume is issued each year, consisting of four numbers, and the price is $20.00 net per volume. Individual copies of the PROCEEDINGS are $10.00.

THE TRANSACTIONS, the oldest scholarly journal in America, was started in 1769. In accordance with the present policy each annual volume is a collection of monographs, each issued as a part. The current annual subscription price is $60.00 net per volume. Individual copies of the TRANSACTIONS are offered for sale.

Each volume of the MEMOIRS is published as a book. The titles cover the various fields of learning; most of the recent volumes have been historical. The price of each volume is determined by its size and character, but subscribers are offered a 20 per cent discount.

The YEAR BOOK is of considerable interest to scholars because of the reports on grants for research and to libraries for this reason and because of the section dealing with the acquisitions of the Library. In addition it contains the Charter and Laws, and lists of members, and reports of committees and meetings. The YEAR BOOK is published about April 1 for the preceding calendar year. The current price is $8.50.

An author desiring to submit a manuscript for publication should send it to the Editor, American Philosophical Society, 104 South Fifth Street, Philadelphia, Pa. 19106.

www.ingramcontent.com/pod-product-compliance
Lightning Source LLC
Chambersburg PA
CBHW082147150426
42812CB00076B/2387